Dalby, Simon.

Creating the second
cold war.

$35.00

DATE			
AUG 2 8 1992			

Creating the Second Cold War

Geography and International Relations series edited
by Peter J. Taylor, University of Newcastle-upon-
Tyne and John O'Loughlin, University of Illinois.

Titles in the series include:

Peter J. Taylor, *Britain and the Cold War:
1945 as Geopolitical Transition*
Hermon van der Wusten and John O'Loughlin,
  A Political Geography of International Relations
Simon Dalby, *Creating the Second Cold War:
The Discourse of Politics*

Creating the Second Cold War
The Discourse of Politics

Simon Dalby

Pinter Publishers
London

Guilford Publications, Inc.
New York

E
872
.D35
1990

© Simon Dalby, 1990

First published in Great Britain in 1990 by
Pinter Publishers Limited
25 Floral Street, London WC2E 9DS

British Library Cataloguing in Publication Data

A CIP catalogue record for this book is available from the
British Library
ISBN 0-86187-871-X

Published in 1990 in the United States by
GUILFORD PUBLICATIONS, INC.
72 Spring Street
New York, N.Y. 10012

Library of Congress Cataloging-in-Publication Data

Dalby, Simon.
    Creating the second cold war.

    (Geography and international relations series)
    Includes bibliographical references.
    1. United States—Foreign relations—1977–1981.
    2. United States—Foreign relations—1981–1989.
    3. World politics, 1975–1985.   4. Cold War.
    5. Rhetoric—Political aspects—United States.
    6. Committee on the Present Danger.   I. Title.
    II. Series.
    E872.D35   1990   327.73   90-3191
    ISBN 0-89862-537-8 (U.S.)

871 29534

Typeset by Florencetype, Kewstoke, Avon
Printed in Great Britain by Billing & Sons Ltd, Worcester

Contents

For Cara

Acknowledgements

Thanks ae due to Michael Eliot-Hurst who guided an earlier version of this study through the Ph.D. dissertation process and to Ed Gibson and Warren Gill who also acted as thesis advisors. Rob Walker, in particular, has offered encouragement and guidance both before and since the Ph.D. writing process. Doug Ross, Rob Hackett, Derek Gregory, Myles Ruggles and Peter Cook offered useful suggestions at various stages. Fred Knelman and Nick Witheford both read the dissertation and provided detailed and pertinent criticisms. Gearóid O'Tuatháil's sympathetic support has also been most helpful. All the usual disclaimers apply, any errors or weaknesses in the text are solely my responsibility.

Thanks also to Peter Taylor for first suggesting that I rewrite the original dissertation in book format for this series, and to Iain Stevenson and Jane Evans for steering the project through the publication process at Pinter publishers.

Parts of this work have appeared in earlier versions in articles in *Alternatives*, 'Geopolitical Discourse: The Soviet Union as Other' (October 1988), in the B.C. Geographical Series, 'Discourses of Peace and War: Toward a Postmodern Geopolitics' (1989); and in *Political Geography Quarterly* 'American Security Discourse: The Persistance of Geopolitics' (April 1990). Thanks are due to Butterworth Scientific Ltd. and to the B.C. Geographical Series, the holders of these copyrights, for permission to use this material. Thanks also to Hodder and Stoughton for permission to print the epigraph taken from John le Carré's *The Russia House*.

On a more personal note thanks are due to my mother, Nina Dalby for long distance support through the years. Cara, as always, has put up with the domestic disturbances of authorship; the dedication is in grateful recognition of her contribution.

List of abbreviations

ABM	Anti-Ballistic Missiles
ASW	Anti-Submarine Warfare
BMD	Ballistic Missile Defence
CFR	Council on Foreign Relations
CPD	Committee on the Present Danger
CPSU	Communist Party of the Soviet Union
DEAD	Destruction Entrusted Automatic Devices
ICBM	Intercontinental Ballistic Missile
MAD	Mutual Assured Destruction
MIRV	Multiple Independently Targeted Re-Entry Vehicle
MPS	Multiple Protective Shelter
NUTS	Nuclear Utilization Theories and Strategies
SDI	Strategic Defence Initiative
SIOP	Single Integrated Operational Plan
SLBM	Submarine Launched Ballistic Missile
TNF	Theatre Nuclear Forces

Preface

To claim that the world is in a state of crisis has become somewhat trite in the age of nuclear winter scenarios, greenhouse effects, debt crisis, arms races and nuclear pollution. But trite or not, the global political situation gives numerous grounds for serious concern. It is increasingly clear that contemporary international political arrangements are often ineffective in offering workable solutions to contemporary problems. Indeed international political arrangements often seem antithetical to a better world, a sustainable future or a just world peace. In this context critical scholarship has a role in charting the dimensions of our current dilemmas and crisis, exploring how we came to our present state of affairs and suggesting how we might act and think differently.

One key to the current crisis lies in better understanding the dimensions of the militarization of political arrangements in the contemporary world. Essential to these processes are how states understand and legitimize their functions in terms of the provision of national 'security'. In superpower terms this theme is related to the larger canvas of geopolitics, of global superpower rivalry on a finite planet.

In the late 1960s and early 1970s the processes of superpower *détente*, arms control and the US withdrawal from the Vietnam imbroglio suggested the possibility of reducing the military dimension in global politics. But the processes of militarization were again accelerated in the late 1970s by the renewal of the Cold War geopolitical contest between the superpowers. Superpower *détente* came to an acrimonious end amid vociferous arguments concerning the danger of the 'Soviet threat' to 'Western' security. Well before Ronald Reagan entered the White House as President, the political mood in Washington had shifted from one of international diplomacy and negotiation to one of harsher rhetoric and military preparation. The USSR was once again portrayed as an implacable foe, an untrustworthy rival who understood only force, a competitor for world domination that would use any means at its disposal to advance its position in the global geopolitical competition with the USA. This process involved shifting political discourse away from matters of international economic interdependence, development and environmental concern. US political discourse in the late 1970s once again specified global politics as an arena of military competition; a harsh world of power, in which the provision of military security was the primary *raison d'état*.

This book is about the arguments of those in the USA who campaigned against *détente* and arms control agreements and who supported the renewal of Cold War and geopolitical competition as the overarching priority of US foreign policy. In particular it investigates in detail the writings of a number of intellectuals connected with the influential political lobby organization, the Committee on the Present Danger (CPD), many of whose members subsequently held important posts in the first Reagan administration. This is not a book about the history of these events, which have been extensively investigated by other authors, nor is it about the details of superpower rivalry in any of the arenas in which the conflict or rivalry was conducted. Instead, this book investigates these matters of geopolitics in the light of the concerns in contemporary social and political theory with the interconnection of matters of discourse and politics.

This study analyses the forms of security discourse the advocates of the second Cold War used in specifying political reality in terms of a Soviet threat and a US response. It investigates the structures of the discourses used and how they were mobilized in the critique of *détente* and the campaign to renew the Cold War. The purpose of the investigation is to draw attention to the intellectual processes whereby the world is specified in particular ways which enable political actors to behave in specific manners with certain political consequences. It is concerned with how politics is made, how conceptions and descriptions of the world, 'geo-graphs' in the current jargon, are constructed and legitimized; how intellectual activity contributes to political practice. It is a contribution to contemporary social theory concerned with critical approaches to geopolitics, international relations and nuclear discourse.

Of particular importance to this book is the exploration of how geopolitical discourse works to construct domestic identities and to exclude foreign 'Others'. It operates to construct certain understandings of who and where 'we' are, and who and where are 'they', the potential if not the actually hostile enemy. These specifications of 'them' and 'us', we and Other, are central to political discourse in the West, where 'we' are usually discursively constructed in antithesis to some 'Other', be it the Oriental, the terrorist, or in this case, the USSR and the threat of 'international communism'.

The task of a critical geopolitics as understood in this study is to investigate how those discursive structures are constructed, to seek their roots in intellectual life in the societies in which they are produced, and in the process show their flaws and (often hidden) assumptions. Critical geopolitics asks questions of how geopolitical discourses might be deconstructed to reveal their complicity in contemporary power relations. As such this text is a very different approach to matters of traditional geopolitics with its surveys of the geographical features of empires or nation states, their 'natural resources', industry, population, political systems and war-making potentials. Instead, it investigates how these modes of knowledge are used to maintain or construct geopolitical spaces. It shows how these specifications were used in the late 1970s to perpetuate and promote militarization in a world where the stakes of military action were already extraordinarily high.

Simon Dalby

'What you don't know is that the colleague couldn't find me when he got back to England. So he gave it to the authorities. People of discretion. Experts.'

Goethe turned sharply to Barley in alarm and the shadow of dismay spread swiftly over his fraught features. I do not *like* experts' he said. 'They are our jailers. I despise experts more than anyone on earth.'

'You're one yourself, aren't you?'

'Therefore I know! Experts are addicts. They solve nothing! They are the servants of whatever system hires them. They perpetuate it. When we are tortured, we shall be tortured by experts. When we are hanged, experts will hang us. Did you not read what I wrote? When the world is destroyed, it will be destroyed not by its madmen but by the sanity of its experts and the superior ignorance of its bureaucrats. You have betrayed me.'

John Le Carré, *The Russia House*

Part One
Context

Introduction

This book draws on contemporary social theory's concern with language and discourse to inform its inquiry into geopolitics. The first chapter begins this discussion with a brief review of the concepts of discourse that are relevant to the subsequent analysis. With ideas of discourse go those of political practice, ideology and hegemony. These concern the use of particular discourses for political ends and the matter of intertexts, the linking together of texts and discourses, in this case, by experts and politicians, to define political positions and policies.

Chapter 2 shows how the perennial themes of dualism and dichotomies in Western philosophy are linked into how discourses construct their objects of knowledge as 'Other'. Discourses of 'Otherness' are important in producing Western metaphysical conceptions and ideological structures. The Other provides a useful way of illuminating the categories of time and space which so fundamentally structure the discourses of social and political theory.

Political theory, in particular the theory of international relations is the subject of the first part of the Chapter 3. As will be made clear there, the central political concept of security is formulated as the exclusion of Otherness, an exclusion that is a geopolitical exercise of power. In part geopolitics is about power and military force and the threats posed to the international order by military threats. But geopolitics is much more than this; Chapter three suggests how geopolitics can be reformulated in terms of discourse.

Chapter 4 shows an example of geopolitical discourse in practice. It presents an analysis of the Committee on the Present Danger's 'threat discourse' in the 1970s in which they constructed the presence of a massive and growing Soviet geopolitical threat to US national security. This chapter shows how their geopolitical discourse is constructed and analyses the ideological moves they make in attempting to render their position the accepted premises for political discussion.

Chapter 1

Social theory and security discourse

'Postmodernism' and global crisis

Amid the numerous reports, commissions and expert panels on matters of the contemporary planetary predicament, the journals of policy analysis and the thinktanks replete with political experts and policy advisers, there is a smaller contingent of critical intellectuals asking far-reaching questions concerning how the philosophical presuppositions of the policy debates shape and limit what it is possible to do and say within the established institutional patterns and structures of political discourse. These critics challenge the conventional formulations, examining the taken-for-granted assumptions of policy advice and the analytical procedures and methodological devices of the practitioners of international politics and foreign policy (Der Derian, 1987; Dillon, 1988; Shapiro, 1988; Der Derian and Shapiro eds, 1989; Walker, 1986), as well as analysing specifically the discourses of nuclear strategy (Chilton, ed., 1985; Cohn, 1987; Klein, 1988; Wertsch, 1987). Concerned with the discursive practices, constructions and strategies of the policy texts these 'postmodern' investigations cast a sceptical analytical gaze on the rhetoric of state policy-makers and the 'advisers to the prince'.

These approaches are concerned with matters of power and discourse, the use of socially organized linguistic and semiotic constructions to mobilize meanings in the service of power. Taking theoretical inspiration, although not a formalized 'method' of inquiry from Frederich Nietzsche, and more recently Michel Foucault, Jacques Derrida and others, the postmodern sensibility questions how the social construction of reality is formulated; and how 'Others' are created as the external antagonist against which internal identity is mobilized. They examine discourse, systematically organized ways of writing, talking, etc. in terms of how concepts legitimate and hence reproduce structures of power. They investigate how discourses operate to foreclose political possibilities and eliminate from consideration a multiplicity of possible worlds.

In particular they challenge the conventional categories of the self-understandings of particular disciplines, subjecting their histories and conceptual structures to a genealogical critique and reconstruction. They show how contemporary cultural structures carry within them the institutional and discursive residues of earlier political struggles. 'Postmoderns' are reluctant to prescribe grand theories, they refuse predictions, rather they open up possibilities, investigate points of struggle and divergence in plural histories rather than chart the unfolding of a univocal History. Above all the postmodern concern is with power, it rituals, its dramas, its modes of representation. Borrowing Klein's (1988) use of Shapiro's phrase, we can say that the postmodern concern is 'to leave power nowhere to hide'. This book is inspired by this postmodern concern with the politics of representation; the use of particular modes of discourse in political situations in ways that shape political practices, implicating political discourse in worldmaking. In dealing with these matters this book draws loosely on a number of important concepts and modes of analysis from contemporary social theory and applies them to tackling the Committee on the Present Danger's geopolitical arguments for the militarization of US foreign policy and the prosecution of Cold War.

Social theory: discourse

Recent social theory is particularly concerned with issues of power and knowledge, with the role of language and particularly, discourse, in the maintenance of political arrangements of domination. In particular the current 'postmodern' concerns are with questions of power and discourse drawing on concerns in linquistics, philosophy and literary theory to critique the contemporary cultural practices of modernity (Said, 1982; Shapiro ed. 1984, 1988). This shift of focus from positivist approaches and epistemological concerns with correspondence rules of truth, involves conceptualizing social existence as human practice. Social life is active creation, albeit within created frameworks of custom, economy, power and language. Social life is understood in and through language, and hence the structures of language reflect and create social life.

But language practices are integrated in specific ways of articulating together linguistic formations. Language is socially structured as discourse. In contrast to hermeneutic approaches, postmodern approaches are concerned with matters of power, how texts and discourses are exercises in power and repression, in addition to just significations (Thompson, 1984; Shapiro 1988). In Foucault's terms discourses are much more than linguistic performances, they are also plays of power which mobilize rules, codes and procedures to assert a particular understanding through the construction of knowledges within these rules, codes and procedures. Because they organize reality in specific ways through understanding and knowing in ways that involve particular epistemoligical claims, they provide legitimacy, and indeed provide the intellectual conditions of possibility of particular institutional and political arrangements.

· The rules governing practices, often implicit and not clearly articulated, but understood by practitioners, are socially constructed in specific contexts. Hence discourses have institutional origins and commitments. The knowledges they produce and encompass are thus political products; discourses are implicated with power. Kress (1985, 85) goes as far as defining discourses in terms of institutions thus: 'Discourses are systematically organised sets of statements which give expression to the meanings and values of an institution. Beyond that they define, describe and delimit what it is possible to say and not to say. . . .' If, for example, one takes an academic discipline as an institution, then the term discourse can apply to the oeuvre of that discipline's practitioners.

Foucault has analysed the discursive practices of medicine, sex and penology, showing how the conception of madness is created in antithesis to reason, deviance to normalcy and delinquent to reformed. His concerns are often with the structuring of identity against the boundary of an external Other.

> Discursive practices are characterised by the delimitation of a field of objects, the definition of a legitimate perspective for the agent of knowledge, and the fixing of norms for the elaboration of concepts and theories. Thus, each discursive practice implies a play of prescriptions that designates its exclusions and choice. [Foucault, 1977, 199]

These 'regularities' transcend single texts or writer's works, and do not necessarily coincide with a recognizable discipline or field of study. Discursive practices change in complex ways that are not necessarily related solely to internal developments.

> The transformation of a discursive practice is linked to a whole range of usually complex modifications that can occur outside its domain (in the forms of production, in social relations in political institutions), inside it (in its techniques for determining its object, in the adjustment and refinement of its concepts, in its accumulation of facts), or to the side of it (in other discursive practices). [Foucault, 1977, 200]

Discursive practices are more than simply ways of producing texts. 'They are embodied in technical processes, in institutions, in patterns for general behaviour, in forms for transmission and diffusion, and in pedagogical forms which, at once, impose and maintain them' (Foucault, 1977, 200). Discourse involves not only language but also practices and social positions which embody power; the psychiatrist who designates who is reasonable and who is mad, the therapist who pronounces on normalcy, the parole officer who judges when the delinquent has reformed. Thus, discourse refers also to the rules by which behaviour is structured, regulated and judged.

Focusing on a particular discipline in terms of its discursive practices involves examining how the discipline constructs its field of study, its object or Other, and hence how it situates itself in relation to its Other (Fabian, 1983). This also involves discussing the internal divisions of that inquiry and how the methodological conventions, and importantly the categorical devices that are used, structure the knowledge that results. These categories and divisions shape the discipline's knowledge, which in turn structures how it is possible to act by defining 'reality' in specific ways. Foucault's analysis makes clear the role of the creation of the Other as the excluded against which behaviour is judged and defined: the mad defines the sane; the deviant the normal. Otherness is inherent in the analysis of discourse. It involves the social construction of some other person, group, culture, race, nationality or political system as different from 'our' person, group, etc. Specifying difference is a linguistic, epistemological and crucially a political act; it constructs a space for the Other distanced and inferior from the vantage point of the person specifying the difference.

Practices function on the bases of these definitions: prisons are built to incarcerate the delinquent; mental hospitals to shut away the mad. Both operate to exclude the Other, shutting Otherness away in regimes where it can be monitored, surveyed and hence known and controlled. In 'security' matters the enemy is specified in a series of security discourses, tied to the functioning of the state security and defence agencies. The practitioners of penology or medicine practise on their objects, prisoners or patients, but they do so in socially constructed positions of authority and power; by regulating the Other they also regulate the rest. Likewise, security discourse, while ostensibly dealing with external Others, has important domestic political effects.

The penologist's and the therapist's positions are justified in terms of moral criteria of reform or cure; their specialized knowledge gives them power to act in positions of authority. To deal with discourses one has to deal with their political conditions, to look at their audience as well as the practitioners, and to understand how the practices of the discourse also legitimize the authority of the practitioner. One looks at how the practitioners delineate their object of study, and how they create and designate the correct norms and rules for dealing with that object. Much of what follows below relates to the processes whereby the CPD attempted to establish their ways of dealing with the USSR as the correct ones. In their discourse the USSR is the dangerous Other that has to be contained, controlled and monitored using their superior and their 'correct' knowledge to ensure the security of the USA.

Readers bring a series of pre-existing discursive practices to a text which are used to operate on the received text and render it meaningful. Thus, for example, a newspaper text on a criminal trial relies on its readers' preconstructed categories of criminal and innocent. Hence discourses also involve the capabilities, in terms of a socio-cultural background, which are used by people to construct meaning. Thus discourse 'is not simply speech or a written treatise on a topic but a set of capabilities, qua rules by which readers/listeners and speakers/audiences are able to take what they hear and read and construct it into an organised meaningful whole' (Agnew and O'Tuathail, 1987, 6). Discourses are about how reality is specified and how social practices are structured in the terms of these realities.

Foucault's focus is on the discourses themselves, in contrast to Marxist approaches to history, class struggle, ideology and, particularly, hegemony. Foucault (1972) is concerned with the analysis of discourses emphasizing discontinuities and ruptures rather than linear totalizing schemes. He is concerned with their structures and practices rather than with their historical evolution; an approach, which in Ashley's (1987, 409) words, 'involves a shift away from an interest in uncovering the structures of history and toward an interest in understanding the movement and clashes of historical practices that would impose or resist structure'. Of particular relevance to this book is the use made of these approaches in the current critical literature in international relations theory, focusing on the discursive practices of international politics, war, peace and security (Der Derian and Shapiro eds, 1989). Theorized in the terms of this contemporary post-modern focus on intertexts; the clashing and melding of different texts in political discourse, this book is in this sense an analysis of the Soviet threat as an intertext: a melding together of a number of specific textual approaches to contemporary world politics.

This study focuses on one specific set of discursive practices – the operations, tactics and strategies of the CPD articulations of security discourse. It is primarily concerned with the structure of the CPD discourse rather than its history. Where it deals with history it is to show that the security discourses have long intellectual lineages, not to argue that there is a necessary historical trajectory over time. These discourses are, in Foucault's terms, available resources of power that can be mobilized for a particular political end. The fact that they have a historical pedigree may, of course, act to enhance their ideological usage by increasing their acceptance in terms of past practice providing a legitimate precedent.

The emphasis in what follows is on how the CPD mobilized the security discourses to support their political project, using their arguments to make their case, and in the process attempting to change the terrain of political debate to exclude *détente* and economic managerial concerns from the discussion of US foreign policy. This focus on the mobilization and utilization of specific discourses for political purposes leads to matters that have often been dealt with in the rather different theoretical terms of ideology and hegemony.

Social theory: ideology and hegemony

Sometimes ideology is defined in terms of a political belief system, in other words as a neutral descriptive sociological term, which equates ideology with a political belief system or *Weltanschauung*. This formulation lacks the critical dimension of the term, introduced by Marx and Engels (Centre for Contemporary Cultural Studies, 1977; Larrain, 1979; 1983, Marx and Engels, 1976; Sumner, 1979) and retained in much recent social theory (Abercrombie *et al*, 1980; Thompson, 1984). In framing ideology as a critical concept, numerous theoretical difficulties arise because it simultaneously bridges matters of power and domination, the social determination of knowledge, and matters of truth and falsity.

The critical dimension of the concept of ideology, as used in this book, refers to its function in maintaining power relations. A cultural practice or a discourse can have an ideological function when it conceals relations of power (dissimulation), presents them as legitimate, or acts to reify or naturalize them by portraying a transitory historical situation as eternal and hence natural. In part ideology functions by limiting what can be said, '. . . ideology allows only certain things to be communicated and discussed. It not only "expresses" but also "represses" excluding certain issues from discussion and creating a "public unconsciousness". Ideology is as it were, the linguistic legislature which defines what is available for public discussion and what is not' (Thompson, 1984, 85). But what is available for public discussion is not necessarily accepted uncritically by the audience. They can resist the proffered discourse and reformulate it. 'The clash of voices is a clash of power, and the analysis of discourse is an analysis of and an intervention in this politics' (Frow, 1985, 213).

Analysing matters in this way maintains ideology's critical edge. 'Given that all discourse is informed by power, is constituted as discourse in relation to unequal patterns of power, then political judgements can be made in terms of particular, historically specific appropriations of discourse by dominant social forces' (Frow, 1985, 204). And so 'Ideology can be seen therefore as the "politics of discourse", marshalling discourses into certain allignments in the cause of larger political aims' (Kress, 1985, 71). Thus ideological analysis can focus on how discourses are appropriated and interconnected in ways that maintain relations of power and do so in ways that delimit what can be said in particular circumstances.

Like ideology and discourse, hegemony is also used in general uncritical ways, and in a more specific critical way within social theory. In the general sense it is analogous with domination and control; in political realist terms, it refers to geopolitical matters of the power exercised by one state over other states (Gill, 1986). The critical sense of the term refers to the Gramscian use of the term (R. Cox, 1983, 1984; Gramsci, 1971; Laclau and Mouffe, 1985; Mouffe, 1979). Gramsci argued that at certain times in history a dominant class exercises its control over subordinate classes by social and cultural leadership rather than by coercion. The establishment of hegemony involves the widespread dissemination by 'organic intellectuals' of commonly accepted, ultimately 'common-sense' conceptions of social reality, which portray the existing economic and political state of affairs as natural, inevitable, legitimate and in the interests of all social groups or classes. This ideological role performed by intellectuals is important in Gramsci's conception because they provide sophisticated rationales for political stances; they act to legitimize particular understandings of social phenomena by writing and teaching in particular ways, even when not explicitly involved in political activity.

The concept of hegemony suggests that 'common sense' is not an ontological given; it is an ideologically produced and repeatedly reproduced series of understandings of the world, ones that operate in ways that support political domination. Thus, in Mouffe's (1979, 181) words a hegemonic class is one 'which has been able to articulate the interests of other social groups to its own by means of ideological struggle'. It is important to note that hegemony is never a static state, it remains a contingent process, open to disputation at all levels. It has to be actively produced and reproduced as political and ideological practice. The concept of hegemony is a powerful theoretical tool but not one without its critics (Anderson, 1976–7). In particular Abercrombie *et al.* (1980) argue that ideological factors are often overestimated in explanations of the social cohesion of societies. The matter of their effectiveness in particular circumstances is a question for empirical investigation. Irrespective of the level of success of particular ideological ploys in maintaining domination and control, it is clear they they are widely used in political struggles in attempts to render particular ideological positions hegemonic.

In critical cultural studies the term hegemonic is often used to refer to ideological formulations that are widely accepted and used to structure social and political life. The term is used in this sense in this book. Used in this way it is not incompatible with the formulation of discourse offered above, although the derivation of the terms come from different theoretical approaches. Here hegemony refers to all political and ideological structures of domination, including therefore the mobilization of discourses to render a political position acceptable, legitimate, common sense. Particular attempts to assert a hegemonic political position can be analysed without necessarily assuming their political efficacy. This book shows how the CPD attempted to render their particular articulation of the security discourses hegemonic, in the sense that they become taken for granted, widely accepted as the appropriate premises from which to discuss matters of international politics. The focus is thus on their arguments, the structure of their discourse, rather than on any detailed attempt to assess their success or failure, although a few comments on this subject are included for completeness in the final part of the book.

The hegemony of security discourse

The rapid growth of state functions in capitalist states since the Second World War, both in terms of their increased role in national and international economic management in the Keynesian era, and in terms of their role in the provision of the welfare state, as well as the growth of what is appropriately called the 'security state', in a perpetual condition of partial military mobilization, has expanded the need for ideological justifications of the functions of capitalist states. Of particular concern to this book are the emergence of semi-permanent, transnational economic and political 'blocs', which also make claims to the allegiance of their respective national populations, and the growth of highly sophisticated and brutally destructive military technology, the most obvious form being nuclear weapons. These perpetual military preparations require the creation of a permanent adversary, an Other whose threatening presence requires perpetual vigilance. The highest political objectives of the state are now phrased in terms of the maintainance of 'national security', a security usually defined in negative terms as the exclusion of the depredations of external 'Others'.

The growth of these new political arrangements and technologies has been accompanied by an expansion of the role of specialized discourses of technical expertise. These discourses act to reduce the role of political discussion by recasting political issues in terms of technical problems to which they can, by using their specialized procedures, find 'correct' or 'optimal' answers. These specialized discourses act to maintain hegemony by reducing politics to a matter of administrating programmes devised on the basis of the definition of social situations contained in these discourses. They depoliticize issues by invoking technical expertise in the place of political decision-making, in the process displacing explicit political discussion and replacing it with expert discourse.

The Cold War period produced many experts, or 'security intellectuals' in Luckham's (1984) apt phrase, in various fields involved in consulting and research for military agencies, the air force's RAND corporation being only the most famous of the new institutions (Kaplan, 1983). In the US public realm these experts often dominate, or attempt to dominate, public debate using their supposedly superior expert, and often classified, knowledge to specify the 'issues' in ways that maintain the foreign policy themes of containment and nuclear deterrence of the 'Soviet threat'. Their discourses interlink to portray the world as a place of dangerous military competition in which nuclear weapons are essential to the protection of US national security.

In particular four fairly discrete but interconnected and often mutually supporting 'security discourses' emerged in the USA in the Cold War period which have dominated much of the debate on 'national security' since the early 1950s. These discourses of 'strategy', 'sovietology', 'realism' and 'geopolitics' were mobilized to describe, explain and legitimate the doctrines of 'containment', 'deterrence' and the provision of 'national security' around the portrayal of the USSR as a dangerous antagonistic Other. The discourses of sovietology, nuclear strategy and a 'realist' approach to international relations were mobilized within an implicit geopolitical framework to create the categories of security which dominate political discourse within the 'Western system'.

Realism dominated discussions of international relations in the post-war period; its key theme of 'interest' understood in terms of power is omnipresent in post-war political discourse. As Richard Ashley (1987, 1988) has argued, the realist discourse also acted to limit the possibilities for critical political intervention precisely by its definitions of community and anarchy; by how it specified the realm of power. Interests are intimately related to security, understood in the sense of preventing a potential adversary invading one's territorially understood space, which in turn relates to physical protection and political alliances at, in the US case, the global scale. The emergence of this security regime simultaneously involved the expansion of the arena of state security to the level of alliance security, and the expansion of the understanding of security in terms of the technological military control of precisely demarcated areas of territorial space.

This enlargement of the importance of military considerations is clear in the emergence of a distinctive nuclear strategic discourse which specified the superpower contest in terms of nuclear coercion and the policy of deterring an aggressive totalitarian USSR. The complex, and at times, arcane discussions of this discourse, premised their analysis on the eternal enmity of the two systems. They supplemented these assumptions with a series of worst-case analyses, where it is always assumed that the other side will do their worst. This form of analysis, coupled with the widespread popular fear and awe of nuclear weapons, supported the continued rapid expansion of nuclear weapons and their 'delivery systems'. The scenarios for the possible use of these weapons in warfare drew on the abstract calculations of game theory much more than detailed socio-political analysis (Freedman, 1983).

Such input as was sought concerning the make-up of the Soviet enemy was drawn from the literature of the then emergent field of sovietology. The methodological consensus of this discourse theorized the USSR as unchanging, driven by internal geopolitical factors as well as the expansionist logic of totalitarianism to expand and hence to threaten US interests around the globe (Cohen, 1985). The totalitarian assumption that the polity was completely dominated by the central party elite, whose ultimate goal was global domination, precluded the possibility of serious or long-term co-operation between the superpowers (Griffiths, 1985). It also reinforced the realist theme of states struggling for domination in an international anarchy. Each of these security discourses relies on expert knowledge to specify reality in particular ways.

The political struggles of the 'new social movements' in the last few decades are often about this 'politics of expertise' challenging the expert discourse by revealing the political assumptions on which their supposed neutrality and objectivity rest (Nelkin and Pollak, 1981). Recently these political struggles are particularly pronounced in matters of war, peace and international relations where this array of specialized discourses of 'security' have developed. These monopolize the state political discourse on these matters, but in recent years they have been repeatedly challenged and criticized by peace movements.

Nuclear technologies and their political arrangements have added an important dimension to processes whereby consent is generated for the maintenance of the political arrangements of Western capitalism. The threat of complete societal annihilation renders the legitimation of the existence of these weapons particularly necessary, while the social and cultural processes of militarization that accompany their deployment simultaneously reduce the scope for democratic decision-making (Falk, 1987). In the West, and the USA in particular, the weapons and their institutions are justified in terms of the omnipresent fear of the external enemy, present in the form of the USSR (Kovel, 1983; Thompson, 1985a, 1985b; Wolfe 1984a).

State mechanisms as well as the organizations within civil society act to defuse threats to the domination of hegemonic formations through what Gramsci terms 'transformismo', often rendered in English as 'co-optation'. Here dissent is channelled into existing structures or marginalized by dismissing it as 'radical' or unrealistic. In the process the overall structures of domination are maintained and rendered secure by the attempted absorption or marginalization of potential positions of opposition. The ideological specification of political identities and acceptable modes of political behaviour is essential to these processes.

As has been made clear by many writers, the numerous contemporary critiques of militarization repeatedly run into problems of the limitations of what can be said in certain circumstances, a process revealing the hegemonic discursive structures of the nuclear state (Bay, 1983; Cohn, 1987; Galtung, 1981; Kovel, 1983; Klein, 1988; NcNair, 1988; Thompson 1985a, 1985b; Walker, 1986; Witheford, 1987). In response to peace movement critiques, 'security intellectuals' use, among others, the ideological device of distinguishing between legitimate 'free speech' and illegitimate protest (Chilton ed., 1985). More important for this book is the use of the widespread and powerful understanding of the USSR as an expansionist foe that requires deterring, to marginalize not only peace movements, but many advocates of *détente* and arms control with the USSR. Dissenters are vilified as giving support and assistance to the external enemy. The Other provides the axis on which acceptable and unacceptable political activities and identities are constructed. Related to this, is the particular 'common-sense' notion of security as spatial exclusion; the Other as threat is specified in spatial terms as inhabiting somewhere else.

Political identity is related to these geopolitical specifications of them and us; their space and our space. Analysing the CPD texts shows how these discourses were mobilized in ideological struggle, against in this case, both the 'global managerialist' and '*détente*' advocates in the USA, and subsequently those in the peace movements who would more deeply challenge the structure of US global military domination. To revamp US military superiority required the CPD to launch a public political campaign to reassert the containment militarist discourses of security as the appropriate premises for discussing political matters, in the process discrediting the *détente* advocates, and those who argued that US leadership required economic management and co-ordination rather than military force.

Reading security discourse

In the USA, and in a more general sense within the 'Western world', the constant preparation for war with the USSR, a perpetual condition captured in the phrase 'the National Security State', requires the consent, or at least some degree of acquiesence, by the population to these political arrangements for war mobilization:

> And we can understand the production of the acquiesence by appreciating the discursive economies within which international strategy and war are represented. As Foucault has shown, the discourses that vehiculate understandings are not simply linguistic expressions to be viewed on the basis of representational adequacy; they are power related resources. In deploying identities for actors and

producing the overall meaning frame within which they operate, they constitute and reproduce prevailing systems of power and authority in general and direct the actions flowing from these systems in particular. [Shapiro, 1989, 75]

This book takes this as its methodological point of departure, focusing on how the discourses of security are articulated together to attempt ideologically to reproduce the Cold War political system.

It focuses on the overall logics of the positions involved rather than on their expression in small segments of text. In doing so it uses the approach taken by a number of writers, very loosely following Foucault, concerned with postmodern international relations theory (Ashley, 1987; Der Derian and Shapiro eds, 1989; Klein, 1987, 1988; Shapiro, 1988, 1989; Walker, 1986), political geography (Agnew and O'Tuathail, 1987; O'Tuathail, 1988), and in literature specifically concerned with the theme of the Other (deCerteau, 1986; Said, 1979; Todorov, 1984). In terms of Foucault's analysis of discursive practices, this book focuses on the operations of definition, the legitimation of the norms of discourse, the exclusion of alternative formulations and the articulation of various discursive practices. It investigates these operations by examining the overall arguments of the texts, seeking out the key ideological moves of each of the security discourses. The emphasis in the detailed explication (in Part Two) is with the application that the CPD makes of the various security discourses and how these are articulated in specifying the USSR as a threatening Other.

This book thus examines the discursive strategies of the CPD arguments, how the Other is defined, how alternative formulations are rendered invalid and how their various concerns within the security discourses are articulated in a geopolitical scheme structured in terms of their omnipresent threatening Other. The other security discourses of sovietology, realism and nuclear strategy contain important geopolitical presuppositions which are often overlooked because they are taken for granted. Informed by a critical postmodern sensibility which insists on challenging the assumptions of hegemonic discourse, this book takes a position that challenges the hegemonic conception of the state as the provider of security by a process of spatial exclusion of Otherness. In doing so it distances itself from the traditional functions of geopoliticians as adviser to state policy-makers and politicians, that is from those who 'practise geopolitics' (O'Tuathail, 1986, 73). It does so by refusing the conventional equation of the state with the provision of security, arguing from a position that states are not natural entities but politically created practices, and their claims to legitimacy ought to be the subject of critical investigation rather than the point of departure for analysis.

Theorizing matters in this way also involves a reconceptualization of the history of geopolitics; one which points to the importance of its discursive practices in US foreign policy before the term itself was coined (Agnew and O'Tuathail, 1987) and in particular after the Second World War, when the term itself fell into disuse (Kristof, 1960; Trofimenko, 1986). The book takes the position that the function of a critical geopolitics is not to provide 'advice to the prince' in terms of using geopolitical reasoning to advise state policy-makers, but rather to investigate how geopolitical reasoning is used as an ideological device to maintain social relations of domination within contemporary global politics.

In this it loosely follows Klein's (1988) suggestions for a 'diremptive' postmodern approach to the strategic enterprise; one that takes seriously the postmodern analytic sensibility to 'the problematic of discourses in making and unmaking of practices'. In particular Klein emphasizes the constituted quality of practices, where 'they create the effects that they purport to be responding to'; strategic discourse as implicating in the practice of violence, not as a passive response to some violence external to the practice of the discourse. This points to the necessity to denaturalize constituted practices to see political processes as historically constituted, and hence amenable to critical enquiry and political challenge. This postmodern approach forces open supposed unities, searching not for some encompassing singular security, but exploring the multitude of insecurities, refusing the spatial representations of security in terms of insides and outsides. To investigate these matters is to challenge the hegemony of political activity currently claimed by states. It demands an analysis of peace and security in terms of global, regional and local concerns, reinventing political life in the spaces forced open by the practices of dissenting politics.

Because of this approach the book's primary concern is not with the history of US foreign policy. Because matters of the historical role of the 'Soviet threat' in US politics, and the historical evolution of the CPD's political campaign have been covered in detail by other writers (Cox, 1982; Sanders, 1983; Wolfe, 1984a), they do not require detailed reiteration in this study. They are not central to this book's argument which concerns the related, but analytically separable, matter of the structuring of the CPD discourse. Neither is this book primarily concerned with matters of whether, or to what degree, the CPD discourse became 'hegemonic' in US politics. Although a few brief comments are included in the final part on this theme, what is of importance to this analysis is how the CPD linked together the various security discourses in ways that attempted to render their position hegemonic. They did this by constructing ideological positions that excluded other possible discourses on international affairs from serious consideration.

This book is not concerned once again to enumerate the errors and inadequacies of the formulations of the 'keepers of the threat', nor their claims that the USA was spending too little on defence (see Aspin, 1978; Cockburn, 1983; Cockle, 1978; Cox, 1985; Dibb, 1988; Garrison and Shivpuri, 1983; Gervasi, 1986; Holzman, 1980; Kaplan, 1980; Komer, 1985; Mack, 1981; Maynes, 1982; Mearsheimer, 1982; Prados, 1982; Simes, 1979–80; Spruyt, 1985; Wolfe, 1984a, 1984b, 1984c). Neither is this study an investigation into the psychological dimensions of international relations, or the making of enemy images (Keen, 1986), where a large literature on policy-makers' perceptions has been accumulated (Boulding, 1969; Hall, 1983; Henrikson, 1980; Holsti, 1967; Jervis, 1970, 1976; Posen, 1987; Tetlock, 1983; Vertsberger, 1982). Nor is this book about constructing an alternative, in some sense, more 'objective' or 'correct' assessment of the global scene. While later sections do point to the flaws, omissions and empirical inadequacies of the CPD case, what is of central importance is the ideological role of the CPD's discourse and how their discursive practices acted to reproduce the world of the 1950s a quarter of a century later.

This study is concerned with the organization of the arguments used to portray the 'threat', a subject that has not received the detailed scholarly scrutiny which, given the profound political consequences that flow from the repeated portrayal of 'the threat', it clearly needs. The concern is with the power of geopolitics, the use of geopolitical reasoning to specify a particular understanding of the world, one that supports, rationalizes and explains the US military buildup in the late 1970s and through the early 1980s. To use Ashley's (1987) phrase, this book is concerned with 'the geopolitics of geopolitical space'; how a particular series of 'security discourses' establishes an ideological space from which to dominate, exclude and delegitimize other discourses, and how this particular formulation of the world constructed the USSR as a threatening 'Other'.

Chapter 2

Discourse and otherness

The Other: identity, difference

The theme of 'the Other' is important in contemporary critical social theory. It provides a focus for this study precisely because the Other involves questions of demarcations between realms of knowledge: how the knower relates to the known; how cultural and political identities are structured; and how discourses are articulated in hegemonic arrangements. How one distinguishes 'Same' from 'Other', the knower from the known, is an epistemological question and, in more pratical terms, a question of politics; it is a relation of power. It is also a move which mobilizes important structuring process of social identity. These three themes are closely interrelated in the sections that follow.

The discourse on and about the 'Other' is concerned with the perennial philosophical debates within the Western tradition concerning identity and difference. In Western thought a bifurcation of reality involves a conception of the Other as difference against which the 'I', 'we' or 'the same' is defined. Aristotle's formulation of political philosophy is premised on a clear distinction between the Greeks, who lived within the 'political space' of the polis, and the Orientals, the outsiders, who inhabited the rest of the ancient world (Dossa, 1987). This bifurcation of East and West is a theme continued to this day, a theme that runs at the heart of rationalist discourse on politics and, as will be shown later, is present in the CPD's identification of the US policy with enlighenment and universal human progress, in distinction from the Soviet system.

Hegel's discussion of the unity of identity and opposition in the dialectical method provides a point of entry into the discussion (Taylor, 1979). In Hegel's discussion of the master/slave relationship, one is defined in terms of the other without whose presence he is undefinable. If there are no masters there are no slaves, and vice versa. By struggling to assert himself against the master the slave creates his identity, the master in turn creates his own identity in attempting to dominate the slave. Sartre's *Being and Nothingness* (1956) analyses in detail the role of the Other in the creation of the subject. Power is related to the Other, whose look turns the subject into an object for that Other, thus threatening it as subject.

It might be argued that other cultural traditions contain similar dualistic structures. The importance of what is rendered in English as 'Ying' and

'Yang' is particularly apposite in this context. What is important here is the repeated theme of the interconnectedness of both Ying and Yang in any phenomenon or activity. In this tradition one is not ultimately collapsible to the other. If one is ascendent, the other acts to compensate and will in turn become ascendent. In Western conceptions, difference is defined in terms of identity, to which it is ultimately reduced in some way. Identity is privileged over difference. In Derrida's terms, self-identity is defined in terms of 'differance', a spatial and temporal deferment of the Other, a move which privileges identity over difference.

Derrida's (1977, 1981) concern is with the structure of Western thought which relies so heavily on dichotomies and polarities. These frequent polar opposites – good versus evil, being versus nothingness, nature versus culture – have distinct valuations built into their formulation. As Johnson summarizes it in her introduction to the English translation of *Dissemination*: 'The second term in each pair is considered the negative, corrupt, undesirable version of the first, a fall away from it . . .' (Johnson, 1981, viii). The first term has priority. 'In general what these hierarchial oppositions do is to privilege unity, identity, immediacy, and temporal and spatial presentness over distance, difference, dissimulation and deferment' (1981, viii).

All this is related to Derrida's broader preoccupation with Western metaphysics based on Being as presence. It also relates to the 'operation of exclusion in a philosophy that permits one group, or value, or idea to be kept out so that another can be safeguarded internally and turned into a norm' (Ryan, 1982, 3). Further it asks 'How might one find what is excluded – something that usually is a variety of difference or repetition in metaphysics – at work determining that from which it supposedly derives' (Ryan, 1982, 3). This project strikes at the heart of Western 'logocentric' social theory based on its privileging of the cerebral, of mind separated from the world which it apprehends through 'senses'; the superiority of theory over practice. The Other is thus a relation of difference, but difference is tied to identity, the Other is defined in contrast to 'I', 'we'; or the same. It is thus a relation of power; 'they' are 'created' as 'them' by 'us'. It is thus a move of power; 'we' can impose 'our' conception of 'them' as being 'them' and act accordingly if 'we' have the capabilities to do so.

The process of exclusion and inclusion is central to feminist concerns, an area where the analysis of the Other and difference, involving the silence and exclusion of the feminine, is particularly developed around the relation of language and power. The denial of female experience in social and political theory is a repeated theme in feminist writings (Clark and Lange eds, 1979). Thus rationality is defined in terms of 'male' criteria where knowledge is tied to domination (Lloyd, 1984). This is particularly clear in the development of science, in terms of the 'mastery' or domination of nature in Francis Bacon's idiom, a development which carried with it political restructuring in which male 'scientific' knowledge came to dominate over female practices (Merchant, 1980).

An important part of the theme of woman as Other is the structure of language; literary criticism is a sphere of increasing feminist concern (Moi,

1985). Initially analysed in terms of the power to 'name' experience, the argument suggests that women are powerless to name and define the terms of their own experience and consequently are forced to discuss their experience in terms produced by men (Daly, 1973). The terms are imbued with a false, because only partial, epistemological significance as universals particularly within 'scientific' study. By defining experience in terms of a language that is at best only partial, female experience is denied. More important is that the possibility of a separate female experience is denied by the assertion of the terms as universal (Spender, 1984). The feminist experience is thus excluded by its inclusion within a systematically distorted discourse; systematically distorted by the reification of male experience as universal. Many feminist efforts have been devoted to attempting a de-masculinize commonly used terms in an attempt to restructure language to reflect the plurality of human experience.

These themes of language and power are present in the feminist analysis of militarism and the structures of power implicit in the discourse about international relations and in particular the ideological assumptions of nuclear physics (Easlea, 1983). In this debate the focus is on the power relations of masculine domination of knowledge, either in the political sphere as in 'international affairs expert' or in the technical sphere as scientist or weapons technician to the exclusion of the women who do not speak the technical languages and, hence, are not considered competent in the fields dominated by the discourses of security (Cohn, 1987). This exclusion goes further in the militarist indoctrination of soldiers to objectify and dominate their own 'female traits', as well as women in general by defining them as Other, different and inferior; hence to be dominated (McAllister ed., 1982; Enloe, 1983).

This focus on the Other ties together a number of themes of modern social theory in a way which directly links epistemological concerns to matters of discourse and power. The formulation of the (separated) object of study is central to epistemological structures which are deeply rooted relations of power expressed, mediated and reproduced in and through discourses riddled with dualistic structures, each of which has hierarchial arrangements of terms which privilege certain forms of practice. As will be elaborated further, these formulations of identity and difference are funda-mental to the structuring of the state system, the essential political category of modernity. Thus, the formulation of fundamental categories of identity and difference structure political life according to difference defined principally in the categories of space and time.

The Other: time, space, geopolitics

As Kemp (1984) argues, the theme of the Other provides a key to understanding Foucault's work. Thus we find in the preface to Foucault's *The Order of Things* a clear statement of the role of the Other in his conceptualization of 'madness', a study which investigated 'the way in which a culture can determine in a massive, general form the difference that limits it' (Foucault, 1973, xxiv). Thus:

> The history of madness would be the history of the Other – of that which, for a given culture, is at once interior and foreign, therefore to be excluded (so as to exorcise the interior danger) but by being shut away (in order to reduce its otherness); whereas the history of order imposed on things would be the history of the Same – of that which, for a given culture, is both dispersed and related, therefore to be distinguished by kinds and to be collected together into identities. [Foucault, 1973, xxiv]

The spatial dimension of Otherness is clear in these phrases. The Other inhabits somewhere else.

The notion of distance in space can be relatively simple and somewhat arbitrary. As Said (1979, 54) puts it:

> this universal practice of designating in one's mind a familiar space which is 'ours' and an unfamiliar space beyond 'ours' which is 'theirs' is a way of making geographical distinctions that can be entirely arbitrary. I use the word 'arbitrary' here because imaginative geography of the 'our land – barbarian land' variety does not require that the barbarians acknowledge the distinction. It is enough for 'us' to set up these boundaries in our own minds; 'they' become 'they' accordingly, and both their territory and their mentality are designated as different from 'ours'.

Identity can be formulated in a negative sense, 'we' are not 'barbarians', hence we are 'civilized'. This theme is present in numerous texts which situate themselves in a spatial arrangement to identify their space in distinction from the space of their object.

Thus, as deCerteau writes of Montaigne's essay 'Of Cannibals' he examines questions of '. . . the status of the strange: Who is "barbarian"? What is a "savage"? In short, what is the place of the other?' (1986, 67). This relationship of text to space is complicated and multi-dimensional:

> One the one hand, the text accomplishes a spatialising operation which results in the determination or displacement of the boundaries delimiting cultural fields (the familiar vs the strange). In addition, it reworks the spatial divisions which underlie and organise a culture. For these socio- or ethno-cultural boundaries to be changed, reinforced, or disrupted, a space of interplay is needed, one that establishes the text's difference, makes possible its operations and gives it 'credibility' in the eyes of the readers, by distinguishing it both from the conditions within which it arose (the context) and from its object (the content). Montaigne's essay functions both as an *Index locorum* (a redistribution of cultural space) and as an affirmation of a place (a locus of utterance). These two aspects are only formally distinguishable, because it is in fact the text's re-working of space that simultaneously produces the space of the text. [deCerteau, 1986, 67–8]

Hence the question of the Other raises fundamental epistemological issues. Many scholarly investigations are premised on formulations of difference which have important implications for the study of social phenomena. How the object is defined as Other in the search for an 'objective' methodology is crucial to social theory. Indeed it goes deeper. The very formulation of an 'object' of study is an exercise in the formulation of difference, a setting apart, deferment, and ultimately a technique which establishes a relationship of power by the knower over the known (Berman, 1984). In terms of the positivist conception of science, it gives the knower power over the known by providing the knower with predictive knowledge and the tools of manipulation and control that flow from that knowledge (Matson, 1966).

In tackling the formation of the Other one inevitably tangles with the central role of dichotomizing and dualism in social theory, and in particular debate is enmeshed in specific conceptions of space and time. In historiography the Other, in this case, is formulated in terms of time.

> Historiography, . . . is based on a clean break between the past and the present. It is the product of relations of knowledge and power linking supposedly distinct domains: on the one hand, there is the present (scientific, professional, social) place of work, the technical and conceptual apparatus of *inquiry* and interpretation, and the operation of describing and/or explaining; on the other hand there are places (museums, archives, libraries) where the materials forming the object of this research are kept and secondarily, set off in time, there are the past systems of *events* to which these materials give analysis access. [deCerteau 1986, 3]

There is thus a line separating the institution and the researcher from that which is researched. There is a *difference* between them 'established out of principle by a will to objectivity' (1986, 3). The space thus constructed separates its 'own' in terms of the present of historiography from the 'Other' which is 'its' past under study. The Other is portrayed as different because it is distant in time.

Time is important in how anthropoloy has constructed its object of study, its Other in ways that ensure the domination of the observer, the Western academic, over the observed, the 'primitive' non-Westerner (Fabian, 1983). In part it has done this by using theories of evolution, often graphically illustrated in terms of dendritic diagrams, which have built in hierarchial arrangements presented in spatialized terms. Thus non-Western peoples are distanced by being both earlier on the time path of 'progress' and also several categories distant in the cultural hierarchy in which the researcher's culture is, of course, at the top. But a simple displacement in time does not complete this relationship. Space is also important, and a particular understanding of space is implicit in Western social and political theory.

Gross (1981–2) argues that the development of many facets of societal existence has led to a radical spatialization of culture in modern capitalism. The rational mind is seen as spatial; the intuitive as temporal. The triumph of the spatial over the temporal is easily seen in the terms used above where one talks of the 'distant' past. Technological modes of thinking are epitomized in Taylorist time and motion studies with their graphic (spatial) representations of motion. A pervasive culture industry emphasizes the immediate and decontextualizes its images in urban landscapes where location is geometric. All this suggests a spatial, and also a technological sensibility. Within Western societies conceptions of space are based on a particular naturalized, uniform Newtonian space (Smith, 1984). This conception of space is crucial to the emergence of modern notions of territorial sovereignty and the territorial state, which is the central political concept in the current political lexicon (Walker, 1984).

More generally Foucault focuses on the crucial links between space, knowledge and power, and the role of concepts with a geographical dimension: 'Territory is no doubt a geographical notion, but its first of all a juridico-political one: the area controlled by a certain kind of power' (Faucault, 1980, 68). But he is prepared to take this much further and link it to his epistemological concerns:

> Once knowledge can be analysed in terms of region, domain, implantation, displacement, transposition, one is able to capture the process by which knowledge functions as a form of power and disseminates the effects of power. There is an administration of knowledge, a politics of knowledge, relations of power which pass via knowledge and which, if one tries to transcribe them lead one to consider forms of domination designated by such notions as field, region, territory. [Foucault, 1980, 69]

He develops these thoughts further in response to additional questions posed by French geographers leading him to conclude that geopolitical concerns are very similar to his own work, although often not explicitly so:

> The longer I continue, the more it seems to me that the formation of discourses and the genealogy of knowledge need to be analysed, not in terms of types of consciousness, modes of perception and forms of ideology, but in terms of tactics and strategies of power. Tactics and strategies deployed through implantations, distributions, demarcations, control of territories and organisations of domains which could well make up a sort of geopolitics where my preoccupations would link up with your methods. [Foucault, 1980, 77]

Combining these themes from Foucault provides a way of theorizing the ideological dimension of geopolitics.

The exclusion of the Other and the inclusion, incorporation and administration of the Same is the essential geopolitical moment. The two processes are complementary; the Other is excluded as the reverse side of the process of incorporation of the Same. Expressed in terms of space and power, this is the basic process of geopolitics in which territory is divided, contested and ruled. The ideological dimension is clearly present in how this is justified and explained and understood by the populations concerned; 'the Other' is seen as different if not an enemy. 'We' are 'the same' in that we are all citizens of the same nation, speak a similar language, share a culture. This theme repeatedly recurs in political discourse where others are portrayed as different and as threats; it is geopolitical discourse.

The Other and world order

These geopolitical processes of cultural dichotomizing, designating identity in distinction from Others, are important in the ways world orders are constructed (Said, 1979; Mazrui, 1984). 'Occident' is contrasted to 'Orient'; 'Christian' to 'aethist'; 'developed' to 'underdeveloped', 'democracy' to 'communism' or 'totalitarianism'. Dichotomies of this kind are relationships of power: thus 'we' are strong, 'they' are weak; 'we' are good, 'they' are evil. This process is in part offset by universalistic tendencies, although these too are often seen in dichotomous terms. Thus, for example, the universalizing principle of Christianity is often interpreted as an attempt to change all 'others' into extensions of 'we'. Here difference is subsumed under the original identity that defined it. The privileged unity is once more imposed; difference is subsumed.

The complexities of intercultural analysis as they appear in international relations literature are beyond this study (see Walker ed., 1984) but the themes of culture and discursive creations of Others are very important. Thus Nandy (1980, 1983, 1984) has investigated the cultural dimensions of colonialism and identity in a number of studies focusing in particular on the Indian subcontinent and how identities are developed in political contexts. The ambivalent reactions and re-interpretations of cultural identities under political domination is a central theme of this work in cultural psychology. He extends these themes in a critique of the ideology of adulthood which links the ideology of colonial domination to the portrayal of the colonized, in this case 'the Other', as infantile and hence inferior and in need of domination and enforced 'education' (Nandy, 1984–5). This is a variation of the use of time as distance in the creation of the Other.

Mazrui (1984) traces the theme of cultural exclusivity through religious notions of monotheism, focusing on Christianity and Islam. He shows also how these notions of cultural difference have been adapted and underlie ideas of development and specifically the role of technology in international relations between North and South. Vincent (1984) has investigated the important role of race in the expansion of European society. JanMohammed (1985) explores the theme of racial difference in colonial literature. Doctrines of racial superiority were endemic in the nineteenth century, providing support for the cause of colonization while also legitimating atrocities against indigenous peoples who were portrayed as less than fully human (Kiernan, 1972). The legacy of these themes remain in racism.

The discipline of anthropology has wrestled with these problems in terms of ethnocentrism in the last two decades, its practitioners alerted to the use of their work to destroy the cultures that they had studied particularly in South-East Asia. The theoretical issues remain important in attempting to come to terms with how anthropology has created its object in terms of assumptions and patterns inherited from the culture of its origin (Sahlins, 1972; Wiarda, 1981). Questions of ideology and the role of anthropology in the process of colonialism have been raised (Asad, 1979) drawing in questions of social structure and the analysis of discourse. Fabian (1983) focuses on the importance of the conception of time in the creation of the Other in anthropology, showing how the evolutionary preoccupations of anthropology allows 'primitive' people to be viewed as inherently inferior to Western culture.

Wolf (1982) has attempted to use the emergence of this critical anthropological sensibility to support his ambitious rewriting of the history of European imperialism. Taking as a point of departure the tendency to 'name' other cultures and deprive them of their history in writing ethnocentric 'universal' histories based on Eurocentric preoccupations, he draws attention to the process of dehumanization of 'different' peoples on a political level. The essence of this matter of Anthropology, Otherness and epistemology is neatly summarized by Paul Riesman thus:

> Our social sciences generally treat the culture and knowledge of other peoples as forms and structures necessary for human life that those people have developed and imposed upon a reality which we know – or at least our scientists know – better than they do. We can therefore study those forms in relation to 'reality' and measure how well or ill they are adapted to it. In their studies of the cultures of other people, even those anthropologists who sincerely love the people they study, almost never think that they are learning something about the way the world really is. Rather they conceive of themselves as finding out what other people's conceptions of the world are. [Riesmann, 1976, 52]

Increasingly that reality from which the anthropologists come is defined in technological terms and the dichotomy of 'the West and the Rest' is understood in the language of modernization and technology transfer (Mazrui, 1984). The ideology of progress has in part replaced by the ideology of technological mastery (Gross, 1981–2). Technological mastery is combined with the enclosure of designated territories in terms of 'private' property and the formal sovereignty of states in the process of 'modernization' whereby capitalism expands (Smith, 1978); technological control involves the incorporation of control over space. As Mandel puts it (1975, 501): 'belief in the omnipotence of technology is the specific form of bourgeois ideology in late capitalism'. Development is discussed in terms of technology transfer, a process of universalizing modernity, absorbing the Other by extending identity, understood in terms of industrial capitalism and the political arrangements of the nation state.

Europeans and others

The single study which most comprehensively incorporates the themes of knowledge and power as they relate to a discourse on the Other is Edward Said's *Orientalism* (1979). It will be discussed in some detail here as it provides a concrete example of the interlinkage of these themes. The notion of the Orient is '. . . one of Europe's deepest and most recurring images of the Other. In addition the Orient has helped to define Europe (or the West) as its contrasting image, idea, personality, experience' (1979, 1–2). But for Said it is not simply a matter of ideas and images:

> The Orient is an integral part of European *material* civilisation and culture. Orientalism expresses and represents that part culturally and even ideologically as a mode of discourse with supporting institutions, vocabulary, scholarship, imagery, doctrines, even colonial bureaucracies and colonial styles. [Said, 1979, 2]

Its most fundamental assumption is the basic idea of an East–West dichotomy. 'Orientalism is a style of thought based upon an ontological and epistemological distinction made between "the Orient" and (most of the time) "the Occident" ' (1979, 2). Orientalism is incorporated in the arena of popular culture as well as academic scholarship.

But much more than an idea or set of images, it is a series of practices and institutions which have power. Orientalism is a 'Western style for dominating, restructuring, and having authority over the Orient' (Said, 1979, 3). This focus on knowledge as power is a key component of Said's analysis. 'Orientalism is implicitly and from the beginning a discourse of power that characterised a particular set of social, economic and political relations between Europe and its colonies' (Mani and Frankenberg, 1985, 177). It is the combination of the three themes of power, knowledge and historical specificity drawn from an amalgam of the works of Faucault (1972, 1973), Gramsci (1971) and Raymond Williams (1973, 1977) that gives Said's work its strength.

Said offers a book that is structured around the themes of Orientalism as a project of domination, as an epistemological and ontological creation and part of material culture, but without a more explicitly worked out methodological project. On a few points, however, Said is fairly clear. First is the centrality of the notion of discourse as used by Michel Foucault. He contends

> that without examining Orientalism as a discourse one cannot possibly understand the enormously systematic discipline by which European culture was able to manage – and even produce – the Orient politically, sociologically, militarily, ideologically, scientifically, and imaginatively during the post-Enlightenment period. [Said, 1979, 3]

The network of interests brought to bear whenever the term 'Orient' appears is the principal subject of Said's text. The subsidiary theme 'tries to show that European culture gained in strength and identity by setting itself off against the Orient as a sort of surrogate and even underground self' (1979, 3).

Said premises his analysis on a number of historical generalizations. He starts with the assumption that the Orient is not an inert entity that is simply 'there'. Using Vico's assertion that men make history, and can know what they have made, Said extends it to geography: '. . . as both geographical and cultural entities – to say nothing of historical entities – such locales, regions, geographical sectors as "Orient" and "Occident" are man-made' (Said, 1979, 5). In this sense Said is concerned with the creation of the discourse of Orientalism, rather than concerned with the correspondence of the Orient with the views of it constructed by Orientalism. This theme of the creation of the Other is important for this book, it is crucial to at all times treat the conceptual categories of identity and difference as contingent *productions*, not as ontologically given categories.

Second, Said is concerned with the configurations of power which shaped the Orientalist discourse. This took place within an overall European hegemony. 'The Orient was Orientalised not only because it was discovered to be "Oriental" in all those ways considered commonplace by an average nineteenth century European, but also because it *could be* – that is, submitted to being – *made* Oriental' (1979, 5–6). Further, it is important not to treat the structure of Orientalism simply as a tissue of lies and myths that can be 'blown away'. Thus it is a created body of theory and practice which has maintained itself for generations in the academies of the West. It is the hegemony of Europe that has given Orientalism its strength and durability. This ascendency of European culture is buttressed by its own structure, the principal component of which is '. . . the idea of European identity as a superior one in comparison with all non-European peoples and cultures' (1979, 7).

Where Said looks East from Europe to the construction of the Orient, Todorov (1984) looks West to *The Conquest of America* by the Spaniards. His analysis is on a smaller scale than Said's but his concerns are similar. Following Levinas's (1969) analysis of the theme of the Other in terms of 'Alterity', Todorov makes the question of the Other the key methodological device for his investigation of how a number of leading European explorers and conquerers constructed the ontological and epistemological categories that facilitated their conquest and domination of the indigenous civilizations of the Americas.

His analysis of Columbus's writings presents a series of discursive practices that he argues (1984, 42) are applicable to much of the colonial experience:

> Either he conceives the Indians (though not without using these words) as human beings altogether, having the same rights as himself; but then he sees them not only as equals but also as identical, and this behaviour leads to assimilationism, the projection of his own values on the others. Or else he starts from the difference, but the latter is immediately translated into terms of superiority and inferiority (in his case, obviously, it is the Indians who are inferior). What is denied is the existence of a human substance truly other, something capable of being not merely an imperfect state of oneself. [Todorov, 1984, 42]

Each of these positions is '. . . grounded in egocentrism, in identification of our own values with values in general, of our I with the universe – in the conviction that the world is one' (1984, 42–3). This metaphysical assumption of a single world is crucial in the whole identity/difference formulation. It relates to the comments of Derrida's critique of Western metaphysics as structured around being as presence, the superiority in the categorical frameworks of numerous discourses of the immediate over the distant. It is crucial because it recurs repeatedly in ways that ultimately privilege unity over difference, requiring the Other to be assimilated, subdued, overcome; ultimately in some manner reduceable to the terms of the identity of the point of origin.

The results of these metaphysical conceptions of a single universe identified with the European, was the creation of the Other on the one hand to be assimilated in terms of Christianizing equals, and on the other simultaneously to be dominated and economically exploited on the basis of the European being superior to the Indian. This points to the complexity of the construction of the Other, it is rarely constructed along a single axis, Todorov suggests that there are at least three axes on which the Other is constructed:

> First of all, there is the value judgement (an axiological level): the other is good or bad, I love or do not love him, or as was more likely to be said at the time, he is my equal or my inferior (for there is usually no question that I am good and that I esteem myself). Secondly, there is the action of rapproachment or distancing in relation to the other (a praxeological level): I embrace the other's values, I identify myself with him; or else I identify the other with myself, I impose my own image upon him; between submission to the other and the other's submission, there is also a third term, which is neutrality or indifference. Thirdly, I know or am ignorant of the other's identity (this would be the epistemic level); of course there is no absolute here, but an endless gradation between the lower or higher states of knowledge. [Todorov, 1984, 185]

Todorov argues that these three levels are interconnected but there is '. . . no rigorous *implication*; hence, we cannot reduce them to one another, nor anticipate one starting from the other' (Todorov, 1984, 185). Thus conquest, love and knowledge are viewed as the autonomous elementary forms of conduct. These three themes then provide a more explicit framework for investigating the Other than that provided by Said (1979), although they are clearly present in his work. Todorov's analysis is important in that it once again shows how identity creates difference, we create the Other in specific discursive practices which structure our behaviour towards the Other in specific ways.

Otherness and US geopolitical discourse

Shapiro (1988) brings many of the themes discussed here together. In a chapter entitled 'The Constitution of the Central American Other: the Case of "Guatemala" ' he starts with Todorov's (1984) analysis because Todorov shows that 'Central America in general and Guatemala in particular were not so much discovered as imaginatively preconstituted by the Spanish Conquistadors' (Shapiro, 1988, 89). Shapiro's concern is to show that a similar mentality underlies US foreign policy in the 1980s. He focuses on the discursive practices of foreign policy-making which support the export of US capital and emphasizes 'the modes of representation abeting this widely orchestrated form of domination by making it acceptable and coherent within the dominant ethos that constructs domestic selves and exotic Others' (Shapiro, 1988, 90).

Not all Shapiro's analysis can be summarized here, but a number of crucial points are of direct relevance to this study, on the theme of how discourses of Otherness are constructed. First, Shapiro notes that foreign policy specialists and academic analysts in the USA usually use similar discursive practices. Second, Shapiro notes how the foreign policy discourse depluralizes and dehistoricizes Guatemalan 'society' by reducing it to a 'fact' where those who lose in political struggles tend to be ignored in the political code. Guatemala was formerly created in Spain's expansion, now it is meaningful in terms of superpower rivalry, never is it understood in the terms of the original inhabitants whose place it once was:

> The geographic 'knowledge' we invoke in our naming helps, in Foucault's terms to put into circulation the tactics and strategies involved in the 'demarcations' and 'control of territories'. Thus, to the extent that one accepts and unreflectively reproduces the security orientated geopolitical discursive practice, one engages in implicit acts of recognition of the existing power and authority configurations. [Shapiro, 1988, 93]

These authority configurations are often difficult to spot because they appear as unproblematic descriptions. Thus we have to examine the terms of descriptions, in particular being sensitive to the representational practices of cartography which designates specific bounded territories, and in the process renders a political creation 'natural', 'delivering up the discursive territory within which legitimate speech about bounded areas can occur' (Shapiro, 1988, 93). Thus the question of who imposes meanings on space is crucial. In O'Tuathail's (1988) terms this 'geo-graphing' is a fundamentally political act. Thus 'Guatemala' in particular and the international system in general 'are parts of a system that has been conjured up in policy-related speech practices over the centuries' (Shapiro, 1988, 95). The point is that these are historic creations; they could have been otherwise.

It is precisely this point that is crucial in the development of a critical theory of geopolitics. This is the investigation of how a particular set of practices comes to be dominant and excludes other sets of practices. Where conventional discourse simply accepts the current circumstances as given, 'naturalized', a critical theory asks questions of how they came to be as they are. But this acceptance of things as they are renders states as static geographic entities rather than as active processes and practices; through this reification the USA becomes a static geographic entity, not the violent conquerer of indigenous peoples. 'The dominant representational practice within which we have a political grasp of the international system is one that sharpens boundaries, national boundaries in this case' (Shapiro, 1988, 98). Hence the 'scientific code' of foreign policy discourse in these areas talks of an 'international environment' providing 'opportunities' for 'management', in a series of practices that act to 'de-narrativize' the discourse. Foreign policy portrays distant places in specific ways through its constitution of Otherness. Foreign policy thus '. . . is the process of making 'foreign' or exotic, and thus different from the self, someone or thing. Given the usual esteem within which the self is constituted, the exoticizing of the Other almost invariably amounts to the constitution of that Other as a less than equal subject' (Shapiro, 1988, 100).

But the creation of Other in distinction from Self, can, as Todorov (1984) points out, be constructed on more than one axis. Thus the construction of Self and Other in moral terms is coupled to the discursive practices of foreign policy-making ('the policy of making foreign') which constitute the international arena as one concerned with power and crucially 'security'. As will be discussed in detail in the next two chapters, political identity in the USA in particular, and more generally the Western world, has constructed political discourse in terms of 'security' or 'national security' and the pursuit of the 'national interest' since the Second World War:

> The making of Other as something foreign is thus not an innocent exercise in differentiation. It is clearly linked to how the self is understood. A self construed with a security-related identity leads to the construction of Otherness on the axis of threats or lack of threats to that security, while a self identified as one engaged in 'crisis management' – a current self-understanding of American foreign policy thinking – will create modes of Otherness on a ruly versus unruly axis. [Shapiro, 1988, 101–2]

Coupling the moral superiority dimension of Otherness to the geopolitical/ security ones 'the foreign policy discourse as a whole becomes a vindication for the US intervention to seek to control another state's steering mechanism for its own moral benefit as well as for purposes of US strategic and domestic interests (Shapiro, 1988, 115).

The security codes also require information to operate, if the Other is potentially a threat then, as was noted above with regard to Foucault and the discourses of madness and criminality, surveillance is necessary, for this covert operations and spying are legitimated. But the construction of Otherness in the Guatemalan case goes further than this. Thus the Kissinger (1984) report on US foreign policy in Central America draws Latin America as a 'rough draft' (Shapiro, 1988, 118) of the US bourgeois culture, an Other which is nearly the same. It suggests that with further economic development it will emerge as the same as US bourgeois society. This move allows the attribution of any 'revolutionary ideas' to 'outside interference' and hence provides the legitimation for intervention and intense surveillance.

This outside interference can come only from across the geopolitical divide, in terms of the USSR and Cuba. The geopolitical dimension thus structures the discourse on Latin America, precisely because of the specification of Otherness as nearly 'like us', but not quite. 'To show *how* such a discourse works requires the assumption that the world does not issue a summons to speak in a particular way but rather that ways of speaking are implicating in world-making' (Shapiro, 1988, 123). Geopolitical discourse constructs worlds in terms of Self and Others, in terms of cartographically specifiable sections of political spaces, and in terms of military threats.

Chapter 3

Security and geopolitics

Political theory, states and security

The geopolitical threat to the USA from the USSR draws on the formulation of that threat as a danger to the preservation of 'national security'. The concept of security is central in international relations although rarely given the detailed theoretical treatment it needs (Buzan, 1983, 1984; Walker, 1988a). The roots of the current literature on international politics and security can be traced from the writings of thinkers like Nicolo Machiavelli who marked the emergence of what, in hindsight, is constructed as the modern political tradition (Walker, 1989). Writing in the early sixteenth century, he marks in many ways the transition from medieval cosmology premised on divine planning and the ultimate compatibility of human actions to a recognition of the new state of affairs in the era in which feudalism gave way to a nascent capitalism, and in which new political arrangements finally transcended the putative authority of the emperor.

These political arrangements were finally codified later in the treaties of Westphalia of the mid-seventeenth century which are often taken as the beginning of the modern political system of international relations. The twin developments – of the emergence of capitalism and the closure of political space – mark the beginning of the 'modern' era which has spread both its dominant political organization; i.e. the nation state, and the interrelated economic organizations of capitalism across the globe (Anderson, 1974; Smith, 1984). This form of the closure of political space in terms of territorially defined states is very important. It involves simultaneously the territorial demarcation of political space within identifiable boundaries and the extension of the concept of sovereignty to one of absolute power, the creation of an international anarchy, in the sense that there is no higher recognized and accepted authority with the power to enforce its will. There remain transnational institutions, religious, commercial and political, but the state is empowered with final authority over matters within its boundaries. Repeated efforts have been made to establish regimes of international law to be observed by all, but, so the argument goes, the related collective security regimes are usually vulnerable to the unilateral operation of national sovereignty. Of course, it never in fact operates quite this neatly, but the rationale of sovereignty is deeply structured into political arrangements.

The centralization of political power in a territorially delimited state was a dramatic change in political organization. Before the emergence of this 'modern' system, codified, as noted above, in the mid-seventeenth century, there had been a multiplicity of authorities, lords and chieftains, bishops and cardinals, cities and empires. The feudal landscape was one of many overlapping claims to allegiance, claims not solely related to the territory that the subject of these claims inhabited. The rise of capitalism and the rise of the modern state with absolute sovereignty were accompanied by the rise of political conceptions based on the individual rather than social collectivities. They also related to the individual as a resident of a particular place. This combination of occurances gave rise to the modern bourgeois notions of citizenship, the state and property, the key structuring concepts of political discourse, of which the state is predominant.

Its intellectual formulation is traceable most clearly to the seventeenth-century political theories of Thomas Hobbes (1968) (original publication 1651) and it relies on a very specific formulation of political theory in terms of isolated human 'individuals' related to each other in terms of contracts. The formation of states is seen in terms of the rational individual trading some of his freedom of action to the supra individual state in return for a guarantee of protection from threats external to the state boundaries, and the regulation of internal matters to maintain order. In Hobbes's terms order means the protection of the rights of owners of property to maintain their possessions.

Within this order the quintessential bourgeois human can then act to maximize his self-interest. It follows from this conception of humans (in fact men) as individuals living within the reification of space of private property at the small scale, and the territorial delimitation of sovereignty, that security is defined in spatial terms of exclusion; enemies are created as Others, inhabiting some other territory. States are thus a form of political container, within which the state provides security. Thus the contract theory of the state relates directly to the creation of Otherness and the political creation of the identities of Self in terms of the state on whose territory one exists.

But this conception of security, and notions of peace, are defined in negative terms. 'Peace as a contract is a right that never becomes a duty – a law that never becomes a moral obligation' (Paggi and Pinzauti, 1985, 6). International politics is thus defined in negative terms. The sphere of diplomacy and inter-state relations is the sphere of state activity; responsibility is designated to the state to defend against other states and dangers from beyond the boundaries of the state. Constituted authority becomes the arbiter of good and evil; a threat is such because it is so designated by the state. Many theories of politics 'have sought to limit sovereignty but have not questioned this authoritarian mechanism resulting from the connection between property, the corresponding system of rights, and political guarantees necessary for their maintainance' (Paggi and Pinzauti, 1985, 7). But this state of affairs requires that the state identify with the interests of the population it supposedly protects. The ideological guise that this identification usually takes is some form of nationalism, whereby the citizens of the state are distinguished as having a common identity (Anderson, 1983; Munck, 1986).

Since the Second World War these conceptions have been complicated by the predominant clash of two social systems, both claiming legitimacy in terms of inevitable historical progress, or the dialectical unfolding of history, and armed with weapons systems that threaten not only the security of each other's state structures but the very existence of humanity itself. Here, however, the negative pattern of security thinking still operates. Otherness is mobilized to support domestic control and progress. The contest between the cultural modernism of the US hegemony or the 'counter modernity' (Klein, 1986) of the Soviet system remains tied into the bourgeois reification of political space in terms of territorial inclusion and exclusion. Identity is still privileged over difference; in Shapiro's (1988) terms foreign policy still involves making foreign, only the scale has now changed.

These divisions of space in turn are predicated on the Newtonian view of absolute space, a view which is related to Gross's (1981–2) analysis of the spatialization of culture discussed in the last chapter. The Newtonian departure theorizes space as apart from matter, a pre-given existence, parts of which are filled with matter. This requires a clean break with earlier conceptions of space which are related in some way to material events (Smith, 1984, 67). Newton theorized a secondary conception of relative space that was related to material events. But absolute space is constructed as the pre-given container of all events which can be designated a position in absolute space. Absolute space receives epistemological primacy, defined as true, relative space, is merely apparent. Space is made into a thing in itself, in Smith's (1984, 70) terms, 'an abstraction of abstractions'.

The primacy of this metaphysical construction is crucial to the construction of the space of states. They are understood as spatial entities, the societies of which they are composed are contained within their boundaries. This privileging of the geometric entity over the real societal practices of the region is based on the spatialization of culture, premised on the epistemologically privileged conception of absolute space. As Shapiro (1988) reminds us, the cartographical designation of states as geometric entities with precisely definable boundaries hypostatizes states and denies large parts of social reality. This discursive practice of reification is crucial to the operation of international relations theory and in particular to geopolitics. But these reifications are historical products, not the universal structures of absolute space in which they are construed.

This whole series of conceptualizations is related to the positivist preoccupations of social science with understanding social phenomena in mechanical terms and in terms of economic commodities (Ashley, 1983, 1984). Thus, international relations are discussed in terms of physics metaphors of equilibrium, dynamics and power. The relationships between mechanics and the commodity form are not accidental. As Sohn Rethel (1978) has argued, the production of abstract space and the development of the commodity form in capitalism are interrelated. The implications of these discursive practices will be expanded below; they structure the discourses of international relations and most obviously nuclear strategy.

Geopolitics, space and power

The relations of space and power are the central theme of discussions of geopolitics, although the term itself presents a multiplicity of meanings, many of which are not spelt out in the numerous texts that use the term. In addition to the relations of space and power, it also refers to superpower rivalry and to the geographical aspects of international relations. It is sometimes equated with the term 'power politics', and it also involves the ability of military technology to traverse territory. The term geopolitics thus has many meanings, often merging one into another, but all have in common a general concern with the interrelationships of space and power. As Brunn and Mingst (1985) make clear, providing a clear definition of the term g 'opolitics is probably impossible; but many authors have tried none the less. McColl (1983, 284) suggests that the term geopolitics '. . . simply refers to geographic factors that lie behind political decisions'. The historical meaning of the term derived from Ratzel's early conceptions of political geography is tied into debates about geographical determinism and geographical 'influences' (Kristof, 1960; Peet, 1985). Sprout (1968, 121) suggests that the term geopolitics can 'denote the areal aspect of any political pattern' and that it can be applied to 'hypotheses that purport to explain or to predict areal distributions and patterns of political potential in the society of nations'.

Thus 'Geopolitics is concerned with the conditions of "order" in a world of sovereign states' (Falk, 1983, 106). This 'order' '. . . has been largely created and sustained by the role great powers have played outside their territories. Thus the geopolitical perspective emphasises inequalities among states, zones of domination, patterns of intervention and penetration, alliances, conflict formations, and the role of military force' (Falk, 1983, 106–7). This conception of order is often in conflict with the notions of order in international law and the normative expressions of international relations theory and the theory of security outlined in the last section. International law is premised on the principles of territorial sovereignty, the state as the sole subject of the system, the equality of states, non-intervention and the right of self-defence. Geopolitics also refers to matters of power politics; the finer points of international etiquette are often ignored in the struggle for power and influence between major powers.

Geopolitics is intimately tied into questions of technology. Power over territory requires some ability to traverse the terrain and if necessary fight for control over it. While some have argued that distance is no longer a factor (Bunge, 1988; Wohlstetter, 1968) and it is clear that technological changes including the ultilization of space have drastically altered military matters (Deudney, 1983), in international affairs the impact of geography on superpower behaviour is still a factor for consideration (Pepper and Jenkins, 1984). Collins (1981) argues that the old geopolitical notions of the importance of land remain valid because the modern high-tech weapons, in particular nuclear weapons, are instruments of obliteration and destruction not weapons which allow their possessors to control territory. Ultimately land provides the bases and resources on which power is built and the logistical complications of friction of distance remain (O'Sullivan, 1986). As O'Sullivan remarks (1985, 30): 'The heavy cost involved in long military supply lines was clear in the Falklands dispute and is the key issue in the why and wherefore of the US Rapid Deployment Force.'

Taylor (1985, 36) distinguishes between imperialism, the dominance relation of major powers over peripheral states, and geopolitics viewed as the rivalry of major powers. Thus the term geopolitical is used as a synonymn for international superpower rivalry. This practice of geopolitics tends to reduce the complexity of the world into a bi-polar competition between the superpowers and obscures the importance of distance in providing security. As O'Sullivan (1985, 29) puts it: 'The received wisdom in matters geopolitical reduces human intercourse to a two sided fight. The maps of Mackinder and his successors are invariably of two classes of territory with a no-man's land between them.' Thus we read the following in *Foreign Affairs*, the leading journal of US foreign policy discussion and debate:

> Geopolitics is, definitionally, the art and the process of managing global rivalry; and success, again definitionally consists at a minimum of consolidating the strength and cohesion of the group of nations which form the core of one's power position, while preventing the other side from extending the area of its domination and clientele. [Jay, 1979, 486]

Geopolitical reasoning of this sort ignores the regional complexities and the geographical circumstances of global affairs and uses a grossly oversimplified metaphor to portray a crude geographic model.

One of the most common geopolitical concepts in the Cold War is that of 'dominoes'. The argument has repeatedly been used to legitimize US intervention in conflicts around the globe on the assumption that 'communism' is a phenomenon that spreads from one area to adjacent territories (O'Sullivan, 1982). Thus when one domino 'falls' (to the communists) it threatens the next adjacent country. Some variations (see Cohen, 1963) complicate this picture introducing minor poles and a complicated series of minor power struggles with 'shatterbelts' interposed between them. In a major textbook DeBlij (1981) credits the domino effect with substantial explanatory power. The domino argument is all based on the assumption that the world is a bi-polar political arrangement where one 'side' is either expanding or shrinking its 'sphere of influence'.

This consideration of geopolitics as global superpower rivalry leads the discussion into a consideration of the classical geopolitical texts. In the works of Mahan, Mackinder and later Spykman these concepts relate to the recurrent themes of the conflict of land power and sea power in British and subsequently US military thinking. In this sense Mackinder simply codified and rendered these themes into geographic language. None the less, by doing so he gave them a specific formulation, which has been repeatedly drawn on since, and one which is essential to the history of political geography, as well as to the understanding of US foreign policy, in particular to the formulation of containment militarism and the deterrence of perceived Soviet expansionism (Sloan, 1988).

Classical geopolitics

As Parker (1985) points out clearly, geopolitical thinking came on the scene at the time of the final closure of political space as the imperial powers of Europe carved up the remaining uncolonized world at the end of the nineteenth century. The geopolitical schemes of the various practitioners reflected their respective national preoccupations in detail but overall there were a number of common features.

First, in recognition of the facts of the final expansion of colonialism and the European state system (Bull and Watson eds, 1984) to enclose all the world's territory, the geopolitical vision of Mackinder encompassed the globe as a totality, all humanity as one, interconnected in one fate by a history shaped, if not quite determined by the facts of geography. The globe was viewed as a whole; the closed frontiers of the new colonies presented a series of new international relationships; humanity was a whole (Kearns, 1984). That was not to see different races and nationalities as in some manner being equal, just that their interconnectedness in the global order of things was realized.

Second, states were conceptualized in terms of organic entities with quasi-biological functioning. This was tied into Darwinian ideas of struggle producing progress. Thus, expansion was likened to growth and territorial expansion was *ipso facto* a good thing. This organicist metaphor was later to appear in the cruder Nazi versions of geopolitics and the argument that vigorous nations were justified in expanding and growing at the expense of less vigorous ones (Paterson, 1987).

Third, there were Victorian ideas of progress in terms of mastery of the physical world uneasily at times coexisting with the ambivalent streams of environmental determinism (see Peet, 1985) and the possibility of freedom of agency to shape the course of events. More generally before the First World War, the current European geopolitical vision linked the success of European civilization to a combination of temperate climate and access to the sea. Temperate climate encouraged the inhabitants to strugggle to overcome adversity without totally exhausting their energies, hence allowing progress and innovation to lead to social development. Access to the sea encouraged exploration, expansion and trade, and led ultimately to the conquest of the rest of the world (Parker, 1985).

The Darwinism of the pre-war days lost its appeal in the carnage of trench warfare. At least in British thinking the pre-war pessimism of the possibilities of the survival of European dominance was displaced by the historical theme of the victory of the maritime powers over continental powers, and the emphasis came to rest on attempts to maintain that recently reasserted supremacy. Parker (1985) argues that Lord Curzon's foreign policy was an attempt to apply his geopolitical ideas on the global stage by establishing a series of buffer zones to protect the British Empire from the encroachments of continental power. The French concerns with international politics emphasized the international diplomacy of the era of the League of Nations. The League as the institution maintaining the supremacy of the victorious powers was to become the target of the new *Geopolitik* of Karl Haushofer.

Some wartime commentaries on the role of *Geopolitik* credit Haushofer as the director of a Munich 'Institute fur Geopolitik'. This organization allegedly produced many tracts which gave support to the Nazi goals of territorial expansion. In the USA it was portrayed during the war as the source of a Nazi master plan for world domination (Sondern, 1941). Recent scholarship has concluded that the institute was a fiction of wartime propaganda and argues that Haushofer's ideas were often at odds with Nazi actions (Bassin, 1987; Heske, 1987; Paterson, 1987). This new world fascination with geopolitics has shaped US foreign policy in terms of theories of containment, doctrines of military strategy (Earle, 1944) and perhaps more indirectly the literature on extended nuclear deterrence ever since. In the last decade the term geopolitics is again in vogue and geopolitical rationales for US foreign policy are frequently invoked, following in part Kissinger's rehabilitation of the term, albeit in a rather different formulation than the classical texts (Hepple, 1986; Sloan, 1988).

The classical geopoliticians wrote with an audience of policy-makers and politicians in mind but did not limit their concerns solely to these people. Many of their ideas have been popularized and widely diseminated. They all wrote primarily for national audiences and in the hope of influencing national policies in ways that enhanced national, or more specifically, state power. Most had an imperial vision which portrayed national survival in terms of territorial expansion, and the development of colonies as a sign of national virility. Above all, geopolitics privileged the European state as the key factor in analysis. Individual states in turn were subsumed under a concern with the overall supremacy of the European, later 'Western', culture. The imperial theme and the rivalry between European powers are sometimes in conflict, but the overall superiority of 'civilization' is unquestioned. This theme in particular is one which has returned recently to geopolitical thinking.

An additional concern to classical geopolitics was the matter of access to resources. This raises the crucial point that the basis of European expansion lay in its technological achievements; its mastery of nature through the application of science gave it a putative superiority over other cultures. The resource question is an important theme in the revived interest in geopolitics in the last decade, reiterating the earlier concerns for access to resources to fuel European economies and their military machines. In its new guise it is concerned with security of oil supplies from the Middle East and minerals from Southern Africa in particular (Haglund, 1986; Krasner, 1978).

The specific dynamism of capitalism which propelled the expansion of European imperialism is not seen as central in either the original geopolitical writing or the new concerns. The national interest is, of course, identified with that of the ruling groups, all submerged in turn in the nation state. Internal political matters were not of significant concern precisely because the key term in the geopolitical lexicon is the state and it is understood in territorial not political terms. Increased power is to be attained by increased territorial acquisition, the conquest, or at least control, of territory is the key criteria for judging national power. Internal conditions are important in some circumstances, but often in terms of national psychological moods or national character rather than in terms of sociological analysis. Thus national will matters, the class structure of that nation is a minor concern, the nation is all, nationalism is the secular religion of the age (Anderson, 1983) and geopolitics is a favoured tool of ardent nationalism.

Geopolitics and containment

The USA rose to global predominance very rapidly in the Second World War. In its aftermath there followed major political debates as to what to do with this predominance, a debate which drew on the wartime thinking of a number of US intellectuals but which quickly became caught up in the emergent Cold War and the containment policy. A key text which emphasized the role of power in international affairs was Nicholas Spykman's *America's Strategy in World Politics* (1942). This was, as Hoffman (1977, 44) puts it, 'more a geopolitical treatise of the tradition of Admiral Mahan or Mackinder than a book about the principal characteristics of interstate politics'. His subsequent *Geography of the Peace* (1944) made the geopolitical theme even more explicit in a series of global maps of the possible configurations of power in the struggle for the Eurasian 'Rimlands' that he foresaw marking the post-war years.

This geopolitical dimension is not always clearly rendered in the 'security' discourses of containment militarism. There are several pertinent points here. First, the term geopolitics was tainted by the association with Nazism, and Haushofer in particular. Hence, there was some reluctance to use it (Kristoff, 1960). Geopolitics is thus associated with the cruder forms of *realpolitik*, and balance-of-power politics which were blamed for the repeated European wars which the USA became embroiled. In addition the territorial control focus, central to the geopolitical conception of power in spatial terms, is reminiscent of imperial policies which the idealist and moral exceptionalist tendencies in the US foreign policy discourse denigrated (Agnew, 1983). Explicitly talking of post-war politics in terms of geopolitics was thus, at least in the early Truman years, potentially politically risky. But as Deudney (1983), Walters (1974), Parker (1985), Sloan (1988) and Trofimenko (1986) make clear, the geopolitical understanding of international relations remains a powerful influence: it shapes the under-standing of the US 'national interest'. The doctrine of containment was explicitly formulated in spatial and territorial terms. If one understands hegemony as relating to the accepted, taken-for-granted elements of political organization, as suggested above, this makes sense.

The USA came to world predominence in the Second World War by military conquest (Ambrose, 1985). The Second World War was marked by the continuous front line and success in military campaigning was related to the conquest of territory. 'Liberation' from the Axis was a spatial process of the advance of US power, a process given frequent cartographical support in the popular press coverage of military actions. In the process of carto-graphically representing the military events whole new regions were created by the military operations (Emmerson, 1984). Coupling this understanding of the representation of US power in terms of the control of territory with the concerns in the post-war period with the necessity of preventing the possibility of a repeat of a Pearl Harbour type surprise attack led to the formulation of 'national security' in terms of forward military defence, understood in territorial terms. Thus the relations of space and power came to be understood in terms of distance providing security, influence requiring the military occupation of territory. Otherness was spatially constrained by containment.

Thus it can be argued that geopolitics did not lose favour simply because of the taints of Nazism, but rather that the spatial understanding of power became so commonly understood, i.e. hegemonic, that explicit reference to them in terms of geopolitics was simply irrelevant. Power was understood in terms of the filling of political spaces which are organized in specific territorial configurations. Hence Gaddis (1982) can discuss containment in terms of 'geopolitical codes', wherein political power is understood in spatial terms, but reject assumptions that Mackinder was the *direct* source of containment ideas.

In addition, the containment theme has more distant resonances in the recurrent theme of the balance of power in Europe (Blouet, 1987). This theme is important in the rationales provided for US intervention in international affairs, and the debates between the isolationists and the interventionists that permeate US diplomatic history (Williams, 1959; Agnew and O'Tuathail, 1987). Also involved in this traditional concern of US foreign policy is the idea of a 'Western Hemisphere' (Whitaker, 1954). Geographical considerations were important in the assessment of the threat posed to the USA by the rise of fascism in Europe; the argument for supporting Britain in particular was often related to the spread of fascist influence in Latin America in the late 1930s and early 1940s (Haglund, 1984).

Thus the 'silence' of geopolitics in the period of containment can be understood in the sense of it having a key structuring role rather than it disappearing from the stage as some histories of political geography suggest (Brunn and Minst, 1985; Hepple, 1986). In particular the key US military strategy textbook of the period is heavily influenced by geopolitical themes

(Earle, 1944). From this perspective there is no need to try to trace the details of the lineages of geopolitics from Mackinder to Kennan, links which cannot be found directly (Blouet, 1987). What is more important is that in its militarized versions containment was understood as geopolitical, even if reference to the geopolitical texts was not made.

Reinterpreting the historiography of geopolitics and containment in these terms requires an inquiry into the broader formulation of security rather than being limited to inquiring into the direct lineages of Mackinder or Spykman's writings. The point is that the policy of containment involves security defined in spatial terms. Mackinder is explicitly present in a few places, and usually implicitly present in discussions of containment and foreign policy, but an approach that limits itself to merely tracing these presences misses the essential point that security discourse is spatial.

Geopolitical discourse

The crucial theme here is the focus, in recent social and political theory as well as in recent geographical writing, on the active creation, or 'production' of space and place. Thus society is seen as active process, in the process of production by human practice, rather than as an abstract series of given 'natural' events or facts. Geographical space is produced, not 'given' naturally (Smith, 1984). Nation states are not natural entities but rather are politically produced territorial demarcations, a point often obscured by the cartographical representations of regional studies (Shapiro, 1988). Thus geopolitics can no longer be taken as a crude form of the geography of international relations, but has to be understood as practice, and as discourse. It involves the political production of geopolitical scripts, texts and procedures that create ways of describing and acting in the world political scene (O'Tuathail, 1988; Agnew and O'Tuathail, 1987).

Geopolitical 'scripting' or 'geo-graphing' is an ideological exercise which in the case of war or the preparation for war pits geographically delimited political organizations against one another. Images of places are crucial to geopolitical scripts. As Hewitt (1983, 253) puts it:

> War also mobilises the highly charged and dangerous dialectic of place attach-ment: the perceived antithesis of 'our' places and homeland and 'theirs'. Sustained in latent if not overt forms in peacetime, this polarisation has produced unbridled sentimentalising of one's own while dehumanising the enemy's people and land. That seems an essential step in cultivating readiness to destroy the latter and bear with progressive devastation at home.

These in turn involve discourses of the Other, how 'their' place is different from 'ours', and as such they operate to situate places in political space, creating other places in specific political relationships to 'our' place (Shapiro, 1988). Crucially the Other is the external threat against which internal identity is formulated.

With these specific delineations of space come political implications, how 'we' act in terms of 'our' geopolitically created knowledge of 'them'. How 'we' are identified is a direct product of how 'they' are differentiated. This is not just a matter of perception which can be compared against some objective knowledge of political reality, but the political creation of the terrain of political debate and crucially of action. Spatial relations are political constructions, and the practices of geopolitics are of central importance to the political construction of space. As such, geopolitical processes are plays of power, central to the hegemonic political discourses of the states and societies in which they occur.

Thus international politics relates directly to internal politics within the boundaries of, in the case considered in this book, the US state, and more broadly the 'Western System' (Klein, 1986). Traditional geopolitics, like the current CPD version, hypostatizes the state, treating states as autonomous spatially defined entities struggling with other similar entities in attempts to enlarge their power by increasing their control of territory. Geopolitics simultaneously concerns itself with the relations of geography to the conduct of international relations, in terms of the struggle for power, while also understanding the ideological role of such a discourse in the creation of external enemies and the related mobilization of domestic political constituencies against the boundary of that external antagonist.

This approach problematicizes the state, rather than taking it as a given; it treats the state as a politically constructed series of practices, including discursive practices, of which the geopolitical creation of Otherness is an important facet. This allows the consideration of the state, the predominant category in political discourse, as a relation of power in a contested political system where fundamental questions of the internal structure within a state are directly related to matters beyond the ambit of a single state. To problematicize the central category is to 'de-centre' the dominant discourses of politics and open up the discourses of politics to critical analysis. Thus political identity is separated from state identity, allowing a critical investigation of matters of state power which does not presuppose the existence of the state (Pasquinelli, 1986).

Here the argument links up with recent developments in international relations theory that are critical of the predominant themes in both the traditional 'realist' approaches and the crude economic interpretations of international affairs (Ashley, 1983, 1984). 'What one needs is a different conception of social reality, a conception which not only recognises the ultimate unity of what we term "political" and "economic", but recognises how this unity is signified and expressed in different human practices' (O'Tuathail, 1986, 83). This forces one to investigate the ideological dimension, not just in terms of 'perceptions' but in terms of how the institutions, in particular the foreign policy bureaucracy, what Barnet (1972) calls the 'national security managers' and the political 'foreign policy establishment' (Sanders, 1983), come to understand their roles.

This re-conceptualization posits geopolitics as discourse (Agnew and O'Tuathail, 1987; O'Tuathail, 1988). The analysis thus focuses attention on how these discourses are used in politics; it thus focuses on their 'discursive practices', or, in other words, how the discourse is constructed, and used. Here geopolitics is understood in terms of discursive practices, 'as part of a series of reasoning processes by which the intellectuals of statecraft constitute world politics and a world political geography' (Agnew and O'Tuathail, 1987, 5–6), and as 'an innately political process of representation by which these intellectuals of statecraft designate a world and "fill" it with certain dramas, subjects, histories and dilemmas' (Agnew and O'Tuathail, 1987, 8).

Put in these terms the central theme of this book is to examine the use of geopolitical reasoning in the discourses used to portray the USSR as a threat. It shows how 'their' place is constructed as different from 'our' place, and specifically how their place is constructed as threatening because of its geographical circumstances. In the CPD discourse on the Soviet threat, geopolitical themes were re-theorized and mobilized for use politically by welding them together with arguments about nuclear strategy, international relations and Soviet history to portray the USSR as a dangerous Other. The USSR was portrayed as different, threatening and crucially as threatening precisely because it was inherently geographically expansionist. The discourse of the Soviet threat thus provided the external antagonist against which domestic political identity was formulated and mobilized. 'They' are constituted as different, threatening, requiring 'us' to act in specific political ways, in this case to militarize international politics through a massive weapons building programme and an interventionist foreign policy.

This discourse of the Other is geopolitical in the sense that it creates an external (threatening) antagonist in a particular way *vis-à-vis* domestic political concerns. It is also geopolitical in that it is a particular exercise in geopolitical 'geo-graphing' which draws on the traditional texts of Mackinder and Spykman to explicate a particular geography of the Other, a geography which is interpreted in deterministic terms. This discourse of the Other is also geopolitical in the sense that it accepts the reification of political power in the particular relation of power and space of territorially defined states. In addition, this analysis shows how the overall logic of the discourse of the Other as constructed through texts on nuclear strategy, international relations and Soviet history is structured on the classic geopolitical conceptions of Spykman and Mackinder, a crucial point missing from other analyses of the CPD and of the Reagan administration foreign policy.

Chapter 4

Threat discourse

Containment militarism and the 'Soviet threat'

At the end of the Second World War the US military, economic and political capabilities were globally pre-eminent. Much of the rest of the world lay devastated; industrial production was seriously disrupted by wartime requirements, where not destroyed by military action. The political arrangements of the pre-war era were outdated by the emergence of Soviet and US military power. Major tasks of reconstruction had to be faced worldwide, and new political arangements devised under the shadow of the US possession of the atomic bomb. Within the USA itself numerous adjustments were made in defence postures and the bureaucratic administration of foreign policy was revamped as part of the demobilization process. Despite detailed planning during the war by the Council on Foreign Relations (CFR), in conjunction with the State Department (Shoup and Minter, 1977), there was no clear consensus on what role the USA was to play in the post-war world, and how the economic system was to be reconstructed. Some with isolationist tendencies were reluctant for the USA to play an active international role, but the Atlanticist and internationalist positions won out; US capital and military power were to dominate the post-war world.

Foreign policy-making in the USA is a complex process. The division of powers in the US state between executive and legislature is further complicated by the presence of powerful economic interests and more general interests reflected in the amorphous term 'public opinion'. The executive branch draws on unelected officials to staff the many policy-making positions. Hence, academics and more recently experts from the 'thinktanks' are drawn into the process to provide specialized knowledge in addition to the traditional source for the foreign policy 'elite' which has drawn heavily from east coast law firms and Wall Street banking firms. Of particular importance to the making of foreign policy towards the USSR is the presence in the USA of *émigré* intellectuals from the USSR and Eastern Europe (Nye, 1984). Many of these people hold very hostile views towards the USSR.

For most of this century the central institution for the formation and discussion of foreign policy was been the CFR, initially set up in the aftermath of the First World War 'to equip the United States of America for an imperial role on the world scene' (Shoup and Minter, 1977, 3). Perhaps best known for its journal *Foreign Affairs*, most high-level policy-makers have been members. Since the Second World War foreign policy has been intimately entangled with defence policy under the overall rubric of 'national security' (Smoke, 1987) and defence policy involves complex technical policy debates, often brought into sharp relief by congressional budget debates over defence appropriations. All of this coupled with the vast post-war expansion of the US role on the global scene has involved an expansion of the political process involved in foreign-policy-making.

Contrary to simplistic conspiracy theories of US foreign policy, corporate wishes among the ruling class of the USA are not usually straightforwardly turned into policy by a process of manipulation because of easy access, although neither is a naive democratic view that public opinion determines foreign policy accurate. The actual process involves complex political manoeuvering, bureaucratic infighting and appeals to 'public opinion' as a way of gaining leverage for particular views. This latter process, including the frequent use of the technique of 'leaking' materials to the press at crucial moments, involves the mobilization of various discourses to provide legitimation to a particular position. In the contentious realm of Soviet-US relations, this is particularly relevant ever since the acrimonius debates in the Truman administration at the end of the Second World War.

The complex political, economic and diplomatic events of the emerging Cold War cannot be discussed in great detail here (see Alperowitz, 1985; Black, 1986; Gaddis, 1978, 1982; Herken, 1980; Pollard, 1985; and Yergin, 1977). Here it is the interpretation of Soviet intentions by the US foreign-policy-makers that is of concern. These intentions were surmised from very little. Before the exchange of diplomatic missions in 1933 the USA monitored internal developments from its Embassy in Riga, and developed an understanding of the regime that has remained the dominant interpretation ever since. Yergin (1977) has termed this view the 'Riga Axioms', in contrast to the more accommodating and friendly 'Yalta Axioms' developed principally by the Roosevelt administration during the Second World War, and named after the summit meeting held in the Crimea in the spring of 1945. The USA had little experience on the world scene of dealing with the USSR, which had been nearly excluded from international society in the 1920s and 1930s.

The US history of the fear of the Russians did not originate in 1917 with the Bolshevik Revolution, although a new dimension was added on in the aftermath of that event, namely the 'communist' dimension. Far from all US historical texts are hostile to Russia and subsequently to the USSR (Anschel, 1974; Grayson ed., 1978). The 'Soviet Threat' has waxed and waned in US political life since the Bolshevik Revolution of 1917. The reasons relate probably more to domestic US political affairs, than to Soviet policies (Cox, 1985; Mack, 1981; Miliband *et al.* eds, 1984). Obviously external developments are not irrelevant, but internal ideological matters (Wolfe, 1984b, 1984c) and the bureaucratic infighting amongst the armed services (Wolfe,

1984a) are important factors in understanding the varying salience of concerns about the Soviet threat in US politics.

The overall direction of US foreign policy crystallized out of the post-war debates around the two key themes of Atlanticism and containment. Atlanticism refers to the global economic system built by the USA and its multinational corporations in alliance with Western Europe which asserted the supremacy of the Euro-American political, cultural and economic arrangements, loosely the political economy of liberal capitalism, through the Bretton Woods arrangements, the International Monetary Fund, the World Bank and the various agencies of the United Nations. This involved extensive intervention in what became known as 'the Third World' to promote 'development' or 'modernization' (Escobar, 1984–5). This was nearly universally accompanied by 'security assistance', designed to incorporate the military structures of Third World states into some form of alliance with the USA in their self-proclaimed global political and military campaign to 'contain' the USSR and more generally 'communism' within the geographical boundaries that demarcated the 'Second World'. This was to be accomplished by deterring it from expanding through military opposition and the threat of nuclear annihilation. Containment was the formal term given to the overall military and political campaign against 'the Soviet Threat'; NATO its most important military and political component.

On these twin ideological pillars successive US administrations built the post-war US global hegemony, a system of international economic, political and military domination which is often termed, '*Pax Americana*', or the 'Western System':

> Deterrence, security, indeed the whole postwar network of military bases, alliance-building and security assistance were part of this attempt to erect globally a stable framework for trade and the internationalisation of capital under the watchful eyes of a whole host of institutions: the IMF, World Bank, GATT, NATO, ANZUS and the like. This is what we call the Western System. Its focal point was the trans-Atlantic network embodied under the auspices of NATO. [Klein, 1986, 4]

NATO and the military alliances were to provide for the security of this arrangement, providing the military power to 'deter' any aggressor from upsetting the smooth functioning of international capitalism. Deterring aggressors requires, so the logic of nuclear strategy says, a convincing military capability either to destroy the aggressor's invading forces or, at least, do damage disproportionate to any possible gains that the aggressor might hope to achieve as a result of military action. Thus security is gained by deterrence (Smoke, 1987), which requires perpetual military preparedness and the ever-present political will to counter the external antagonist, in this case the USSR and its satellites, with all means up to and including global nuclear war.

This formulation of US foreign policy as containment and deterrence in the late 1940s and in particular in the early 1950s during the Korean war in military terms, is termed 'containment militarism' by Sanders (1983). The term is used in this book because it accurately encompasses both the geopolitical dimensions of geographical encirclement, as well as the use of military alliances, bases and the continuous US military mobilization which marked the following two decades of US foreign policy. This military framework provided the necessary political organization for the expansion of US business around the world.

The complex formulations of containment militarism have played a key role in the structuring of post-Second World War US foreign policy. But the consensus on containment militarism was not established easily, it was vigorously contested in the late 1940s by supporters of isolationism and by fiscally conservative Republican politicians. Crucial in the consolidation of the containment militarist position was the debate over National Security Council document number 68 (*Report by the Secretaries of State and Defence on 'United States Objectives and Programs for National Security'*, April 1950), which is probably the most important single post-war statement of US foreign policy (Wells, 1979). This document clearly defined the global political situation in terms of a bi-polar world in which the USA was pitted against an expansionist totalitarian USSR. It insisted that a rapid military buildup was essential to prevent a future Soviet military superiority that could be used to intimidate the USA into withdrawing from a dominant position in world politics. Once firmly established in the early 1950s, the containment militarist hegemony remained effectively unchallenged until its policies led to practical difficulties in Vietnam and Cambodia.

There were additional institutional reasons within the USA for the development of the 'Soviet threat'. These related to the immediate post-war question of unification of the forces under a single department of defence, and the question of budgetary allocations in the restricted fiscal environment of demobilization. In particular, the navy and the air force were each pushing their own views of their future roles, and having a credible foe was seen as improving one's arguments in the budgetary and bureaucratic infighting (Wolfe, 1984a). Electoral politics inevitably involve discussions of the Soviet threat as the pre-eminent concern of US foreign policy, and the 'politics of defence contracting' (Adams, 1982; Kaldor, 1982; Melman, 1988) ensures that defence intellectuals will always be found to raise the alarm about some new Soviet military technology (Cockburn, 1983).

Coupled with these electoral political arguments has been a series of high-level analyses, often conducted in secret, which have portrayed the USSR in grim terms. In the late 1940s the 'Dropshot' plan for nuclear war with the USSR anticipated a Soviet offensive in 1957 (Cave Brown ed., 1978). A little later the NSC68 document anticipated Soviet superiority in the mid-1950s. The RAND vulnerability studies and the subsequent Gaither Committee investigations (Halperin, 1961) also followed the pattern of suggesting an imminent Soviet nuclear superiority (Freedman, 1986). In the 1960s there were scares about the superiority of Soviet ABM technology. In the 1970s the Team B intelligence review provided alarmist accounts of Soviet potentials (Prados, 1982), and Albert Wohlstetter (1974a, 1974b, 1975) renewed concerns about the strategic adequacy of the US forces.

Subsequently Lee and Staar (1986) have updated this argument, suggesting that the period of greatest danger will occur in the 1990s. Hence the series of defence 'gaps' that have plagued US politics. Bomber gaps and missile gaps were followed in the late 1970s by the 'Window of Vulnerability' connected to the CPD concerns with US strategic inferiority.

There has not been a consistent evolution of the Soviet-US relationship since the Cold War began; there have been fluctuations between periods of intense antagonism and periods of relative calm. Halliday (1983) suggests a periodization of post-war US–Soviet relations into four phases. The first from 1946 to 1953 he terms the first Cold War. This is followed by a long period of what he calls 'oscillatory antagonism', stretching through the Eisenhower, Kennedy and Johnson eras to 1969 when the decade-long period of *détente* commenced. Following this the fourth phase from 1979 to the present occurs, which Halliday terms the second Cold War. Many of these fluctuations are due to what Kennan (1983) calls the 'instability' of the US–Soviet policy. There have been a number of attempted accommodations with the USSR and also periods of greater hostility, accompanied by the ideological mobilization of various themes of the 'Russian threat' (Wolfe 1984a). The *détente* period involved the temporary demise of the 'Soviet threat' (M. Cox, 1984; Williams, 1985) which the CPD and other New Right groups subsequently attempted to re-insert at the centre of US political debate.

In the early 1970s the domestic US political situation presented alternatives in terms of *détente* and arms control replacing military supremacy in containing the USSR and later the shift of focus from military matters to the economic management of international capitalism. In the aftermath of OPEC and the collapse of the gold standard, in part under the strain of the military operations by the USA in Asia, the economic aspects of Atlanticism became more pronounced, particularly in terms of trilateralism and the institution of regular economic summit meetings among Western governments. This decline in the emphasis on security matters, in a period with some Soviet interventions in the Third World, was challenged by many right-wing and neo-conservative politicians and movements. These included neo-conservative 'thinktanks' (Easterbrook, 1986), militant evangelical religious groups, sometimes preaching doctrines linked to the theme of imminent nuclear holocaust (Halsell, 1986), a whole network of right-wing political groupings (Saloma, 1984) and defence lobby organizations (Gervasi, 1986).

The CPD provided the high-profile personalities and foreign policy expertise for the New Right political movement, and the later Coalition for Peace Through Strength. The CPD 'went public' at a press conference on 11 November 1976 just after Jimmy Carter's election as US President. At the conference the CPD presented the text of its major policy statement, 'Common Sense and the Common Danger', a document which Kampleman (1984, xv) calls 'our manifesto'. 'Common Sense and the Common Danger' went through thirteen drafts during the organizational phase of the CPD in 1976 before its 'going public'. These drafts were produced during the period of the Team B intelligence review. 'The intellectual basis for the Committee grew out of the work of the now famous Team B which presented its view that the CIA had consistently underestimated the massive Soviet military effort' (Kampleman, 1984, xv). The membership of the CPD and Team B overlapped. In many ways the Team B intelligence review operated in a similar manner to earlier high-level reviews of the Soviet threat, galvanizing the hawks into public political action. Coupled with their second (4 April 1977) statement, 'What is the Soviet Union Up To?', these two documents outline the basic concerns of the committee.

'Common Sense and the Common Danger'

The opening statement in this 'manifesto' is a blunt warning to the audience: 'Our country is in a period of danger, and the danger is increasing. Unless decisive steps are taken to alert the nation, and to change the course of its policy, our economic and military capacity will become inadequate to assure peace with security' (CPD, 1984, 3). The audience is the wide readership of mainstream news media, the policy statement is presented at a press conference with the specific aim of reaching that audience through the intermediaries of the press. It attempts to capture the audience's sympathy in a series of ideological moves in the rest of the opening section.

Key among these is the explicit use of 'common sense', a term placed in the title. As was pointed out in Chapter one, common sense suggests both being common, i.e. widely prevalent and sensible, in the sense of thought out and reasonable. But it also refers in the Gramscian sense to hegemonic ideas, conceptions of how the world is that contain implicit structures of power which are naturalized, taken for granted, hegemonic precisely because they are unchallenged, often unconscious. In Thompson's (1984) terms, they are ideological because they are dissimulated, moves of power hidden from view. Given its title, the whole document claims to be common sense. By positioning itself as such it suggests that other viewpoints are neither common nor sensible. It thus appeals to a conception of global order that is the received wisdom of containment militarism, which is far from a natural or an inevitable state of affairs, but a politically constructed arrangement to assert US global hegemony. Now a quarter of a century after its initial formulation in NSC68 this particular formulation is rendered as 'common sense'.

The second paragraph of 'Common Sense and Common Danger' starts with a device to reassure the audience that the analysis presented is not too alarmist, and yet provides the possibility to the audience that it is not at fault for being unaware of the threat. Thus 'the threats we face are more subtle and indirect than was once the case'. This is why 'awareness of danger has diminished in the United States' and elsewhere. It clearly suggests that the audience probably shares this (common-sense) assumption. The remedy is available through a mobilization of 'political will' to revive alliances and to 'restore the strength and coherence of our foreign policy' and on the basis of this revival to 'seek reliable conditions of peace with the Soviet Union, rather than an illusory detente' (CPD, 1984, 3). It goes on to argue that only on these conditions can a 'just and progressive world economy' be developed. The framework within which these things can be made possible is crucial to understanding the ideological position of the discourse on the Soviet threat, and it will be returned to later.

The final sentence of the opening section carries a direct attack on the then perceived future agenda of the forthcoming Carter administration: 'In that framework, we shall be better able to promote human rights, and to help deal with the great and emerging problems of food, energy, population, and the environment.' Thus it identifies the CPD's goals as similar to the 'liberal' agenda which Carter advocated during his election campaign. This is a double ideological move, simultaneously suggesting that these are desirable ends and hence diverting possible criticism on the grounds of stated political ends while arguing that the methods advocated by the Carter campaign are naive and misguided.

This move puts the CPD in a space of superior knowledge. It is aware of the real state of the world, not taken in by an 'illusory *détente*'. Reality is thus defined as a military strategic one. Political *détente* is unreal, illusion. The CPD alone understands the presence of the as yet unnamed 'threat' which lurks unseen on the world stage. The implication is that those currently in charge of government policy are likely to make serious blunders because of their failure to appreciate the impending threat to the USA. The only solution is the adoption of the CPD 'common-sense' perspective. Those who do not see the 'danger' are not portrayed as deliberately malevolent, this is impossible given the implication that many of the audience accept the 'liberal' perspective and its goals, which the CPD has also aligned themselves with, but rather they are in need of education and a change of political direction. Having suggested that a problem exists, that it is solvable, although those in power may be incapable of doing so without being pushed into doing so, and having made a clear attempt to identify itself with the concerns of its audience, only then does the document turn to specify the threat that is alluded to in the opening sentence. Thus the policy statement carefully cultivates the position of being politically 'reasonable' by phrasing its arguments in terms of 'common sense' to an audience to which it attempts to ingratiate itself.

Having accomplished this, the second section starts with a dramatic statement of the problem: 'The principal threat to our nation, to world peace, and to the cause of human freedom is the Soviet drive for dominance based upon an unparalleled military buildup' (CPD, 1984, 3). No equivocation here; this sentence stands alone as the opening paragraph of the second section of the text. The critique of *détente* is immediately added to by an assertion that 'The Soviet Union has not altered its long-held goal of a world dominated from a single center – Moscow' (CPD, 1984, 3). The evidence presented points to the classic concerns of the geopolitical perspective with the domination of territory beyond national boundaries. 'It [i.e. the USSR] continues, with notable persistence, to take advantage of every opportunity to expand its political and military influence throughout the world: in Europe; in the Middle East and Africa; in Asia; even in Latin America; in all the seas.' (CPD, 1984, 3). Not only does it continue 'to take advantage of every opportunity' but the 'scope and sophistication' of its 'campaign' has 'increased', 'and its tempo quickened'. It encourages divisive tendencies while acquiring a network of positions 'including naval and air bases in the Southern Hemisphere which support its drive for dominance in the Middle East, the Indian Ocean, Africa, and the South Atlantic.'

Worse than this the USSR has been 'enlarging and improving' both its strategic and its conventional forces far more rapidly than the United States' (CPD, 1984, 4). This, we are told, is not explicable by interests of self-defence, presumably a legitimate activity, but rather is part of what 'its spokesmen call "visible preponderance" ', which their spokesmen explain will 'permit the Soviet Union "to transform the conditions of world politics" ' (CPD, 1984, 4). The device here is simply to use the words of the unidentified Soviet spokesmen and take them at face value. This legitimates the CPD assertion of their aims by shifting the burden of proof onto the Russians.

Not only are the interests and political independence of Allies and friends threatened by direct attack, but they are also in danger from 'envelopment and indirect aggression'. The danger of a Soviet-dominated Middle East is of special concern to Europe and Japan as well as to the USA. 'Similarily, we and much of the rest of the world are threatened by renewed coercion through a second round of Soviet-encouraged oil embargoes' (CPD, 1984, 4). The association of the two concerns of Soviet domination and of oil embargoes is hardly accidental. Although the CPD is careful not to charge the USSR directly with causing the OPEC oil embargo three years earlier, they manage to get tarnished simply by the association of these ideas. This adds to the unacceptability of Soviet 'domination' of the Middle East.

In summary, the third section of this statement offers the following encapsulation; 'Soviet expansionism threatens to destroy the world balance of forces on which the survival of freedom depends' (CPD, 1984, 4). There follows a dramatic ideological shift which links up with the opening paragraph thus: 'If we see the world as it is, and restore our will, our strength and self confidence, we shall find resources and friends enough to counter that threat' (CPD, 1984, 4). Presumably after the last few paragraphs outlining a global threat that is accelerating and expanding, the reader will have forgotten that in the opening sentences this phenomenon was described as 'subtle and indirect'. There is little subtle about the threat that the CPD describes.

How the 'awareness of danger' could possibly have 'diminished' in the USA as the CPD asserts it has, if the threat is as massive as they portray it to be, is ignored. This gaping hole in the logic of the argument is simply left aside. There appears to be a political calculation here suggesting that investigating this too closely before building a firm constituency might alienate potential support by challenging too directly the integrity and intelligence of that potential support. In other words, you do not call potential friends 'dummy' until they are firmly on your side. Having first brought them on side you can only then inform them of the errors of their ways. None the less this major logical contradiction remains in the text; common sense may be common but in this case it is not sensible in terms of being coherent.

The logical contradiction provides a dramatic example of what Kress (1985, 74) writes of in terms of texts providing opportunities for intervention at points of unresolved discursive difference. Here the differences between the theme of massive threat essential to the urgency of the CPD appeal to action runs counter to their textual strategy of addressing the audience in the first few paragraphs. Either the audience was blind to the obviousness of the threat or else the whole status of the threat is exaggerated; either possibility gets their text into trouble. Their solution is simply to ignore the incoherence.

The appeal to action is not made simply as a self-interested defensive reaction to an external threat, that presumably would be lowering oneself to motivations not entirely unlike those of the enemy. Rather 'There is a crucial moral difference between the two superpowers in their character and objectives.' Having just outlined the USSR's global ambitions, in contrast, and using in Barthes's terms the rhetorical device of 'the innoculation' (Barthes, 1973, 154) we are informed that 'The United States – imperfect as it is – is essential to the hopes of those countries which desire to develop their societies in their own ways, free of coercion' (CPD, 1984, 4). In Todorov's (1984) terms, the Other is different on the axiological axis. This is a restatement of the traditional US position of moral exceptionalism which runs through so much of US thinking on international affairs (Agnew, 1983; Williams, 1959). The statement of difference could not be clearer: they are expansionist and power hungry; the USA is simply an uninterested observer now compelled out of the moral supremacy of its vision to support the freedom of other countries to develop 'in their own ways'.

The suggested remedy for the 'danger' of the Soviet threat lies in a revamped foreign policy, economic and military strength, and a 'commitment to leadership'. More specifically:

> We must restore an allied defence posture capable of deterrence at each significant level and in those theatres vital to our interests. The goal of our strategic forces should be to prevent the use of, or credible threat to use, strategic weapons in world politics; that of our conventional forces, to prevent other forms of aggression directed against our interests. Without a stable balance of forces in the world and policies of collective defense based on it, no other objective of our foreign policy is attainable. [CPD, 1984, 4]

The military is seen as the linchpin on which all else rests. But a complex and diverse military buildup is needed. The balance of forces is primary. The collective defence can only be built up once that balance is assured. Thus leadership does not lead to improved collective defence, rather US forces restore the balance and the rest follows according to the CPD.

This will require an expansion of the military budget in the USA which, they argue, is at a twenty-five year low in terms of percentage GNP. As a sop to those who criticize the Pentagon for wasteful spending, they insist that with 'feasible efficiency' this is 'well within our means'. Here the rhetorical device is the use of the domestic analogy: prudent household budgeting requires 'living within one's means'. Here domestic 'common sense' is grafted onto the enormously complex matter of national economics in a way that renders the complex mundane and familiar to the average US middle-class member of the audience, and so acceptable (Hook, 1985), or 'common sense'. This, we are promised, will provide a strong foundation from which all other things will follow, including, of course, 'hardheaded and verifiable' agreements to control and reduce armaments.

The alternative is bleak:

> If we continue to drift, we shall become second best to the Soviet Union in overall military strength; our alliances will weaken; our promising rapproachment with China could be reversed. Then we could find ourselves isolated in a hostile world, facing the unremitting pressures of Soviet policy backed by an overwhelming preponderance of power. Our national survival itself would be in peril, and we should face, one after another, bitter choices between war and acquiesence under pressure. [CPD, 1984, 5]

The geopolitical theme of gradual retreat in the face of increasing Soviet gains is the old stuff of the Cold War ideology, making a clear reference to the experience of appeasement in the 1930s but now identifying the USSR rather than the Axis powers as the aggressor. Here it is rehearsed once again with the sonorous phrases of 'unremitting pressures' and 'overwhelming preponderance' inserted to assure the predicament is understood in all its seriousness.

The CPD ends its manifesto with a call to educate public opinion so that it can 'reach considered judgements and make them effective in our democratic system'. Finally, a few sentences from the end, the document is placed in its political context by its authors in their call to rebuild the bipartisan consensus on foreign policy weakened by 'Time, weariness, and the tragic experience of Vietnam'. In conclusion, the CPD announces to the world that it has established itself to promote a better understanding of the main problems confronting 'our foreign policy'. The use of 'our' and particularly 'we', the word that opens four of the last six sentences in the text, cements the process of ideological interpellation between the audience and the authors of the statement begun more circumspectly in the opening sentences. This repositioning is clearly present in an attempt to invite support and promote this ideological agenda.

This ideological agenda is nothing less than a rebuilding of the doctrine of containment militarism and with it the reassertion of US hegemony in global affairs, a situation that is common sense after all. The common-sense approach to solving international problems is most clearly evident in the opening paragraphs where the committee outlines its 'solution' to the danger which it has not even specified at this stage. It combines a large dose of moral exceptionalism with a dangerous Other to provide a blueprint for the future, which is in fact a rerun of the Cold War position of US supremacy within the world economy. But it is an authoritarian blueprint in the extreme. It is also very simple, common sensical, in fact, and herein lies the key to much of what follows. Here common sense is the received ideological consensus of NSC68 and the Cold War.

Thus to return to the opening section of 'Common Sense and the Common Danger':

> There is still time for effective action to ensure the security and prosperity of the nation in peace, through peaceful deterrence and concerted alliance diplomacy. A conscious effort of political will is needed to restore the strength and coherence of our foreign policy; to revive the solidarity of our alliances; to build constructive relations of cooperation with other nations whose interests parallel our own – and on that sound basis to seek reliable conditions of peace with the Soviet Union, rather than an illusory detente.
>
> Only on such a footing can we and the other democratic industrialised nations, acting together, work with the developing nations to create a just and progressive world economy – the necessary condition of our own prosperity and that of the developing nations and Communist nations as well. In that framework, we shall be better able to promote human rights, and to help deal with the great and emerging problems of food, energy, population and the environment. [CPD, 1984, 3]

These two short paragraphs summarize the CPD position. They are based on a series of powerful ideological moves.

First, there is the division of the world into the Other, different, distant, threatening, malevolent, here unspecified, but fairly obviously the USSR, and 'us', who wish for peace and security, despite the implied machinations of that Other. But 'we' are not alone. There are friendly countries out there who can support us through our concerted diplomacy and provide support in deterring the Other. But 'we' are defined in contrast to that Other. Otherness structures the discourse. Political will can 'restore' the coherence to foreign policy, assuming that it was coherent in a forgotten golden age. From this one draws the conclusion that the alliances are in place, simply awaiting US leadership. Nothing has really changed from the good old days, at least nothing that a bit of good old-fashioned know-how and common-sense leadership cannot remedy.

The further crucial assumption inscribed in this text is that the other nations' interests really do parallel those of the USA. The geopolitical divide of the planet into a bi-polar arrangement of 'them' and 'us' is clear. The possibility that other 'industrial democracies' might have interests other than supporting the USA in its campaign against the USSR is neatly excluded. Further, it is asserted that the interests of the 'developing nations' are the same, a 'progressive economy' is universalized as an interest even of the 'communist nations'. Hence, if 'we' have the political will to pull together now all will benefit. This vision of a general good is surely enough to overcome mere partial interests. The general good is simply defined in US terms. Common sense tells 'us' that what is good for Americans is good for everyone else; the whole ideological structure is defined in precisely these terms. The particular is universalized to legitimate the stance taken.

This also relates to the last sentence, where global problems are to be tackled as the 'liberal' agenda of ends demands. Thus we are told that military strength must come first; only with that established can all the other things be dealt with. Here the primacy of strategic over political matters is bluntly called for, giving primacy of force and military considerations over all other aspects of political relations. The discursive practices of realism and strategic discourse are privileged. They are defined in a clear move of exclusion. Liberal ends are secondary; the only legitimate perspective is the geopolitical concern with rivalry and military power. Security is defined purely in military terms, and in terms of military control over territory.

The implication in this is that there is no possibility of the USSR offering any help in terms of the problems identified by the liberal agenda. Human rights is put first here; the association with the USSR as a system that is antithetical to human rights is implicit, but this association is also implied to the final concerns with environment, etc. Making this move re-inscribes the USSR as the primary concern: first it has to be dealt with; then the other problems can be cleared up. If any nations do continue to hold out against the CPD view of the world, then they either are still suffering from illusions which will be removed by enough public education or they must be malevolently plotting with the USSR to upset the happy state of global harmony projected in this view of world order. Except that it is not a world order; it is a US or even more precisely, a CPD order. By universalizing their particular interests, the CPD has denied any other nation or country, or for that matter their opponents within the USA or the 'alliances', a say in how international affairs might be ordered. Other positions have been neatly excised from serious consideration by their failure to perceive the 'true' nature of the present danger; one known only to the more knowledgeable and informed members of the CPD, who 'know' the true nature of the Other.

But this knowledge is a knowledge specified using the discursive practices of security discourse premised on a very specific designation of Otherness. The ideological moves in this document are of realism, in terms of power being the primary concern of international affairs, of understanding the Other in terms of military and strategic terms as a geopolitical threat, the threat from its military capabilities being directly linked to its perceived geopolitical advances. Power and the threat are understood in terms of territorial gains made albeit often with indirect aggression. In Foucault's terms, the agents of legitimate knowledge are the practitioners of the security discourses of geopolitics, realism, sovietology and strategy, who through their mastery of these discourses can truly identify the state of the world and specify the 'true' nature of the Other.

'What is the Soviet Union Up To?'

The nature of this Other is the topic for the second of the CPD's policy statements. Here the CPD constructs this Other by explicit references to how the USSR is different. 'We strove to contrast the radical differences between our two societies and to illustrate the danger the Soviets constitute to the United States and to other democracies' (Kampleman, 1984, xix). The logic of this statement and much of the rest of the CPD literature rests on the connections made between difference and threat.

The differences are the key to the danger; 'they' are dangerous specifically because of how 'they' are different. The paper is structured around these twin themes and their interlinkage. Otherness is presented in numerous ways, but Todorov's classification, (mentioned above) of Otherness in terms of axiological, praxaeological and epistemological axes, is clearly present. The CPD relies on its expertise to legitimate its position. The epistemological dimension is emphasized; the CPD 'knows' the Other. This is the central premise of 'Common Sense and the Common Danger' and 'What is the Soviet Union Up To?' Their argument is that the mistaken policies of *détente* are followed because their practitioners fail to understand the true nature of the USSR, one known to the CPD.

'What is the Soviet Union Up To' starts with a brief summary of 'common' conceptions of how 'A rich, democratic and seemingly secure country such as the United States' conceives its 'national aspirations', to which 'at home and abroad, our open, democratic society, with its many centres of decisionmaking and limited constitutional government' (CPD, 1984, 10) is committed. These, we are told, tend to be focused domestically on such things as 'full employment, less inflation, better health care, a higher standard of living and improved opportunities' (CPD, 1984, 10). These are supplemented by broadly conceived international aspirations such as 'enduring peace, preservation of human rights and a freer flow of people and goods' (CPO, 1984, 10). Again, in the first sentence of this passage, the ideological device of universalizing the particular conceptions of the USA, in this case as being just one of a number of rich democratic and seemingly secure countries, is slipped in to support the ideological position taken. In other words, the USA is not alone, it is one of a (superior) kind. Having thus hopefully acquired the tacit support of the audience by this reiteration of standard ideological themes of the US polity, otherwise known as common sense, difference is bluntly presented.

'The Soviet Union is radically different from our society. It is organised on different principles and driven by different motives' (CPD, 1984, 10). On the axiological axis of Otherness its 'motives' are clearly distinct from the 'liberal' values in the previous paragraph. On the epistemological axis, the point about failure of understanding is reiterated immediately: 'Failure to understand these differences and to take them seriously constitutes a grave danger to the democratic societies' (CPD, 1984, 10). The danger lies in the process of 'mirror imaging', that is, of thinking 'of others as being like ourselves and likely to behave as we would under similar circumstances'

(CPD, 1984, 10). This habit leads 'many Americans to ignore, to rationalize or to underestimate the Soviet challenge; (CPD, 1984, 10). Thus at the praxaeological level the CPD insists on a distancing, emphasizing the need to avoid identifying with the Other.

Difference is primarily 'rooted in . . . history and geography, its economic conditions and structure, and its political system and ideology' (CPD, 1984, 10). In a usage that will be returned to in detail later, geography gets first mention among these factors and, in a passage that smacks of determinism, it is given an important, although not complete, role in explaining the CPD scheme:

> Notwithstanding its vast territory and rich mineral resources, the Soviet Union can only with difficulty support its population. Its extreme northern latitude makes for a short agricultural season, a situation aggravated by the shortage of rain in areas with the best soil. Its mineral resources, often located in areas difficult to reach, are costly to extract. Its transportation network is still inadequate. These factors have historically been among those impelling Russia – Tsarist and Soviet alike – toward the conquest or domination of neighbouring lands. No empire in history has expanded so persistently as the Russian. The Soviet Union was the only great power to have emerged from World War II larger than it was in 1939. [CPD, 1984, 10]

Without any further discussion of the nature of the Soviet economy, we are informed, in the sentence that follows this quotation, that the deficiencies in the economic system are aggravated by the regime and its attempts to maintain power. The totalitarian interpretations of sovietology are rehearsed here. Apart from the *non sequitour* and the determinism, there is no possibility of an alternative explanation; no mention of the numerous invasions of the USSR in history, no possibility that the option of *détente*, using Western technology to overcome the transportation difficulties, to develop the mineral resources and to strengthen the economy, might be a less hazardous course for Soviet policy than building up armed forces and threatening neighbouring countries.

Crucially in the last sentence of this passage the USSR is presented as unique because of its territorial expansion. Here the geopolitical theme in security discourse is introduced. The understanding of power in terms of territorial factors is explicit. The ruling elite, it seems, is caught in the same determinist geopolitical trap as its Tsarist predecessors. This is made clearer later when we learn that 'it is driven by internal, historical and ideological pressures towards an expansionist policy . . .' (CPD, 1984, 14). This 'ruling elite' is the key to understanding the USSR. It maintains itself in comfort 'while the remaining 250 million citizens not only have few material advantages but are deprived of basic human liberties' (CPD, 1984, 10).

This state of affairs is maintained because the elite manages to keep the population 'under effective control'. But the elite sees itself as the leaders of a 'revolutionary society' and their ultimate objective is 'the worldwide triumph of Communism' (CPD, 1984, 11), which 'would give the Soviet elite ready access to the world's resources, both human and material' as well as doing away 'with all external challenges to its privileged position by eliminating once and for all alternative political and social systems'. The authoritarian regime in the USSR allows the Politburo to 'exercise total control of the country's political institutions, economic resources and media, and set for itself short-tern as well as long-term objectives, disregarding the wishes of its own population' (CPD, 1984, 11). It can thus pursue its objectives in 'an organised and decisive manner, taking advantage of every opportunity to enhance its power in the world'. While it may have to rest content with a 'polycentric' communist order in the end, 'the notion of a stable world order in which nations based on differing political principles cooperate rather than contend is alien to Soviet psychology and doctrine' (CPD, 1984, 11). Thus, 'peaceful coexistence' is a strategy to pursue its ends in a nuclear era when prudence is called for in the pursuit of global objectives.

To accomplish these global objectives the USSR follows a 'grand strategy' with the ultimate aim of isolating the USA and 'reducing it to impotence'. Their means include 'economic, diplomatic, political and ideological strategies against a background of military strength' (CPD, 1984, 11). Thus the USSR will trade with the West while simultaneously conducting 'politico-military campaigns to outflank and envelop centres of non-Communist influence'. These include the 'long and patient Soviet efforts to penetrate and dominate the Middle East' (CPD, 1984, 11–2), and the 'drive, supported by client states, to establish regimes friendly to Soviet domination in Africa' (CPD, 1984, 12). This evidence is important to the argument. The grand strategy is encapsulated within its historical context and geopolitics is linked to nuclear war thus:

> The peoples of the Soviet Union have suffered enormously in past world wars. Their rulers would doubtless prefer to gain their objectives without another. But they believe they can survive and win a war if it comes and therefore are not unwilling to risk confrontation in order to attain their objectives. [CPD, 1984, 12]

Within this grand strategy four medium-term objectives are itemized. They are: first, the strengthening of the Soviet economy as an essential prerequisite to expanding military capacity; second, increasing links with Western Europe while attempting to cut it adrift from the USA; third, cutting links between the Western world and the Third World, assuming that removing the raw materials sources for the capitalist economies would 'throw the industrialised democracies into a series of fatal convulsions' (CPD, 1984, 13); and, finally, attempting to isolate and contain China, feared as a long-term threat. As a backdrop to these moves is Soviet military power.

In another reiteration of a vintage NSC68 theme, we are told that although the USSR is behind the USA in overall productive capacity and is less technologically sophisticated in weapons production, it is not inhibited internally in how it deploys its forces and consequently it can effectively use them to intimidate potential opponents and influence the actions of 'client states'. Further, because of the nature of the Soviet system, the USSR can devote larger proportions of its resources to military uses. All of these 'inherent advantages cause the Soviet leadership to rely heavily on military policy as an instrument of grand strategy' (CPD, 1984, 13) and to invest heavily in a military buildup. By focusing on the Soviet armed forces as players in the international arena the debate is shifted into the terms of military strategy.

We are informed that 'The Soviet buildup of all its armed forces over the past quarter century is, in part, reminiscent of Nazi Germany's rearmament in the 1930s' (CPD, 1984, 13). It reaches to all branches of the armed services, and 'in addition Soviet Nuclear offensive and defensive forces are designed to enable the USSR to fight, survive and win an all-out nuclear war should it occur' (CPD, 1984, 13). In italics they state that the SALT I agreements have not had any visible effect on the buildup, omitting to mention that the negotiated ceilings on weapons were much higher than the existing Soviet arsenal at the time of the negotiations. They further argue that the USA has restrained itself in areas where it held an advantage while the Russians have apparently not restrained themselves. 'Neither Soviet military power nor its rate of growth can be explained or justified on grounds of self-defense' (CPD, 1984, 13).

But they take the argument further into nuclear matters, arguing that 'by its continuing strategic military buildup, the Soviet Union demonstrates that it does not subscribe to American notions of nuclear sufficiency and mutually assured deterrence' (CPD, 1984, 13). From these assertions the CPD concludes that 'Soviet strategists regard the possession of more and better strategic weapons as a definite military and political asset, and potentially the ultimate instrument of coercion' (CPD, 1984, 13). Added to this are 'intensive programs of civil defence' and the 'hardening' of command posts against nuclear attack, all of which suggests 'that they take seriously the possibility of nuclear war and believe that, were it to occur, they will be more likely to survive and to recover more rapidly than we' (CPD, 1984, 14). This is the third mention of this point, in as many pages.

All this leads to a consideration of what was to become a key point in subsequent CPD materials: the role of nuclear superiority. They argue that in real terms the USSR had been increasing its military expenditures by 3–4 per cent while the USA had been decreasing its expenditure by 3 per cent per annum. If past trends continue, the CPD warns, 'the USSR will within several years achieve strategic superiority over the United States' (CPD, 1984, 14). This superiority could 'enable the Soviet Union to apply decisive pressure on the United States in conflict situations. The USSR might then compel the United States to retreat, much as the USSR itself was forced to retreat in 1962 during the Cuban missile crisis' (CPD, 1984, 14). Thus,

Soviet pressure, when supported by strategic and conventional military superiority, would be aimed at forcing our general withdrawal from a leading role in world affairs, and isolating us from other democratic societies, which could not then long survive.

Thus conceived, Soviet superiority would serve basically offensive aims, enabling the USSR to project its power in various parts of the globe without necessarily establishing a major physical presence in any single country. Soviet strategic superiority could lead the USSR to believe that should it eventually succeed in isolating the United States from its allies and the Third World, the United States would be less likely, in a major crisis, to lash out with strategic nuclear weapons, in a desperate attempt to escape subjugation. [CPD, 1984, 14]

The CPD then reiterates that despite major internal difficulties the USSR's goals are global in scope, and *détente* has not provided any reasons to suppose that their drive for global hegemony is in any way reduced. Thus they conclude that 'there is no alternative to vigilance and credible deterrence at the significant levels of potential conflict. Indeed, this is the prerequisite to the pursuit of genuine detente and the negotiation of prudent and verifiable arms control agreements that effectively serve to reduce the danger of war' (CPD, 1984, 15).

The implication, also clearly drawn earlier in 'Common Sense', is that the USA has to impose its set of conditions on the global scene. Given the unchanging nature of the USSR, bent on world domination, there is no other logical possibility, the USA has to strive to impose its conceptions and order on the rest of the world. All this is premised on the nature of the USSR as expansionist, devious, ultimately immoral. All the pieces of the global scene fit together around this theme. The geographical pressures of the Soviet location coupled with a power-seeking political elite not subject to internal political restraint are joined to a view of Soviet foreign policy with a distinct agenda of geopolitical expansion to be helped along by the imminent attainment of nuclear superiority.

There is no possibility of political compromise here; the whole notion of a stable world order is ruled out by asserting that the USSR does not recognize the possibility of such a situation, other than by the triumph of its system. The possibility of internal change in the USSR is not given serious consideration, although internal problems are allowed for, as are temporary setbacks. Consistent with the bi-polar dimensions of geopolitical thinking, social change elsewhere in the globe is defined in terms of whether it helps or hinders the USSR's plans for global domination; the possibility of non-alignment does not appear anywhere in this scheme.

Thus there is only one possible response to this global situation: a military and political offensive by the USA. The ideological straightjacket is seamless, indigenous conflict and internal contradiction defined out of existence, by being collapsed into the context of a bi-polar contest. It is this reduction of complexity which provides the CPD ideological position with its mobilizing power. The reduction of complexity to a two-sided fight suggests an analogy with a sports contest, with two sides and an eventual winner, a zero-sum game in which one side's gain is the other's loss. This oversimplification of political conflict is a recurring ideological formulation in US political discourse (Shapiro, 1989).

The whole exercise is inscribed within a manichaean portrayal of axiological difference. We are virtuous; they are evil. We are responding to an evil threat and therefore, even if we are doing exactly what we accuse them of (i.e. intervening around the world and building massive military arsenals) it is legitimate for us to do these things. Our ends are, after all, justified in the cause of freedom; theirs are evil and even when apparently noble they are a cover for the real goals of power. Thus the CPD draws on the theme of Otherness in many ways to construct their Other in the USSR. In Todorov's (1984) scheme, they use all three axes: the axiological, in terms of the manichaean contest; the epistemological, in terms of how well the CPD 'knows' the Other; and the praxaeological, in that the CPD supposedly avocates a policy of distancing themselves from the USSR – except that their logic drawn from the other two axes prevents them from doing that. Their distinctions lead them to policy recommendations that are identical with that to which they object in the Other. In psychological terms projection operates with a vengeance (Shulman, 1984), forcing them to advocate a massive arms buildup and an interventionist foreign policy. In praxaeological terms, they are in fact exceedingly close to the Other, a position the axiological rhetoric strains to obscure.

CPD discourse

This chapter has surveyed the principal points on which the CPD built their position. They argue for a common-sense position, one that takes for granted the inevitable 'natural' order of political affairs to be one of international strife. Specifically they represent the themes of containment militarism as 'common sense'. This reality is defined in terms of a military and strategic situation. This reality is one that the CPD claims it is uniquely privileged to enunciate. Because of its expertise, the experience of its members in policy formulation and academic study of these matters of strategy, foreign policy and sovietology, the CPD 'knows' the 'true' nature of the USSR. Its position is free from the 'illusions' of *détente*.

They argue that the USSR is involved in a campaign for global supremacy, searching out influence in the Third World to gain military bases with which to threaten Western interests. It is morally different, motivated entirely by power sought in its own interest, which sets it apart from the USA, defined in turn as a morally principled actor in the tradition of 'moral exceptionalism'. Not only this but the global interests of humanity are invoked as the rationale for US policy. But because of these high moral standards, the USA is in danger of appeasing the USSR, repeating the mistakes of the 1930s because it is lulled into complacency by the illusion of *détente*. The clearest signs of this are in the geopolitical retreat of the 1970s and the imminent danger of the USSR gaining strategic superiority.

The agenda of neo-realism is clearly present in the CPD writings; all 'liberal' agendas are deferred until the military threat is dealt with first. This deferment is implicit in all the literature on the Soviet threat that the CPD was involved with, all other political agendas are subsidiary. The necessity of this is constantly reiterated by the CPD because it 'knows' the true nature of the Other. The Other, however, is known in the discursive practices of security discourses. The knowledge of the Other depends on these practices.

As will be argued in the rest of this book, the discursive practices of security produce an Other that is threatening. These security discourses produce a USSR whose actions are at least partly determined by its geographical location and the major influence this has had on its history; here is the theme of classical geopolitics. Totalitarian regimes strive for total control; this is the theme of sovietology. The USSR seeks global control by a long-term well-thought-out grand strategy which privileges military power as a key player; this is a theme of realist power politics. Nuclear weapons, as the weapons of greatest power, are the linchpin in all this; nuclear strategy is crucial.

Hence the necessity to focus on the strategic implications of the SALT process. If the USSR gains an undeniable strategic superiority, so the argument continues, then it will be able to expand its geopolitical reach, gradually taking over a series of strategically important states and in the process unravelling the US alliance system and eventually isolating the USA. Thus the whole concern for military supremacy is tied into the primary concern for geopolitical control over the Third World as well as Europe.

The two initial statements by the CPD reviewed in this chapter contain the key elements of the CPD position and the themes that they reiterated in the following years. The position is one that ties the themes together within a framework whose central organizing theme is geopolitical. The other parts of this position are all organized through the geopolitical framework of an expansionist USSR which can be thwarted in the last resort only by military power. Many of the CPD's later arguments were over the minutiae of military statistics: they were to play 'the nuclear numbers game' repeatedly, but the overall coherence of their case is held together by their geopolitical theme. But the prerequisite of this is the nature of the USSR. Otherness and geopolitics are intertwined at all stages of the argument. As was made clear in Chapter three, this is inevitable in that the political theory of the state that underlies international politics and security discourse is a negative one; security is defined as the territorial exclusion of Otherness and, in its current guises in neo-realism, as the management of threats.

Part Two
Text

Introduction

The arguments in the CPD statements concerning the Soviet threat draw on numerous themes in US political discourse to shape and support their position. This part of this book is a detailed 'unpacking' of the logic of the security discourses used by the CPD. Chapter five investigates the nature of the USSR as understood through the analysis of totalitarian sovietology. Chapter six investigates the themes of appeasement and geopolitical progress showing how the concern over the 'present danger' is intimately concerned with geopolitical developments. Chapter seven discusses the themes of geographical determinism in Russian and Soviet history and shows how the Mackinderian tradition of geopolitics was updated to add strength to the CPD's geopolitical arguments. Finally, Chapter eight deals with the CPD arguments about SALT and nuclear strategy, which, it will be shown, are clearly decipherable only if their geopolitical premises are understood. Given the high profile of the CPD opposition to the SALT II treaty this dimension of their thinking is very important.

More specifically each chapter focuses on how the discursive practices of these security discourses use ideological moves that define security and Otherness in geopolitical terms and use structuralist interpretations to reproduce ideologically the political patterns of the past. Each of the discourses of security thus acts to perpetuate its institutional arrangements supporting the militarization of politics. The discourses *in toto* act to re-inscribe politics within the USA and elsewhere in the West into the categories of containment militarism.

Chapter 5 shows how Richard Pipes, the CPD's leading sovietologist, argues for the superiority of a 'historical method' focused on internal developments within the USSR and Tsarist Russia, in interpreting Soviet activities and, crucially, their intentions. The historical approach Pipes takes is determinist and draws on geographical formulations to justify his interpretation of Russian and Soviet history in terms of 'patrimonialism'. This construction of patrimonialism is congruent with the interpretation of Soviet behaviour in terms of totalitarianism; both interpretations suggest the impossibility of political compromise with the USSR. This conclusion is Pipes's essential contribution to the CPD.

Chapter 6 shows the more detailed working out of the CPD's realist logic, a position that excludes all except military power from consideration in international politics. Crucially, the CPD does this by conflating this concern with power with an explicitly geopolitical understanding of the global situation. Defining power in terms of military control over territory is coupled to the collapse of the world into a bi-polar struggle, one which reduces all matters solely to their significance in the geopolitical rivalry of the USSR and the USA.

The CPD attempt to reassert its military and geopolitical viewpoint as the hegemonic position in Washington is supported by the updating of Mackinder and Spykman's theories of geopolitics. This theoretical justifica- tion for their position is clearly present in Colin Gray's writings. Chapter 7 shows how this spatial preoccupation is relevant to their concerns of 'present danger'. Later Gray links up these geopolitical writings with Pipes's concerns with the 'patrimonial' interpretation of Russian history in deriving his 'imperial thesis' of Soviet behaviour. This determinist account is an explicitly geographical model of the functioning of the Soviet state apparatus. Here patrimonialism, geopolitics and realism are interlinked, each discourse supports the others.

Chapter 8 shows how the strategic rationale developed to support the CPD call for a military buildup is premised on these discourses of geo- politics, realism and sovietology. Coupled with these are the arguments that the USSR was planning to fight and win a nuclear war, presented most forcefully by Pipes, and arguments by Paul Nitze, in particular, that the USA was moving into a situation of strategic inferiority *vis-à-vis* the USSR and hence would be 'self-deterred' in a crisis. Colin Gray drew on each of these and on his 'imperial thesis' to develop his 'theory of victory'. This theory of victory is an important part of the literature on nuclear war-fighting strategy which indirectly provided many of the rationales for the Reagan adminis- tration's nuclear weapons procurements.

Chapter 5

Sovietology

Sovietology and totalitarianism

Sovietology as a recognized field of academic specialization in the USA dates, like nuclear strategy and international relations, from the late 1940s and early 1950s. The field of Soviet studies which spread to over one hundred campuses in the USA, often in the form of Russian–Soviet area studies, drew on political science and history. Methodologically the emphasis was on the political developments of the Bolshevik Party, in particular in the upper levels of its leadership (Schapiro, 1985). The broader social and economic contexts were downplayed, merely offering a backdrop for the real explanation which lay in the internal nature of the political development of the communist movement.

Sovietology was created at the time of the McCarthyist crusades in the USA when considerations of loyalty and security were important. There was also an intellectual backlash against the new deal and many academics were vilified as communists (Caute, 1978). This was not an era when many critical perspectives flourished. The fear of being seen as 'soft on communism' undoubtedly shaped the subsequent development of scholarship in this field. It quickly came to a broad academic consensus on the overall framework within which the USSR could be understood. Scholars 'embraced as axiomatic a set of interrelated interpretations to explain both the past and present (and sometimes the future) of the Soviet Union' (Cohen, 1985, 4). This was the totalitarianism school which dominated, to the virtual exclusion of any other interpretative scheme, the field of Soviet studies well into the 1960s. These scholars were drafted into government service repeatedly as consultants and advisers, and hence shaped foreign policy and in turn brought concerns of government policy directly back into the academy.

The basic tenets of the totalitarianism school's account of Soviet society included the following: in 1917 the Bolsheviks, an already, or at least nascent, totalitarian party, usurped power and betrayed the Russian Revolution. The totalitarian dynamics of the Communist Party, personified in Lenin, of monopolistic politics, ruthless tactics, ideological orthodoxy, discipline and centralized bureaucracy then inevitably shaped the subsequent history of the USSR. They won the civil war by ruthlessness and organization. Exhaustion forced a tactical retreat in the 1920s and the liberalization of the

New Economic Policy allowed the party to reorganize. Then the party, under the leadership of Stalin, reassumed the totalitarian agenda. This took the form of enforced collectivization and industrialization through expanded bureaucratic control and terror. The party totally took over the state apparatus. The war of 1941–5 forced some relaxation but it re-emerged full blown in the late 1940s as a monolithic terroristic society.

> Historical analysis came down to the thesis of an inevitable 'unbroken continuity' throughout Soviet history, thereby largely excluding the stuff of real history – conflicting traditions, alternatives, turning points, and multiple causalities. Political analysis fixated on a regime imposing its 'inner totalitarian logic' of an impotent, victimised society, thereby largely excluding the stuff of real politics – the interaction of governmental, historical, social, cultural, and economic factors; the conflict of classes, institutions, groups, generations, ideas and personalities. [Cohen, 1985, 7]

The predominance of policy concerns in sovietology seriously limited the intellectual possibilities. All research took on the quest for 'lessons' and the search for knowledge that would predict Soviet policy. Thus this was a political, or perhaps more accurately, a policy scholarship – overly utilitarian, with a built-in attitude of hostility towards its object of study. Interpreting the Soviet experience in these terms led to a foreign policy of resistance and a politics of punishment. The nuclear doctrine of 'massive retaliation' was justifiable morally, and certainly intellectually, by this image of unrestrained evil. If it was so monolithic and impervious to normal political considerations, then obviously the only thing that could possibly control the USSR's actions was the threat of massive violence.

The denial of history has had serious political repercussions (Cohen, 1985). By portraying the totalitarian ethos as unchanging and as inevitably successful, once the initial Bolshevik takeover of power was complete, it denies the multiplicity of the themes in the Russian revolutionary process. The New Economic Policy of the 1920s is dismissed as a tactical retreat, its potential as a possible model for other social formations is ruled out; the upheavals of the Khruschev period can also easily be dismissed as insignificant. Related to this is the assumption that any socialist revolution will inevitably become totalitarian. This has been a powerful ideological weapon in the repression of national liberation movements in the Third World.

Crucially, this denial of history removes from serious consideration any possibility of co-operation with the USSR to reform the international order. If the system is as the totalitarian conception says it is, then the system will not change by inducement or contact with the West. Any apparent changes are either dismissed as cosmetic, not substantive, or else as a ruse to lull the West into complacency, hence making it more vulnerable to plots to subvert it. The totalitarian interpretation thus contains within it a crucial ideological move that delegitimates all other interpretations. It defines other interpretations as false by requiring the totalitarian state to attempt to dupe Western leaders into accommodations that it will exploit to its unilateral advantage.

Thus, totalitarian discourse contains as a central tenet a move that precludes other discursive practices about the USSR.

The notion of totalitarianism was used widely in popular and political discussions. It was a mainstay in the anti-communist ideology of the 1950s. The intellectual climate of the 1950s was one of fear and suspicion; the academy was no exception (Caute, 1978). There were, of course, exceptions in Western scholarship, Isaac Deutscher being an obvious example, while in Britain E.H. Carr (1966) was at work on a mammoth history of the USSR that was more sympathetic. But the old notions of totalitarianism never left the field, they were to re-emerge to prominence in the late 1970s in the critique of *détente*, notably in the CPD literature. Different opinions were to come to the fore later in the 1960s and 1970s as critical perspectives on the totalitarianism schools developed in the light of the experiences of the 1960s and longer perspectives on the events of the 1920s emerged. Despite these revisionist efforts of the 1960s, Welch's (1970) survey of academic views of the USSR found them heavily skewed towards the 'hard' perspective on the USSR.

As the worst of the Cold War receded, tensions relaxed and scholars on both sides started to view the other side as less monolithic and as more complex. Griffiths (1985) argues that, at least in terms of political scientists, this occurred in three distinct phases. During the Cold War both sides were gripped by a totalitarian image or model of the other side. In the Soviet view the US state apparatus was wholly dominated by the super rich monopoly and finance capitalist stratum of the ruling class who used the state to ensure their profits. Militarism and aggression were part and parcel of this process. The totalitarian school of sovietology was in turn peddling a view of the USSR as completely dominated and controlled by the Politburo. The totalitarian thesis was used in both superpowers to mobilize support for Cold War policies and to legitimize the economic costs of military buildups. This was later complemented by a 'conflict' model of either side where the basic tenets of the totalitarian image were retained but the role of factional strife amongst parts of the financial elite in the USA and the Politburo in the USSR was also taken seriously. Although this model still had clear propaganda uses, in the domination of the other side by a small group, it muted the conflict between the superpowers by allowing a consideration of policy options. The Americans came to distinguish between 'hawks' and 'doves' while the USSR distinguished between 'militarist-aggressive' and 'sober-moderate' (later 'realistic') Americans.

The assumptions that both states were controlled by small groups came under attack in the 1960s and 1970s. Griffiths terms the resulting images a 'quasi-pluralist' perspective. The field of participants in policy formulation was widened. In the Soviet conception of the USA the state was no longer seen as directly controlled by the interests of finance capital, but within a looser framework with some autonomy to control the social system in the general interests of the bourgeoisie. The interest group analysis on the US side argued that there was a number of professional and bureaucratic interests in the USSR which engaged in the political process, making for a more complex analysis of Soviet policy.

Obviously, in Cold War terms, the propaganda uses of these approaches are minimal, however they are useful approaches for the 'operational requirements of collaboration among adversaries' (Griffiths, 1985, 11). This was the era of *détente* and these more complex models heightened hopes that each side could mobilize 'allies' on the other side to further co-operative behaviour. Despite these developments in sovietology, the theme of the USSR as totalitarian remains potent in political discourse. The term totalitarian was used by the Reagan administration frequently to justify foreign policy interventions in the Third World (McMahan, 1985). In the literature of the New Right the term is repeatedly used in connection with the USSR. It is present in the CPD texts in many places.

CPD Sovietology

The CPD's foremost sovietologist clearly was Richard Pipes, who has had a distinguished academic career as a historian at Harvard; among his many publications are a number of volumes on Russian and Soviet history (Pipes, 1960, 1963, 1964, 1974). He directed the Harvard Russian Research Center from 1968 to 1973; currently he is Baird Professor of History at Harvard. During the 1970s he broadened his academic interests to include concerns with contemporary US foreign policy and in addition to serving as a consultant he chaired the Team B intelligence estimate review panel. He is most notorious for his 1977 *Commentary* article titled 'Why the Soviet Union Thinks It Can Fight and Win a Nuclear War'. Subsequently in the Reagan administration he served as director of East European and Soviet Affairs in the National Security Council in 1981 and 1982. He has continued to write political papers since, and a major book on these themes titled *Survival Is Not Enough* appeared in 1984. Eight of the most important of his political papers from the 1970s were collected as *US–Soviet Relations in the Era of Detente* (Pipes, 1981). These papers provide a clear picture of the thinking of the CPD's leading sovietologist. His influence is clearly present in the CPD interpretation of Soviet foreign policy and its geographical roots present in 'What is the Soviet Union up to?'.

Pipes has a reputation as a Russia-phobe (Scheer, 1983, 55); his Eastern European origins from an *émigré* family are undoubtedly a factor. Pipes's position draws on his academic experience with Russian history developed as part of this discourse on sovietology, to which he later adds concerns with nuclear strategy. Pipes introduces an element into the analysis that is sometimes played down elsewhere, that of the continuity across the 1917 Revolution. He argues that there are historical themes that run back into early Russian history that are important in understanding current developments. This provides him with a way to criticize the developments in sovietology that are reflected in the policy of *détente*. Although he limits himself to criticizing the policy aspects, rather than engaging in debate with the newer sovietological perspectives, these are clearly also his target.

It was his prestigious position as a Harvard scholar that elevated him to prominence in policy-making circles. His ideas of the USSR as expansionist, often discussed in terms of a global Soviet strategy rather than specifically in terms of geopolitics, have a distinct geographical perspective. This chapter focuses on a number of his key papers which elaborate on the themes that are present in the CPD statements reviewed in the last chapter. Kampleman (1984, xx) notes that Pipes made a 'major contribution from 1977 on'. His pen can clearly be seen in the CPD documents, nowhere more so than in 'What is the Soviet Union up to?'.

Specifically, the following sections deal with his construction of differences between the USSR and the USA, differences that lie deeply in their respective histories and their cultural traditions. Crucial, in Pipes's opinion, to these factors is the geographical position of Russia and subsequently the USSR. Drawing on these historical factors and the crucial geopolitical tendency to expansion, Pipes then constructs a series of arguments about the conduct of Soviet foreign policy and uses these to criticize US advocates of *détente*. This chapter closes with a summation of the ideological positions created by Pipes's interpretation of the USSR. It shows how the ideological moves he uses structure the Other in specific ways and act, in Foucault's terms, as moves of exclusion legitimating his particular series of discursive practices.

Soviet–US differences

The expression of the 'radical differences' between the superpowers was the central purpose of the CPD's 'What is the Soviet Union up to?'. Pipes's writings repeatedly reiterate variations on this theme which he usually traces to some historical difference, and which in turn is used to explain differing approaches to foreign policy. Two aspects of his approach are particularly important. First, is the assumption of a continuity of political organization through the events of the Bolshevik Revolution. Second, is the focus on this organization in terms of a 'patrimonial' political system. Both these themes are clearly delineated in the preface to *Russia under the Old Regime* (Pipes, 1974).

Pipes's analysis of Russian history suggests that the old feudal regime had by the late nineteenth century effectively been superseded by a police state form of ruling apparatus; the Bolshevik movement simply continued this mode of ruling when they consolidated their power. The patrimonial system in Russia operates in terms of state sovereignty being unlimited. Pipes points to the relationship of sovereignty and property as being crucial here:

> Anyone who studies the political systems of non-western societies quickly discovers that there the lines separating ownership from sovereignty either do not exist, or are so vague as to be meaningless, and that the absence of this distinction marks a cardinal point of difference between western and non-western types of government. One may say that the existence of private property as a realm over which public authority normally exercises no jurisdiction is the thing which distinguishes western political experience from all the rest. [Pipes, 1974, xxi]

Pipes argues that the distinction has not emerged clearly in the USSR to this day. Hence the conflation of the spheres of sovereignty and ownership in the USSR suggests to Pipes that the patrimonial system is still intact. In it all privilege and material benefits are held by individuals at the pleasure of the state. This mechanism of the granting or witholding of these privileges continues to provide the key to how the USSR is ruled. These historical positions underlie all that follows in Pipes's political essays.

They draw on this essential specification of the difference between 'the West and the rest': the West as modern, liberal enlightened; the rest as, if not primitive then despotism of some variety. Thus, in Pipes's terms, the theme of patrimonialism is a form of what has often been termed 'Oriental despotism' (Wittfogel, 1957). Specifying Otherness in these terms brings with it the axiological assumption of Western superiority, the premise of most Western social science and consequently the rationalization for intervention and imperialism (Wolf, 1982).

In 1970 Pipes published an essay originally prepared for an audience of historians, entitled 'Russia's Mission, America's Destiny', in *Encounter*. The basic division of the world into 'us' and 'them', the omnipresent feature of the later CPD literature, is present here in rehearsal, it might seem, for the later criticisms of *détente*. At this time Pipes's particular target was the 'convergence' thesis that underlay some conceptions of *détente*. But this paper is worth commenting on in detail because it reveals many of the arguments that were subsequently to appear repeatedly in CPD discourse. In various versions the convergence thesis argues that both superpowers have histories that derive from Europe, but have strong elements in their make-up that reject crucial aspects of their European heritage. But Pipes argues that the differences outweigh any superificial similarities that might be deduced from this historical commonality.

The Russian rejection of Europe, Pipes argues, is traceable to the adoption of Christianity from Byzantium rather than Rome. 'From Byzantium, Russia absorbed a singularily conservative, anti-intellectual, and xenophobic ethos' (Pipes, 1981, 2). Viewing Christianity as a perfect achievement, the Byzantine church was inherently conservative. This cultural legacy lasted in this interpretation until just before the accession of Peter the Great to the throne. Following this there was an era in which Russia was Europeanized, at least to the extent of the adoption of military techniques and social customs among a sizeable portion of the nobility. The other social groups in Russia remained hostile to the European ways. Pipes argues that the Bolshevik Revolution of 1917 and the subsequent civil war meant the end of the Westernizing influence in Russia. Along with the monarchy and private property went 'the Westernized elite which for two centuries had served as Russia's link with the West, and through it, with the world at large' (Pipes, 1981, 5). The administration of the country was taken over by the petty bourgeoisie which had been excluded from power before the Revolution, 'elements characterized by resentment, conservatism, anti-intellectualism, and xenophobia' (Pipes, 1981, 5). Because of this Pipes argues that the regime fell back on old Muscovy as the cultural base for its new orthodoxy of 'communism'.

Thus, as Pipes puts it later in 'Detente: Moscow's View', the government and its service class see the land as belonging to them and that they administer it as they see fit without accountability to anyone. The communist regime has in Pipes's view, simply reverted to this traditional pattern, albeit dressed up in a new language, and despite somewhat different intentions on the part of its founders. 'In communist Russia, as in Muscovite Rus, the government as represented by the bureaucratic and military elites owns the country. No comforts or privileges in the USSR can be acquired save by favor of the state: and none are likely to be retained unless that state remains internally frozen and externally isolated' (Pipes, 1981, 68). Thus the ruling elites in Russia are traditionally illiberal and anti-democratic, an inevitable result of their patrimonial heritage. Pipes argues that in capitalist countries the state operates as a break on the propertied elites' enjoyment of property through regulation, taxation and the threat of nationalization, while in the USSR the state owns all the property which it dispenses at will, hence the elite has a direct interest in maintaining the power of the state. Therefore it is suspicious of all but direct state-to-state interactions. Democratizing impulses and the private ownership of property are a threat to the state structure and elite privilege.

In contrast, Pipes argues, the USA has isolationist sentiments, although not among those who make foreign policy. The rejection of the European heritage in the USA is limited to the rejection of feudalism, and reliance on landed wealth as the source of authority. The US policy in foreign affairs is the logical out-growth of the values of the liberal middle class. 'It derives from the religious-philosophical conviction that there is a right and wrong in every action and that man must constantly make a choice between the two' (Pipes, 1981, 7). The isolationist tendency in the USA is one that is based on an assertion of nations' rights to try to solve their own problems. 'It is an isolationism qualitatively different from that sense of exclusiveness pervading the Musco-vite and Soviet ruling elites, which tends to confound nationality and historic mission: as different as Liberal Protestantism is from Greek Orthodoxy from which the two isolationisms, respectively, derive' (Pipes, 1981, 7).

Having outlined the cultural bases of the difference between the two powers' political systems, Pipes turns to the historical roots of the conduct of foreign policy. These he likewise asserts are fundamentally different, based on the sharply different histories of the states. Thus, the Russian way of dealing with international affairs is based on their historical isolation from the rest of the world state system coupled with their imperial administration of the many colonized peoples that made up the Empire. Pipes argues that the process of nation building and Empire building were one and the same in the Russian experience, as opposed to the separate stages that European states supposedly went through.

Thus Soviet foreign policy is established in a way very different from that of the USA, which is based on its 'commercial and manufacturing background' (Pipes, 1981, 8).

A country whose governing apparatus has learned how to deal with foreign peoples from what are essentially colonial practices is not predisposed to think in terms of 'a stable international community' or of 'the balance of power'. Its instincts are to exert the maximum force and to regard absorption as the only dependable way of settling conflicts with other states especially those adjoining one's borders. There is little need here of theory, because the options available concern tactics rather than strategy or objectives. [Pipes, 1981, 9]

Pipes also argues that the Soviet system continues the patrimonial system of administration. This applies also to foreign policy where it is pursued solely to benefit the privileges of the service elite. The granting of privileges to sections of the administered populations has, Pipes argues, operated as an effective method of co-optation and integration. He argues that this is the policy used to incorporate the Eastern European states after the Second World War; in this case by entrusting power and privilege to a new 'class', the communist administrators.

Pipes argues that another apparent similarity between the two super-powers lies in their rejection of the idea of balance-of-power arrangements as an acceptable basis for the conduct of international relations. However, Pipes argues that the USA in fact conducts its policy on precisely these grounds; interventionism is simply the operation of a restorative measure in the context of an upset in the balance. The faith in this principle is proved to Pipes's satisfaction by the decision to allow the USSR to attain strategic parity with the USA on the assumption that once it had done so it would 'play the game', an unprecedented voluntary renunciation of superiority, according to Pipes.

The final difference which Pipes draws is one between agrarian and commercial societies. In this conceptualization the USA is the latter, the USSR the former (Pipes tells us that half its population lives on the land). The commercial ethos implies bargaining and division of profit. Producing goods does not teach the art of compromise, disputes over land are settled to one side's gain and the other's loss. 'It is not the production of goods, in other words, but their exchange that infuses the habits of civilised life, that teaches individuals and nations alike to respect the rights of others on the ground that their well-being is the precondition of one's own prosperity' (Pipes, 1981, 16). Thus it follows that until the USSR trades 'in earnest' internally and with the outside world it will not learn the value of compromise.

In conclusion, Pipes argues that there is not much hope for agreement between two such fundamentally different political traditions. 'The notion of what is "good" and what is "self-interest" is not the same for those who make policy in both countries' (Pipes, 1981, 17). Hence the international agree-ment of equilibrium, which was codified subsequently as *détente*, did not come about as a result of some acceptance of the world order by the USSR. The axiological differences ensure an incompatability of conduct.

As seen from there (Moscow), the cosmos consists not of majestic planets revolving according to the laws of nature, each in its allotted orbit, in the midst of which man has been placed on earth to prove his worth. The vision there – when it is not drowned in cycnicism – is one of chaos in which wondrous and terrible things happen, and God, in the guise of History, renders implacable Final Judgement. [Pipes, 1981, 17]

With such dramatically different histories the implication is clearly that conflict is inevitable. The Russian/Soviet system is antithetical to what Pipes argues are the central themes of Western culture, it cannot be assessed in Western terms and hence the conceptualization of it that underlies *détente* is fundamentally flawed. The xenophobia and the lack of internal political freedom combine to present a threatening system which only really knows how to deal with outsiders by conquering them. Each part of this analysis suggests that the Soviet foreign policy is inherently expansionist. Each distinction that Pipes draws relies on the construction of a menacing USSR facing a benign USA.

But the crucial ideological move in all this, which is repeated over and over again later in Pipes's writings, is to argue that Soviet foreign policy is a matter of historical determination, not a matter of policy choice by the holders of high office in the Kremlin. By making this move Pipes excludes the legitimacy of the *détente* position; he constructs an epistemological terrain where such considerations are excluded. Here we find the roots of the argument used by the CPD that only they are competent to provide foreign policy guidelines because they alone know the truth of the Soviet system, a system beyond the possibility of fundamental political change, one compelled by the historical logic of its geopolitical condition to attempt to expand.

The failure of 'liberal' thinking to understand this nature of the USSR was a target in a paper written some years later for the Stanford Research Institute. It appeared as the introduction to a collection of papers edited by Pipes in a book entitled *Soviet Strategy in Western Europe*, which appeared in 1976. While Pipes observes that probably all cultures are inherently ethnocentric to some degree, he argues that the liberal perspective assumes a particular culturally blinkered approach that prevents its from understanding other cultures. What follows deserves lengthy quotation, as it is a stinging attack on the basic assumptions of liberal thinking, and provides Pipes with a position from which to develop his critique of *détente*. Specifically:

> The idea of human equality, the noblest achievement of 'bourgeois' culture, is also the source of great political weakness because it denies *a priori* any meaningful distinctions among human beings, whether genetic, ethnic, racial, or other, and therefore blinds those who espouse it to a great deal of human motivation. Those differences that cannot be ignored, the commercial-liberal mind likes to ascribe to uneven economic opportunity and the resulting cultural lag. [Pipes, 1981, 64]

This is related also to the need to provide legitimation for the liberal political order and its trading profit arrangements.

The most probable cause of this outlook, and the reason for its prevalence, lies in the contradiction between the 'bourgeois' ideal of equality and the undeniable fact of widespread inequality. Such an outlook enables the 'bourgeois' to enjoy his advantages without guilt, because as long as all men are presumed to be the same, those who happen to be better off may be said to owe their superior status to personal merit. [Pipes, 1981, 64–5]

In turn these ideas and outlooks spill over into intellectual matters and into practical political relations with the rest of the world.

The various theories of 'modernization' that have acquired vogue among American sociologists and political scientists since World War II, once they are stripped of their academic vocabulary, say little more than that when all the people of the globe have attained the same level of industrial development as in the United States, they will become like Americans. [Pipes, 1981, 65]

These assumptions have direct impact on the conduct of US foreign policy because:

It is probably true that only those theories of international relations that postulate a fundamental convergence of all human aspirations with the American ideal have any chance of acceptance in the United States. It is probably equally true that no major power can conduct a successful foreign policy if such policy refuses to recognise that there exist in the world the most fundamental differences in the psychology and aspirations of its diverse inhabitants. [Pipes, 1981, 65]

That being the case, then it is incumbent upon foreign policy practitioners to examine closely these different psychological and aspirational factors. Specifically, the US foreign-policy-makers need to examine the roots of the Soviet system to understand the motivations of its foreign policy and how to respond. In Pipes's analysis, the geographical factor in Russian history is pre-eminently important.

Geography and patrimonialism

Pipes's major history of Russia, *Russia Under the Old Regime* (1974) starts with a chapter entitled 'The Environment and its Consequences'. Pipes argues that environment is the essential factor in the formation of pre-industrial societies. From this all else follows.

Men living in the pre-scientific and pre-industrial phases of history had and continue to have no choice but to adapt themselves to that nature which provides them with all they need to sustain life. And since adaptation implies dependence, it is not surprising that the natural environment, the subject matter of geography, should have had a decisive influence on the mind and habits of pre-modern man as well as on his social and political institutions. [Pipes, 1974, 2]

The Russian environment with its mismatch of rainfall and soil type (good soils either get too little rainfall or get it in the wrong seasons for reliable crop production) provides a particularly precarious situation we are informed; poverty drastically limits the social and political options.

Hence, in 'Detente Moscow's View' Pipes argues that the patrimonial system is 'accounted for' if not completely 'determined' by geographical factors.

Climate and topography conspire to make Russia a poor country, unable to support a population of high density: Among such causes are an exceedingly short agricultural season, abundant rainfall where soil is of low quality and unreliable rainfall where it happens to be fertile, and great difficulties of transport (long distances, severe winters, and so on). The result has been unusually high population mobility, a steady outflow of the inhabitants in all directions, away from the historic centre of Great Russia in the taiga, a process that, to judge by the census of 1959 and 1970, continues unabated to this very day. The movement is partly spontaneous, partly government sponsored. It is probably true that no country in recorded history has expanded so persistently and held on so tenaciously to every inch of conquered land. [Pipes, 1981, 70]

And further: 'It is estimated [Pipes does not specify by whom] that between the middle of the sixteenth century and the end of the seventeenth, Russia conquered territory the size of the modern Netherlands every year for 150 years running' (Pipes, 1981, 70). This is followed by the assertion that the USSR was the only imperial power that refused to give up its colonial possessions but increased them 'by the addition of new dependencies after the war in Eastern Europe and the Far East. Nothing can be farther from the truth than the oft heard argument that Russia's expansion is due to its sense of insecurity and need for buffers' (Pipes, 1981, 70). Still on geographical themes, Pipes continues:

Thanks to its topography (immense depth of defence, low population density, and poor transport) Russia has always been and continues to be the world's most difficult country to conquer, as Charles XII, Napoleon, and Hitler each in turn found out. As for buffers, it is no secret that today's buffers have a way of turning into tomorrow's homeland, which requires new buffers to protect it. [Pipes, 1981, 70]

He argues that Eastern Europe is just the lastest buffer, acquired with Western acquiescence, but that 'it is far better to seek the causes of Russian expansionism in internal impulses springing from primarily economic conditions and the habits that they breed' (Pipes, 1981, 70).

A final point on the theme of expansion is that the migrating populations have learned how to subjugate and dominate the populations that they came in contact with through exploiting the political weaknesses of their neighbours before annexation. 'No other country has a comparable wealth of accumulated experience in the application of external and internal pressures on neighbours for the purpose of softening them prior to conquest' (Pipes, 1981, 71). Pipes makes the link particularly clear in his later paper (1980a) in *Daedalus* on 'Militarism and the Soviet State'. The paper begins with another warning against the dangers of mirror-imaging by Western scholars, in which the argument is presented that the USSR arms massively in defence of its territories as a result of insecurity and fear of invasion.

Thus Pipes argues that the assumption that economic resources spent on military expenditures is wasted, as Western economics might suggest, is not true because of the historical experience of Russia, as well as because of the exigencies of Marxism–Leninism. Pipes argues that historically the vast majority of the Russian state budget was spent on the military, and it often operated to conquer adjacent territories. There is a cycle of poverty necessitating conquest, involving large military forces which impoverish the state.

At the root of this poverty is geography, as the CPD texts reviewed above, have also argued.

> Russia's traditional expansionism and the militarism to which it gave rise were primarily caused by economic factors. The northern forest zone (taiga), which was the homeland of Russians in the formative period of statehood (thirteenth to sixteenth centuries), is an inherently poor area with a substandard soil and an extremely brief agricultural season. [Pipes, 1981, 197–8]

This results in low crop yields.

And then in a passage which provides an essential key to the whole geopolitical conception that underlies Pipes's (and, as Chapter seven shows, Colin Gray's) position, we read that:

> A prominent nineteenth century German geographer has estimated that the natural conditions in a region like northern Russia permitted, on the average, a population density of twenty five inhabitants per square kilometer, whereas the countries of industrial Western Europe were able to support a density ten to thirty times as great. It is a consequence of mounting population pressures, and the related tendency to cultivate the available soil to the point of exhaustion, that the Russian people have exerted constant pressure on their neighbours. [Pipes, 1981, 198]

The prominent German geographer is none other than Friedrich Ratzel; Pipes gives the second volume of *Anthropogeographie* (Stuttgart, 1891, 257–65) as the source of his calculations.

Thus, population pressure led to Russian expansionism and militarism. The military also provided a crucial internal service to the Tsarist regime, that of ensuring internal order. As Pipes hastens to point out, it was the defection of the troops in Petrograd at the end of February in 1917 that finally led to the demise of the Tsar. While the communist state that came later had different ideological concerns they 'inherited the same land with the same traditions and many of the same problems: it would be surprising, therefore had it entirely discarded that or any other legacy of Russia's past' (Pipes, 1981, 200).

Much later Pipes returns to these figures for agricultural production, in his *Survival Is Not Enough* (1984). Rejecting arguments that Russian expansionism can be explained in terms of defensive reactions to foreign invasions, Pipes suggests that 'More serious explanations of Russian expansionism take account of concrete economic, geographic and political factors' (1984, 38). Under the heading of economic factors we read that

> Scientific estimates indicate that the soil of northern Russia, the homeland of the Russian state, cannot support more than 25 inhabitants per square kilometer; this figure compares with some of 250 inhabitants per square kilometer for the climatically more favoured Western nations. Population growth has made it necessary to acquire ever new land to accommodate the surplus peasantry, and this requirement, in turn, called for a large army, first to conquer territory and then to protect the settlers who colonized it. [Pipes, 1984, 39]

No reference is given to the sources of these 'scientific' figures, but they are consistent with those derived from Ratzel.

This passage could not be clearer. Here Pipes has reiterated the link between a cold climate, poor soil and military expansion. But he does so in a quasi-determinist fashion, one which excludes liberal concerns with international harmony, international trade, etc. It is quasi-determinist because Pipes does not suggest that all northern peoples are militarist, although that implication is clearly present in some of the passages above, but he interprets it as a process of militarization that established itself early and has developed a self-reproducing dynamic since.

The focus on military expansion and an aggressive foreign policy is a repeated theme in CPD writings, Pipes has developed a series of arguments that connect the patrimonial nature of the Soviet regime with the geopolitical tendencies to expansion, through which he attempts to alert US policymakers to the inherent dangers of not understanding Soviet policy in his terms. These he has assembled in a number of writings where he talks of the 'operational principles' and the 'grand strategy' of Soviet foreign policy and in 1980 simply 'Soviet Global Strategy' (Pipes, 1980b).

Militarism and Soviet foreign policy

'Some Operational Principles of Soviet Foreign Policy' (Pipes, 1973) starts with the Soviet concept of operations in warfare to develop its argument. As Pipes notes, Soviet military writers use the conception of operations to bridge the gap between strategy and tactics, neither of which they consider complete enough to encompass the complexities of military 'operations'. He argues that the language of Soviet politics is riddled with military terms, and that this notion of operations is important. He traces its origins to the analysis by the Russians of the campaigns of the German general Ludendorff in the First World War, 'whose masterful conduct of "total" war seems to have exercised a greater influence on Communist political practices than the writings of Karl Marx and Friedrich Engels combined' (Pipes, 1981, 21). Hence war involves the successive conduct of a series of operations designed to destroy the enemy's forces by constant uninterrupted pressure.

Pipes uses this as his point of departure for the analysis of Soviet foreign policy, arguing that the use of military terms and the language of struggle is not accidental but essentially reveals how the USSR conducts its foreign policy. 'The whole concert, with its stress on co-ordinated, uninterrupted assault intended to bring mounting pressure on the enemy, admirably describes what is probably the most characteristic feature of Soviet foreign policy' (Pipes, 1981, 22). Thus diplomacy is only one part of the overall operation of Soviet foreign policy, and it must be seen in terms of the larger context of Soviet activity. Pipes extends the argument about the importance of operations and the militarization of politics by arguing that Lenin was attracted to Marx and Engels because of their conception of class war. He argues that Lenin was the first statesman to amalgamate politics and military activity and that Clausewitz's insistence that politics and warfare are not antithetical was an important part of Lenin's thinking. He argues that Lenin's ideas are important because the Soviet leadership finds itself (in the early 1970s, the time of writing) in a similar situation to that which Lenin left at his death: 'that is devoid of a popular mandate or any other kind of legitimacy to justify its monopoly of political power except the alleged exigencies of class war' (Pipes, 1981, 23).

The leadership of the USSR is a self-perpetuating group isolated from new ideas by its own bureaucratic interests in the perpetuation of its control. There is little possibility of change without a major upheaval. It follows what Pipes calls 'a "total" foreign policy which draws no distinction between diplomatic, economic, psychological or military means of operation' (Pipes, 1981, 24). The USSR does not differentiate between foreign and domestic policy, which is why in Pipes's opinion the Foreign Affairs Minister is not normally a member of the Politburo, where all important decisions are made, and why there is so little Soviet literature devoted to the analysis of international relations per se. In addition, agencies like the KGB and the GRU have a greater role in foreign affairs than the Foreign Ministry. There is thus a 'total' foreign policy which is seen as a direct extension of domestic policy conducted by a multiplicity of agencies, not a single Foreign Affairs Ministry.

Pipes moves on from there to discuss the central theoretical notion of the 'correlation of forces' which refers in his reading to the 'actual capability of the contending parties to inflict harm on each other, knowledge of which allows one to decide in any given situation whether to act more aggressively or less, and which of the various means available to employ' (Pipes, 1981, 26). While the USSR maintains a militant foreign policy in the sense that it is active and vigilant, assuming expansionist aims where possible, although usually unprepared for reverses, military force is applied only when the risks are minimal and the chances of success large, i.e. when the correlation of forces in the particular sphere is strongly in favour of the USSR. Military force is preferred as a method of blackmail rather than as a direct threat. It is this overall militant stance that Pipes argues those in the West overlook when searching for piecemeal solutions to international problems in which the USSR is involved, and more generally in its dealings with the USSR in terms of *détente*.

While Lenin learnt from Clausewitz, Pipes argues that Stalin learnt his international politics from a study of Hitler's treatment of France and Germany. Pipes suggests that in Stalin's opinion the failure of Hitler's policies came because he did not know when to stop, and because he failed to analyse the correlation of forces adequately. Thus 'The quality common to Nazi and post 1946 Soviet methods of waging political warfare is the practice of making limited, piecemeal encroachments on Western positions to the accompaniment of threats entirely out of proportion to the losses the West is asked to bear.' (Pipes, 1981, 29).

The primary target of such threats is public opinion, to so disorient it that 'it refuses to follow the national leadership and by passive or active resistance forces the government to make one concession after another' (Pipes, 1981, 29). A recent addition to the Soviet threat techniques is, Pipes argues, the use of the line that Third World friends and allies are volatile and likely to go to war despite Soviet wishes. This has been used in the Middle East in particular, Pipes argues, to good effect, because it allows the USSR to appear like a responsible mature world power but the threats can be delivered anyway. The case of Egypt is mentioned in particular, but the implication is clearly that its allies are under Soviet domination and that they are incapable of acting against Soviet wishes.

Threats are also related to deception: Khruschev's deception with the number of strategic bombers and later ICBMs being the classic cases which helped to undermine the USA's sense of invulnerability and force it into accommodations with the USSR, a significant advantage to the USSR. The existence of the massive Soviet arsenal has not succeeded in the dismemberment of NATO but Pipes argues it has led to a paralysis of will among Western public opinion, while within the USSR the leadership, by depriving its population of 'the good things of life', keep it 'lean, hungry and alert' (Pipes, 1981, 31).

Putting all the above together Pipes argues that the multi-faceted nature of the Soviet foreign policy can be likened to the role of military reconnaissance, probing strength, and drawing fire to assess dispositions and intentions. But above all the Soviet foreign policy has a single priority: 'The very first objective of Soviet foreign policy is to make certain that all the territory which at any time has come under Russian or Communist rule remains so: in other words, that whatever changes occur in the world map affect the holdings of the other camp' (Pipes, 1981, 39). This is a continuation of the historical policy of subjugation and incorporation that Pipes argues marks the development of Muscovy into the Russian Empire. As will be discussed in detail in Chapter seven, this argument can be extended to provide the basis for a more comprehensive theory of geopolitical expansion. Thus, what the USSR holds is territory that is not up for discussion; 'what is mine is mine, what is your is negotiable' sums up the position for Pipes. He argues that it has applied particularly recently to Eastern Europe and East Berlin where the Russians have taken over what they controlled and negotiated on everything else.

In his later paper, '*Détente*: Moscow's View' (1976), Pipes pulls together his analysis of the key factors that shape Soviet foreign policy. Somewhat playing down the militarist interpretation, he relates the overall conduct of Soviet foreign policy to four internal factors within the USSR which, when combined, he argues, go a long way to explaining the expansionist and combatative foreign policy stances, and reveal *détente* to be a convenient tactical ploy rather than a genuine attempt at a superpower *rapprochement*. Pipes emphasizes internal Soviet factors here. In criticizing the Nixon–Ford–Kissinger policy of *détente*, he charges that 'The administration appears to assume the primacy of international politics (that is the decisive impact of international relations on a country's domestic politics) and to ignore historical experience in favour of a "behavioural" response to the immediately given situation' (Pipes, 1981, 67). This is a repeat of his argument that the USSR is effectively immune to political negotiation at the international level.

First, he emphasizes the patrimonial theme in Soviet politics, the argument outlined in 'Operational Principles' and earlier in this chapter, that the Soviet elite maintains itself in power by granting and withdrawing privileges and in maintaining a monopoly on all political decision-making. The second crucial historical factor is the geopolitical one, the 'persistent tradition of Russian expansionism', whose sources lie not in a cultural tradition of 'imperial fantasies' but in 'the economic and geopolitical factors that account for Russia's peculiar tradition of government' (Pipes, 1981, 69). The third and fourth historical factors necessary to put the *détente* policy into perspective are really a single factor: the peasant background of the current Soviet elite and their training during the worst of Stalin's purges which ensured that only the most brutal survived in positions of power. The peasant background supports this assertion because Pipes argues that the vast majority of serfs survived only by 'exercising extreme cunning and single-mindedly pursuing their private interests' (Pipes, 1981, 72). Combined, these experiences

> blend to create a very special kind of mentality, which stresses slyness, self-interest, reliance on force, skill in exploiting others, and, by inference, contempt for those unable to fend for themselves. Marxism–Leninism, which in its theoretical aspects exerts minor influence on Soviet conduct, through its ideology of 'class warfare' reinforces these existing predispositions. [Pipes, 1981, 72]

The argument continues with Pipes suggesting that only a major cataclysm can change these historical traditions and force a new way of approaching the world on Russian society: 'Unless and until that happens, one can ignore Russia's historical tradition only at great risk' (Pipes, 1981, 73). What kind of great cataclysm might be needed is not specified, but it can be inferred from the text that neither of the world wars in this century accomplished the task. This historical tradition is one of military conquest and subjugation, what Pipes asserts remains the long-term trajectory of the USSR. It is with these matters in mind that Pipes joined political debate on the theme of *détente*. Given the position he outlines here, one which argues that the Russian experience and the insecure political position of the elite in the USSR inevitably drives the USSR to be expansionist, his oppposition to *détente* is entirely predictable.

'*Détente*: Moscow's View' presents a long summary of the history of *détente* since Khruschev's initiation of the policy of 'peaceful coexistence' in 1956. Pipes argues that despite the expressions of 'peaceful coexistence' and the diplomatic and trade agreements of the early 1970s, the long-term goals of the 'total' Soviet foreign policy remain expansionist; *détente* was forced on the USSR as a necessary policy to exploit the contradictions in the West from its position of relative weakness in the correlation of forces. Thus there is no contradiction between the *détente* policies and the continued involvement of the USSR in an arms race and proxy wars in the Third World. They are all parts of the same attempt to exploit weaknesses in the West. As clearly visible evidence of this assertion he enumerates continued Soviet involvement in Third World events; propaganda offensives linking the USSR with the concepts of peace; economic initiatives with the West, necessitated by the relative backwardness of Soviet technology but directed in ways that attempt to make Europe dependent on the USSR and distance it from its crucial raw materials suppliers in the Third World.

Pipes charges that the West consistently underestimates the Soviet willingness and ability to pay for a large and up-to-date military establishment. This is because the military is the only tool that the USSR has that has a clear record of winning for the regime. The economy is not likely to inspire emulation, the political doctrines of communism have lost much of their ideological appeal, only the military is untarnished. The regime's survival in the early days and its ultimate emergence has been determined by the success of the Red Army. Its continued buildup is, it seems, central to the Soviet system.

> The Soviet leadership seems to strive to obtain a marked superiority in all branches of the military, in order to secure powerful forward-moving shields behind which the politicians can do their work. To reach this objective, the Soviet Union must have open to it all options – to be able to fight general and limited conventional wars near its borders and away from them, as well as nuclear wars employing tactical and/or strategic weapons. [Pipes, 1981, 94]

Finally, Pipes suggests that the *détente* policy has had two clearly unfavourable outcomes for the Soviet rulers. The break with China is a major loss; the Chinese refused to play second fiddle to the USSR as it elevated itself to superpower status leaving China out in the cold. The second debit has been some loss of internal control, by reducing the danger of the external threat. Overall, Pipes argues that the USSR has gained superpower status, 'smashed' the alliances forged by the USA during the Stalinist period of the Cold War, NATO now being in 'disarray', continued support for national liberation movements and proxy wars with reduced risks, legitimated, through the Helsinki accords, its conquests in Eastern Europe and gained considerable economic benefits. Thus the USSR will continue its policy of *détente*, 'because as now defined and practised, detente primarily benefits the Soviet Union' (Pipes, 1981, 102).

Totalitarianism rehabilitated

Pipes argues in a fashion that is typical of the totalitarian school of analysis, but he emphasizes the historical continuity across the events of 1917. This supports the whole contention that the totalitarian system of Soviet communism is unreformable by any means other than by confronting it with so much force that it is compelled, it is hoped without a major nuclear war, to turn inwards and address internal matters in ways that will fundamentally alter the nature of its political system, and the resulting political arrangements will, it is also hoped, be more amenable to genuine 'peaceful coexistence'.

The 'Russified' version of the totalitarian thesis leads directly to military concerns. International politics is thus reduced to military force. Politics is denied in the process, those who seek to change the USSR by policies of *détente* are thus dupes if not worse. Internally the Communist Party is compelled by the logic of its position as an insecure patrimonial structure without internal legitimacy among the populations of the Empire to maintain itself. Reform is impossible because it would admit the lack of legitimacy of the status quo and unloose social tendencies that would be impossible to control.

'They' are evil and beyond compromise. Power is the only goal of the party, but even if it wanted to change, because of its historical development it cannot do so. Choice is removed, the current political position is inevitable, determined and consequently can only be lived with not changed in any way except by brute force. *Détente* is truly an illusion because the USSR is incapable of reform. This is the central ideological move of Pipes's contribution to the 'present danger'. But it goes further than this, crucially he offers the next key element in the ideological position, the link to geopolitics. Precisely because of the historical determinations of the Soviet system, it is not only unreformable by political methods but it is also inherently expansionist. The geopolitical premises are part of Pipes's patrimonial interpretation of totalitarianism.

Hence the USSR is a monolithic system, the possibilities of internal reform are discounted because of the economic interests of the Soviet leaders in the maintenance of their economic privilege. This view of history and politics in the USSR denies internal bargaining and power struggles between parts of the system (Cohen, 1985). Internal tensions within the Communist Party of the Soviet Union and the structural economic problems within the Soviet economy are simply ignored in their political implications by the model of iron control from the centre. Pipes does argue that the policy of 'peaceful coexistence' somewhat complicates this picture, but he argues that it is only a tactic forced on the USSR by the exigencies of the Cold War and the 'spiritual exhaustion' of Stalinism. But the overall trajectory is one of expansion and the impossibility of change other than by external pressure of which the military aspect is crucial.

But there is none the less a very important political element to Pipes's and the other CPD writings on the USSR. This is the separation of the *nomenklatura* from the larger Soviet population. The distinction between state and society is clearly demarcated in ways that argue that conflict between two separate spheres is inevitable. Cohen's (1985) critique of the totalitarian thesis provides the key to unravelling all this. He argues that the Soviet system has a party of millions of members and an economic structure that not just the *nomenklatura* at the top of the structure have a vested interest in maintaining. Thus the economic and political structure of Soviet rule is widely dispersed through the society. The argument suggests that a complex industrial and urbanized society cannot be run by a small policy apparatus unaided by at least a fairly widespread tacit consent. More specifically political policies will benefit some groups at the cost of others, hence there is a genuinely political process of social struggle within the system (Colton, 1986).

If the totalitarian assumption of a small political elite running a vast society with an apparatus of repression as its main mode of rule, a model possibly plausible in understanding the Stalinist 1950s but hardly appropriate for the 1980s, is relaxed, then politics is allowed back into the picture and the possibility of reform is open in terms of the struggles between different interests within the society causing social change. With this comes the possibility of political compromise with sectors within the Soviet system that are open to accommodation with some aspects of Western arms control and *détente* policy (Holloway, 1983).

Given the absence of potential alternative political institutions within the USSR capable of serious political action, it seems inevitable that in the immediate future political compromise is essential with the existing power structure in the USSR. The totalitarian thesis, coupled with Pipes's and Gray's more specific geopolitical interpretations of the formation of Soviet policy, excludes by definition these kinds of political compromises necessary if any form of *détente* or political relaxation of tensions is possible. It acts here as a crucial ideological weapon against arms control by defining the USSR as a political system that by its very nature cannot compromise. The bleak alternative is a continued military buildup and nuclear war-fighting strategies.

But Pipes extends his argument further than many of the 'totalitarian' positions commonly take. He does this by arguing that the roots of the Soviet system are more Russian than Marxist. His announcement in the preface to *Russia Under the Old Regime* (1974) makes this eminently clear. The modern Soviet system is simply the Tsarist patrimonialism plus police state apparatus with a new ideological rationale, albeit one that is important to maintaining what very limited legitimacy the regime has. Thus the internal development of the USSR, from a peasant agricultural system with a small capitalist industrial sector at the time of the 1917 Revolution to an industrialized and much more urbanized society under communist organization, is effectively dismissed as not having any serious consequences. The patrimonial system is simply reimposed and history develops nearly as if the Revolution had not occurred.

Within this approach Pipes sees no problems with arguing that late nineteenth-century calculations of agricultural productivity can be used a century later to argue that this is still a relevant consideration in the expansionist nature of the Soviet system. No more recent evidence on the agricultural potential of this area is referred to; apparently it is irrelevant, or at least unnecessary. Hence Pipes quotes Ratzel as a source of agricultural productivity calculations in his 1980 paper. In *Russia Under the Old Regime* (1974) Pipes uses a 1963 German source of figures on agricultural production to make the same point and refers the reader to Parker's (1968) historical geography of Russia for background on the Russian environment. Other more recent sources available to Pipes in Harvard would surely provide more convincing evidence. But whether the source of his calculations is from this century or the last is apparently of no concern to Pipes, preoccupied, as he is, with the long-term determinants of geopolitics.

In Pipes's version history is, after all, about continuity. Innovation, change, the stuff of political life is mere surface appearance and not real. Here is the deep structure argument; the distinction between reality as permanent and deep in contrast to transient circumstance. Reality is defined as structure; practice is mere epiphenomenon. The use of this division is important in all that Pipes writes, its ideological power clearly revealed in how he uses the argument to exclude all positions that are different. This structuralism is the key to its ideological function.

In Foucault's terms, what Pipes does is to draw on a series of historical interpretations of the USSR in ways that define the legitimate approach to international relations and the USSR in particular in terms of history. But it is a history in which deep determining structures are at work, structures that are far too powerful to be changed by mere transient political initiatives. This a classic move of exclusion, other approaches are invalidated on both their ontological and epistemological bases. Not only are they inadequate conceptions of reality but their knowledges cannot be legitimate because they derive their positions from false assumptions about how the world really is. The superiority of the historical method is invoked; its permanence is relied on to give it certainty and to disallow the claims of all other positions.

This move of exclusion brings with it the fatalism of perpetual conflict because it 'knows' the Other as a perpetual adversary, forced to be so by its history. Once one 'knows' the world in this manner the evidence for Soviet behaviour to confirm this knowledge is easily 'found'. This 'tragic' view of the USSR dovetails nicely with the realist assertions that what is eternal (hence real, please note) in international political affairs is power and conflict. Thus the sovietological discursive practices are easily articulated to the realist concerns with power and international developments as military events.

Chapter 6

Power politics

International relations and realism

It is only in this century that a specific academic discipline of international relations has emerged. Before its emergence matters of international politics were dealt with principally by diplomatic historians, scholars of international law and military writers. International relations as a separate academic discipline has been dominated by US thinking. The reasons for this are at least threefold. Hoffmann (1977) suggests that the combination of suitable intellectual predispositions, political circumstances and institutional opportunities explains the pre-eminently US nature of the discipline of international relations.

The political circumstances of the US supremacy on the world scene attracted scholars to the study of international relations because the US was playing the pre-eminent role on the international scene. Foreign policy formulation involved effectively all of the international scene; former interests in domestic politics, in particular in the formation of foreign policy, became translated in the new circumstances into interests in the global scene. A scholarly fascination with power was provided with a vast canvas for investigation. Institutional opportunities were provided by foundation grants which were forthcoming for research. Access to the policy-making process was also available as academics gradually took over many of the roles previously performed by career diplomats and lawyers. Unlike many other foreign policy establishments academics were able to move between government and academia on a regular basis, both as office holders and consultants.

Of particular importance in the immediate post-war years was the coalescing of pre-war concerns with defence and foreign affairs, formerly often considered separately, into an overarching consideration of national security. The military emphasis has been pervasive, but it subsequently incorporated within its ambit concerns of geopolitics, economics as well as intelligence activities and traditional diplomacy. This concern for 'national security' has ensured the maintenance of the USA in a partly mobilized military stance ever since the Second World War. Its concerns with protecting the 'national interest' have been used in justifying numerous military interventions in the Third World.

The discipline has been preoccupied with policy matters, and the overlaps between the disciplinary pursuit of international relations and the study of

US foreign policy as well as the field of 'strategic studies' have influenced its formation and history (Smoke, 1987). But despite all this, or more probably because of its genesis in these conditions, the central tenets of international relations have a poorly developed theoretical tradition. Security studies in particular have concentrated on the empirical and the immediate policy questions to the exclusion of more theoretical reflections (Buzan, 1983). Foreign policy issues also suffer from similar deficiencies, but the dominant theoretical framework of international relations in the USA, and consequently around the world, is that of realism, often distinguished from a loose collection of concerns and approaches labelled idealism.

These distinctions are part of Carr's influential *The Twenty Years Crisis: 1919–1939*, originally published in Britain at the outbreak of the Second World War. It contained a polemical critique of the 'utopian' school which emerged in the aftermath of the First World War. His critique focuses on the naivety of these approaches which in his opinion emphasized international legal arrangements to the virtual exclusion of power. Thus it was a doctrine for the satisfied powers, i.e. the winners of the First World War. By ignoring the interests of the defeated powers, and proclaiming the universal validity of the international system focused on the League of Nations, this tradition, so the argument goes, laid the seeds of much of the conflict which emerged when the defeated powers, in particular Germany, regained their power in the international arena. By focusing on international legal and administrative arrangements to the exclusion of the interests and, crucially, the power of aggrieved powers, Carr blames this utopian tradition for many of the failures of peace-keeping in the twenty years crisis. Although Carr's text contains many other points, it is the insistence on the focus on power that was picked up after the Second World War by the school that became dominant particularly in the USA – the so called realists.

Morgenthau's seminal text *Politics among Nations* first appeared in 1948 and provides something approaching a codification of the realist credo as well as the founding text of the US discipline of international relations. In the first chapter he outlined six principles of political realism in international relations which succinctly summarized the realist position. First, the realist believes that society is governed by objective laws with their roots in 'human nature'. This 'tragic view of history' provides the realist with the epistemological terrain on which a rigorous theory can be built. Second, the principle most often remembered, is the conception of interests defined in terms of power. Third, this concept of interest is universally valid, indeed the key term in politics. Fourth, the tension between moral action and the expedient requirements of political action are noted. Fifth, realism refuses to 'identify the moral aspirations of a particular nation with the moral laws that govern the universe' (1978, 11). Sixth, the realist argues that its perspective is distinct from other perspectives, maintaining the autonomy of the political sphere, and in the process subordinating other standards of thought to the political.

This approach is based on many of the precepts that the earlier utopian or 'idealist' thinkers had tried to refute. It rejects the idealist postulate of a changeable human nature, and the possibility that the 'right' institutions could bring out the best in humanity. Where the League of Nations postulated a community with common interests, the realists argued that the international system was a brutal anarchy where power was exerted in the promotion of national interests, a position reminiscent of Hobbes's rather different concerns with the state of nature. International law, morality and opinion count for little, at best tempering the excesses of power politics but not seriously constraining the usually brutal practice of power. Martin Wright (1979) argued that international politics is the arena of recurrence and repetition, the 'modernist' project of societal improvement is limited to national boundaries. This clear separation of the international sphere from the considerations that apply to domestic politics is a hallmark of the realist school where it is often raised to the status of a methodological device (Walker, 1980). Thus, different parameters are taken to operate in the international sphere, justifying different approaches.

Where the realist school thinks in terms of power and interest and tends to define national security in terms of the power to promote a state's interests in an international anarchy, the idealist approach and its offshoot 'peace research', focuses on war as the central issue. War is the major threat presented by the international system and solutions to the problem of war are its prime concern. These two approaches have dominated international relations through its history. While other concerns have imposed themselves on the international scene, international relations has remained preoccupied with matters of peace and power (Buzan, 1983; Holsti, 1985).

The approach of idealism emphasizes peace and international co-operation often linked to concerns of international law. Notions of collective security and international institutions are also more important here than in a realist focus on the distribution of power between states. The idealist approach argues that more than power motivates states, indeed war is seen as an unfortunate, and preventable, condition. Power struggles are interpreted in terms of security and fear of attack rather than simply attempts to gain and maintain dominance in the international arena. The idealist approach is more explicitly interested in the possibilities of international organizations in regulating inter-state affairs. In addition, its analysis emphasizes the international security system as an appropriate level of analysis rather than an exclusive focus on national policy alone. Hence it operates with wider concerns than the realist focus on the fuzzy conception of 'national security'.

The US foreign policy establishment has effectively used both these themes to base a foreign policy on idealist principles as well as on realist concerns with power politics and the national interest understood sometimes in economic terms. US foreign policy is riddled with idealist elements, from Wilsonian principles of self-determination and non-intervention to notions of 'moral exceptionalism' (Agnew, 1983). They interact with ideas of isolationism and with US interventions abroad in a complex series of historical and policy situations (Hoffmann, 1982). As Chomsky's (1982) trenchant critiques have repeatedly revealed, these idealist themes often provide the ideological cover for a 'realist' US foreign policy. However, the realist logic is also used to justify international militarization, usually on the grounds that the USSR acts as a realist power, advancing its self-interest at the expense of all others, deterred from further expansion only by the might of the US global military presence. Indeed, often idealism and realism meld together into a single entity; power politics is based on idealist principles and these in turn are used to legitimate power politics. Thus the distinctions between idealism and realism are usually blurred in the practice of international politics, although the focus of idealism on peace and realism on power remain as useful distinguishing factors.

The realist approach, a doctrine of power seen often in military terms, appeared at precisely the time when the USA had gained pre-eminent power on the global scene. It provided a perspective through which US interests could be interpreted in terms of power, and which provided a framework for interpreting Soviet actions in terms of attempts to extend Soviet power. The realist discourse's power comes in part from the assertion that only power can resist power: aggressors must be resisted by military power adequate to thwart their ambitions. From here it was but a short step to the geopolitical doctrines of containment. These themes from the first Cold War period are again strongly in evidence in the late 1970s and in particular in the CPD's focus on the balance of power and its relationships to what they portrayed as the USSR's geopolitical expansion.

The emergence of the CPD was part of a larger ideological shift against humanistic concerns and modes of thought (McMurtry, 1984; Said, 1982) which marks the rise of the New Right, and the neo-conservative ideological onslaught of the 1970s and early 1980s. In this attempt to change the terms of political debate notions of welfare, equality and justice are sacrificed to power. Freedom is redefined in terms of free enterprise. In international relations the reactionary mood of neo-conservatism is reflected in the much more sophisticated 'neo-realist' literature (Gilpin, 1981; Keohane ed., 1986; Waltz, 1979). This in turn has been criticized for its failure to account for the historical conditions of its object of study, the international state system (Ruggie, 1983) and in more strident polemical terms as 'a self-enclosed, self-affirming joining of statist, utilitarian, positivist and structuralist commitments' (Ashley, 1984, 228) which operates to 'naturalize' the international status quo and severely limits the discourse on international politics. 'What emerges is an ideology that anticipates, legitimizes, and orients a totalitarian project of global proportions: the rationalization of global politics' (Ashley, 1984, 228).

The neo-conservative world view was not particularly new or internally coherent (Ajami, 1978) but it attracted considerable following often outside the universities. Most noticeable in the USA was the emergence in the 1970s of a number of well-funded private 'thinktanks' which attempted to shape the international policy of the US government in line with the neo-conservative agenda (Saloma, 1984). The largest and most prestigious is the Center for Strategic and International Studies situated in Washington and associated with Georgetown University (Easterbrook, 1986). The 'thinktank' emphasis is on strategy and an old-fashioned geopolitics which combines with a global militarization of international politics and in places an unabashed championing of political realism in the formulation of US foreign policy (Gray, 1976a). These discourses of power politics and geopolitics were important to the CPD and its attempts to reimpose the containment militarist hegemony in Washington.

Détente and appeasement

While Carr (1946) had critiqued the utopian political proposals of the 1920s and 1930s for their lack of consideration of the factor of power in international relations, many of the CPD members were to echo the critique in the 1970s. They argued that the focus on *détente* had obscured the growing risks of an expansionist USSR. They argued that *détente* was a policy of appeasing the USSR, a policy that ran tremendous risks because, just like the British in the late 1930s, the *détente* policy-formulators had seriously misread the international political situation, and above all had misinterpreted the motives of their adversary.

One of the key founding members of the CPD was Gene Rostow. He was responsible for drafting the initial 'Common Sense and the Common Danger' policy statement. Rostow spent many decades within the foreign policy establishment and the CPD was sometimes viewed as Rostow's organization (Sherrill, 1979). In books, articles and interviews (Whitworth, 1970) Rostow had long argued that containment militarism was the essential task of US foreign policy. His earlier arguments, in particular in *Peace in the Balance* (1972) and *Law, Power and the Pursuit of Peace* (1968) are less shrill and much more measured in tone than later texts which were written with more particular political tasks in mind. In the mid-1970s he unashamedly championed the case of realism over the more-idealist approaches inherent in *détente* and arms control. Gene Rostow's basic argument was that in history weak leaders and ideas of appeasement led ultimately to many wars, including the American Civil War and in the case of British leaders to both world wars. This argument is put bluntly in Rostow's article in *Strategic Review* in 1976, entitled 'The Safety of the Republic: Can the Tide be Turned?', which was also reprinted as the opening essay in a book edited by Rostow for the National Committee on American Foreign Policy and the Middle East (1976).

He is concerned by the isolationist sentiment generated, by the 'tragic setback' in Indo-China. This has led to the belief that there must be an 'easier way to defend the nation' (Rostow, 1976, 13). There is, he argues, a yearning to return to the isolation of the nineteenth century, a phenomenon aggravated by governments that refuse to tell the people the truth.

> One cannot expect the nation to take the threat of Soviet policy seriously when our leaders tell us that things are getting better; when they argue about how much to cut the defence budget, and fire the best Secretary of defence we had for years

because he balked at accepting the cuts proposed by the president, nor equally can we expect Congress or the people to carry out executive functions which only the Presidency can perform. [Rostow, 1976, 14]

Overcoming this and returning to the traditional state of affairs with a bipartisan support for a consensus foreign policy is the situation that Rostow advocates.

To 'turn the tide' in Rostow's view requires that the US culture's peaceful attributes and puritanical guilt be set aside in favour of a clear recognition of the need to view the world in terms of power politics. Thucydides's warning that the growth of Athenian power rather than the episodes of conflict prior to it was the cause of the Peloponnesian war is invoked. Here is the clear call to realism, power politics is the only acceptable way of understanding international affairs. Immediately after Thucydides, Rostow invokes Solzhenitsyn's warnings that the Soviet Union is well on its way to taking over much of the world. More specifically he adopts Solzhenitsyn's terminology which posits that the USSR has effectively won the 'Third World War' in that 'Europe, the Middle East, and many other parts of the Third World are passing inevitably into Soviet control' and that the 'Fourth World War, for America itself' was already underway (Rostow, 1976, 15). Thus, power politics is a matter of control over the Third World; it is about geopolitics.

In a section entitled 'The Balance of Power', we are told that Solzhenitsyn's prognosis can be reversed if 'the leaders of Europe, China, Japan and a few other countries including Israel' do the right things. But they will be decisively influenced by what the USA does. Rostow argues that the European peoples have not abandoned their 'will for independence' and quotes 'the extraordinary assertion of will of the people of Portugal, who are struggling – thus far effectively – to insist, despite massive Soviet efforts . . . that the Portuguese revolution must evolve in the direction of European pluralist democracy' (Rostow, 1976, 15). The Soviet challenge can be met, we are assured, but time is very short. Rostow thinks that the US public is concerned that something is badly wrong with US foreign policy but 'the silent faith of patriotism, the deepest and strongest force in our public life' (Rostow, 1976, 17) can, he argues, be mobilized to counter the policy of *détente*. 'The claim that detente with the Soviet Union has been achieved is an absurdity from start to finish, half public relations and half wishful thinking' (Rostow, 1976, 18). This is true because 'Soviet policy is exactly what it has always been, except that its pressures are greater and more diverse than ever, more sophisticated in style, and more difficult to deal with' (Rostow, 1976, 18).

He criticizes President Ford's argument that *détente* is a working relationship and that problems arise because both the USA and the USSR are superpowers. First, Rostow retorts that the problems are because the USSR is expansionist, not because it is a superpower. Second, he argues there is no working relationship to reduce tensions and avoid confrontations. On the contrary he argues that the USSR broke pledges to the Nixon administration and has been involved in international affairs at points of tension. Third, Rostow argues that a genuine *détente* is desirable, what is at issue is the assertion that the international relationship can be termed *détente*. 'Alas, the Cold War has never stopped. We have simply stopped talking about it. Its pressures today, in Lebanon, Israel, Portugal, Spain, Angola, and a good many other places are far greater and more important than those of the Berlin Airlift' (Rostow, 1976, 19).

In March 1978, in his contribution to a CPD panel discussion, Rostow summarizes his argument and applies the analogy of the 1930s British appeasement of Hitler to the 1970s. Here he issues a warning that the same historical mistakes are likely to be repeated by leaders in the USA unless drastic changes are made. One of the key reasons for the formation of the CPD was, he argues, the perceived need to 'arrest the slide toward chaos before it explodes into war'. This may happen if

> we feel ourselves threatened and coerced; if we sense that the last vestige of our power to govern our own destiny is slipping out of our hands; if the Soviet Union takes control of one strong point after another, and achieves domination in Western Europe or Japan, or in a number of places whose power in combination spells hegemony. We can never recall too often Thucydides' comment that the real cause of the Peloponnesian War was not the episodes of friction and conflict which preceded it, but the rise in the power of Athens, and the fear that this caused Sparta. [CPD, 1984, 29]

We are left in no doubt that 'Soviet imperial ambition, backed by a military buildup without parallel in modern history, are threatening the world balance of power on which our ultimate safety as a nation depends' (CPD, 1984, 29). And later, 'The pressures of Soviet policy have been greater since 1970 or so than ever before. The agreements for peace in Indo-China were torn up and disregarded. The Soviets supported aggressive and large scale war in Bangladesh, in the Middle East, and in Africa. There has been alarming slide toward chaos' (CPD, 1984, 30). Turning to the British experience in 1913 and 1938, Rostow concludes his remarks by arguing that the British could afford to be weak and fail to provide firm leadership, because the Americans were the ultimate guarantor that they would win in the end. But the USA in the 1970s 'has no sleeping giant to save us from our folly' (CPD, 1984, 31).

Two years later the CPD updated this argument when they turned their attention to the Carter Presidency's record in 'The 1980 Crisis and What We Should Do About It'. They argue that the Carter administration 'has, by words and acts of restraint, taken one unilateral step after another in the hope that the Soviet Union would accept such a policy of restraint for itself' (CPD, 1984, 172). But they state that the USSR has continued its expansionist programme and supported 'flagrant violations of the Charter of the United Nations' in episodes including 'support of North Vietnam's attack on South Vietnam, the Vietnamese invasion of Cambodia, the Palestine Liberation Organization's attacks on Israel, the use of poison gas against the Meo tribesmen in Laos, and the Soviet direct and inspired attacks on

Afghanistan, Angola, Ethiopia, Somalia and North and South Yemen' (CPD, 1984, 172). All of this is likened again to the 1930s and the policies of appeasement of Hitler, except that the USSR's expansionist programme is 'even more ambitious than that of Hitler' (CPD, 1984, 176). The final paragraphs of this statement read like a Ronald Reagan election speech, as they soon, indirectly, became:

> The tides of war are once again rushing the world toward general war. The United States and its allies still have time to protect their vital national interests by the methods of peace, but that time is growing short.
> The American people are ready to answer a call to action and, where necessary, sacrifice. Will their leaders chart an adequate programme – and will they do so in time? The answers to those questions will determine whether the 1980 crisis is the forerunner of catastrophe for the non-Communist world or whether it marks a turning point toward restoring peace with security and freedom. [CPD, 1984, 177]

This argument was not Rostow's or the CPD's alone; Walter Laquer (1978) argued a similar case in his 'Psychology of Appeasement' and CPD member Richard Perle (1979) wrote in terms of 'the lessons of the 1930s'. Later the arguments of the CPD were rehashed by Norman Podhoretz (1980a) in the March 1980 issue of *Commentary* where he published his own expression of concern about the then currently perceived malaise in US foreign affairs, under the title 'The Present Danger' taken from the CPD. Written a few months after the seizure of the US Embassy in Tehran and the Soviet intervention in Afghanistan, a topic for much geopolitical commentary in itself (Halliday, 1982; Kazanzadeh, 1980; Laquer, 1980, 1983, Luttwak, 1983), it sounded a warning in keeping with its title. The strident tone is in keeping with the CPD positions and underlying his analysis is the same geopolitical view of the world.

The article was revised and lengthened with the addition of material from his earlier *Commentary* article 'Making the World Safe for Communism' (1976) in a book published later that year by Simon and Schuster (1980b), which added the subtitle 'Do we have the will to reverse the decline of American power'. This book contains the critique of *détente* and what became known as 'the Vietnam Syndrome', in Podhoretz's terms the rise of a new isolationism and a new pacifism born out of the frustration of the Vietnam imbroglio. The arguments were substantially the same as those made by Rostow and Pipes as well as in the CPD materials. There was a call to view the world in terms of power politics, and a critique of the 'culture of appeasement'. Issued in 1980, this book, which took its title from the CPD, was effectively an election manifesto, concluding with a call for a return to policies of containment, a serious focus on the nature of communism, and a military buildup to ensure that the USA would never be intimidated in a crisis in the Third World. In combination, these themes were a clear call for a return to a form of realism as the basis for discussing US foreign policy, and prominent among the advocates of realism was Colin S. Gray.

The rationale for realism

The argument in favour of a realist perspective on foreign policy was strenuously made by Colin Gray in 'Foreign Policy – There is No Choice' (1976a), where he focused his attack on a series of what he argued were fallacies of liberal foreign policy. The article was published as a critical response to an earlier article by Thomas Hughes (1975) on US foreign policy. Gray argues that there are three fallacies running through Hughes's and the *Foreign Policy* editors views of US foreign policy. The fallacies are those of variants of idealism, the response is to make an appeal to realism, the only possible interpretation of events.

Gray's first target is 'moral exceptionalism'; the assumption that the USA is 'a uniquely principled actor in international politics'. Gray asserts that the Americans are no better or worse than any other nation in their international affairs. Political actions are thus the product of necessity, not moral choice, except for those states that are marginal to the overall patterns of global power who can act according to the dictates of their moral standards because they are protected by larger powers. Thus tensions between expediency and morality are not uniquely a US phenomenon. 'The major reasons why the problem of mutually accommodating practice and principle appears to be a very American dilemma, are the facts of geopolitics and the unwillingness of many American intellectuals to come to terms with the nature of the world in which they live' (1976a, 116). While different states in different geographical locations and reflecting different historical memories have different policy styles: 'International politics comprises one game only, with rules common to all foreign policy players' (1976a, 116). This game is power politics in which countries do what they have to do and morality rarely is a major consideration. 'The creed of *realpolitik* is often brutal and unattractive, yet it remains the only creed appropriate to the conduct of foreign relations. Power politics, to resort to a quite unfairly denigrated term, is the only game in town. The only choice open to the United States is between playing it effectively or ineffectively' (1976a, 120).

The second fallacy Gray draws attention to is the demand that the USA establish some harmony between the values of domestic life and foreign policy. This is related to the first fallacy and is dealt with in a similar manner. We are reminded that 'a substantial number of people continue to deny the fact that foreign politics is really quite unlike domestic politics' (1976a, 121). In particular Gray takes issue with Hughes's assertion that the USA has indulged in confrontation politics arguing that in places like Korea and Vietnam the only alternative to confrontation was acquiescence in military conquest. On the related charge that the USA has followed narrow self-interest in its foreign policy, Gray argues that the Western Europeans have been supported at tremendous cost to the USA in their folly of refusing to take their own defence seriously. Further, the activities of the KGB provide the rationale for US counter-intelligence activities of dubious legality in that the 'KGB and other illiberal and non-populist agencies' have to be opposed by effective counter-measures. International politics is 'an arena where no holds are barred' (1976a, 123–4). Ultimately, the argument comes down to this: 'If democracies are not prepared to slay and maim the innocent, then they had better accept the logical consequence – that they are surrendering their values to any state willing to do these things' (1976a, 125).

The third fallacy that Gray wishes to attack is that there is an alternative to *realpolitik*. In a polemic against the trends in international relations that had by the mid-1970s pushed realism aside, as a serious method of analysis in the discipline he argues that 'power politics, or realpolitik, is not merely one approach – and a very unfashionable one at that – among many. Realpolitik, for all its ambivalences of the central concepts of power and interest, is the enduring condition of international politics' (1976a, 125). In case this point is not clearly enough made Gray continues his tirade against the academic study of international relations with the following observations: 'To secure a measure of empathy for the problems of those conducting foreign policy, students would be better advised to read Thucydides' *Peloponnesian War* that a dozen tomes on system, cybernetics, and other dadist concepts purportedly relevant to an understanding of international political life' (1976a, 125–6). Global institution building is dismissed as 'globaloney'. The USA has to realize that its uniqueness lies in its 'global power balancing potential' not in its high moral character or purpose, because 'power must be balanced, interests must be secured, and – if necessary – force must be threatened and applied' (1976a, 127).

The arguments presented are sharply worded, and thrown into relief by the polemical phrasing. The reassertion of *realpolitik* could not be clearer. The focus on power as all that ultimately matters in the global order of things underlies all of Colin Gray's writing. In this position of *realpolitik* considerations of morality are at best subsidiary, at worst actively ridiculed. Gray is right in the middle of the cruder versions of the realist position, unashamedly promoting a view of an amoral international anarchy of competing states regulated solely by matters of power principally in terms of the use or the threat of the use of military force. But, as will be made clear in the next chapter, like the rest of the CPD members he understands realism as geopolitics.

Realism and geopolitics

The CPD focus on 'the present danger' in terms of power politics phrases the international political situation in terms of military confrontation and geopolitical expansion. In October 1978 the CPD released the first of a series of lengthy analyses of the US–Soviet military balance. 'Is America Becoming Number 2?' started its analysis with a section entitled 'Facing Basic Facts', which deals with the CPD's overall conception of the global situation. The first basic fact Americans have to face is that the historical situation pertaining to US security before 1917, 'when, behind the screen of the British fleet, we enjoyed something close to immunity from the fact or the threat of external attack' (CPD, 1984, 39) no longer holds. This situation arose from the remoteness of the USA from any possible locus of hostile attack 'and Britain's success in maintaining the European balance of power'. Now 'it is an unwelcome novelty for Americans to have to pay sustained attention to military factors as the ultimate basis of national security' (CPD, 1984, 39). Again, the geopolitical theme is present.

The USA and the USSR are the two major forces in international politics, European nations are important only 'as allies and partners of the United States or as satellites of the Soviet Union' (CPD, 1984, 40). The difference in status between East and West could not be clearer: in the East they are 'satellites' under domination and control, held in orbit, by the USSR; in the West they are allies and partners. Japan is in a largely similar position 'because of the logic of nuclear power' (CPD, 1984, 40). Not surprisingly the next sentence reminds us once again that the

> two superpowers have utterly opposing conceptions of world order. The United States, true to its traditions and ideals, sees a world moving towards peaceful unit and cooperation within a regime of law. The Soviet Union, for ideological as well as geopolitical reasons, sees a world riven by conflict and destined to be ruled exclusively by Marxism–Leninism. [CPD, 1984, 40]

The superpowers are the only countries powerful enough to confront each other militarily, and this confrontation has been the primary consideration for US national security since the Second World War. This conflict 'also deeply affects the relationship between the industrialised democracies as a group and the developing nations of the southern hemisphere' (CPD, 1984, 40). This is a crucial dimension of the global struggle according to the CPD because

> The Soviet Union has sought to exploit difficulties among the developing nations, and between them and the industrialized nations, in order to gain positions of strategic importance in its drive for global dominance. The Soviet Union, driven both by deep rooted Russian imperial impulses and by Communist ideology, insists on pursuing an expansionist course. In its endless, probing quest, it attempts to take advantage of every opportunity to enlarge its influence. [CPD, 1984, 40]

As an essential part of its programme the USSR 'seeks to outstrip the United States and its allies in every category of military power' in order to 'maintain and increase the momentum of its expansion'. This is followed by a short passage which graphically portrays the binary nature of the Cold War discourse.

The strategists and political planners of the USSR

> are trained to understand that military power is the essential guarantor to expanding political influence. It is the first object of their policy to assure that guarantee.
> Thus, it would be irrational as well as imprudent to ignore the military element in the Soviet-American relationship. Although the political, economic, and human aspects are each important, the military dimension is fundamental and potentially decisive. [CPD, 1984, 40]

As argued earlier, the specification of Otherness in the CPD literature leads it to a praxaeological specification of Otherness which leads the CPD to advocate precisely what it deprecates in the adversary. Thus we have to comply with the instructions of those in the USSR who teach their political planners and strategists. The viewpoint of the expansionist planners who view the world in conflictual terms is thus elevated to the rational view; those who advocate the pursuance of the USA's goals of a peaceful world order in a regime of law are thus, despite the ritual obeisance to these themes further up the page, delegitimized as irrational. Ultimately, to the CPD what counts is military might, all else is secondary. The implication from all this is clear; all those hated, reviled Russians are really right, the arms controllers, all who work for other goals are dupes or suffering from naivety. Realism is back with vengeance; there is only power defined in military terms. The most important factor in military matters is strategic nuclear weapons, and the means of delivering them to their targets. This is the ultimate power in international affairs.

From this all else follows in the CPD conceptualization. Thus the USSR's goal is to translate this preponderance in nuclear weapons which they are attempting to acquire into political predominance without having to fight a nuclear war. Having a preponderance of nuclear power will limit the diplomatic and political possibilities of any adversaries, forcing them to concede in a crisis. From this the argument points to the need for the USA to have enough forces 'to deter military aggression throughout the spectrum of armed conflict with forces appropriate to the threat' (CPD, 1984, 41). Thus a strategic nuclear arsenal is not enough on its own.

> Consistent with their doctrine, the Soviets have long maintained non-nuclear, or conventional, superiority in the European theatre and may well be more willing to use that superiority either for war or for coercive diplomacy in the event they achieve significant strategic nuclear supremacy. The Soviets are moving toward a capability, if diplomacy fails, to prevail in Europe without destroying it, using more accurate weapons of lower nuclear yields. [CPD, 1984, 43]

Moreover, they have built up chemical weapons as well in Europe, 'again, a potential means of winning battles and taking territory without destroying its assets' (CPD, 1984, 43). In contrast, the USA neglects chemical weapons, and pursues 'unenforceable agreements to outlaw chemical warfare' (CPD, 1984, 43). In contrast, the USA 'appears to be retreating for both policy and budgetary reasons to a posture of "finite deterrence", perhaps even to a "fortress America" ' (CPD, 1984, 43).

'Is America Becoming Number 2?' then proceeds to itemize the roles of the USSR's formidable standing array of forces' against China and Western Europe. They argue that the USSR's assertion that their large conventional and nuclear forces in Europe are to prevent any repeat of the historical pattern of invasion from there is false. The CPD asserts that these forces cannot be explained in terms of defence but rather present 'a clear and present danger to the political independence and indeed to the territorial integrity of Western Europe', the principal strategic goal of Soviet Policy being 'to bring Western Europe under its control' (CPD, 1984, 43). If this were done 'they believe, China and Japan would draw obvious conclusions. The global balance of power would be transformed to Soviet advantage, and the United States would be left isolated in a hostile world' (CPD, 1984, 43).

Likewise, the forces facing the Chinese are rationalized by the Russians, according to the CPD as 'necessary because China is traditionally antagonistic and currently re-visionist in Soviet eyes'. Thus the USSR 'claims its huge deployment of forces against China is essentially defensive. To the Chinese, of course the Soviet deployment is threatening' (CPD, 1984, 44). Note the phraseology: the Soviets claim the weapons are defensive; they *are* of course threatening to the Chinese. The possibility that historical claims by the Chinese to parts of what is now the USSR and the presence of a growing Chinese nuclear arsenal, with no obvious enemies except for the USSR, might be taken seriously as a long-term threat by the Russians is simply defined away.

The remaining concerns are the maintenance of Soviet hegemony in Eastern Europe, the Middle East, which they regard as their 'most important geopolitical target. They believe that control over the space, the waterways, and the oil of the region would be a major and even decisive weapon in permitting them to dominate Europe, Africa, and large parts of Asia' (CPD, 1984, 44). The denial of oil supplies, or the threat thereof, is a desired means of putting pressure on the USA and Europe. Finally, the USSR supports 'wars of national liberation' and therefore requires the capability to 'project power throughout the Southern Hemisphere' being 'particularly interested in positions which out-flank the Middle East or China' (CPD, 1984, 44). This notion of 'outflanking' is again present and is elaborated later in this statement thus:

> If the Soviet Union gained control of a small country in Africa, that fact might be a matter of concern to us, but not in itself a threat. If Soviet control spread throughout a large part of Africa, however, and began to outflank the Middle East and raise questions about our capacity to control sea lanes leading to the Persian Gulf, to obtain access to raw materials, and to project power where necessary, our security problem would greatly magnify. [CPD, 1984, 66]

Finally, the CPD takes aim at the interpretation that the USSR is now (in the mid-1970s) a conservative power run by an elderly bureaucracy which is inherently conservative, arguing that this view is falsified by Soviet behaviour.

> In recent years, the elderly bureaucrats of the Kremlin have undertaken programmes of expansion far beyond Stalin's dreams. Stalin probed toward Turkey, Greece, Berlin and Korea, and pulled back when the risks became serious. His successors have sponsored wars of far greater magnitude – the breach of the 1973 agreement for peace in Indo-China, for example; the Arab aggression in the Middle East of October 1973; and the current campaign in Africa. It is an illusion to suppose that the Soviets do not mean what they say. It is folly to ignore how they act. [CPD, 1984, 44]

Thus, in conclusion, this section argues that the USSR is convinced of the use of military power in international affairs and diplomacy and uses it whenever it can. Thus, with its strategic buildup and its plans to fight and win a nuclear war, it presents a grave threat to US security.

There are many other significant references to the geopolitical theme in later papers which link the notion of theatre (regional) nuclear deterrence and naval power to the larger scheme. In a sentence worthy of Spykman, we are told 'Theatre deterrence must also be maintained because continued Soviet encroachment could isolate the United States from the political and military affairs of a Soviet-dominated Eurasian landmass' (CPD, 1984, 87). This is also of concern in the naval sphere, where 'the Soviet navy has developed into a major threat to vital sea lanes and as an important diplomatic instrument to expand and consolidate Soviet power' (CPD, 1984, 91). This naval presence is seen as offensive because the 'Soviet Union is a continental power with secure interior lines of communications and an autarkic economic system' (CPD, 1984, 90). This is in contrast to the USA being a power based on sea trade routes and raw materials supply routes. The Soviet navy therefore is seen as offensive and supported by Soviet land-based airpower is assigned the tasks of destroying the US navy and disrupting its global maritime communications. Other roles are not considered.

Later Paul Nitze was to return to these geopolitical themes in his policy paper 'Is SALT II a Fair Deal for the United States?' released by the CPD on 16 May 1979. Again, the concern with power projection as it had come to be called in the area of the Rimland was prominent in Nitze's concerns. Since the Second World War the US navy had enjoyed 'unchallenged control of the seas. This assured we could project our power, wherever needed, on the periphery of the Eurasian landmass' (CPD, 1984, 159). Nitze expresses alarm that the Soviet buildup of intermediate-range nuclear weapons is on its way to developing such a capacity. Reiterating the now familiar refrain that the Russians do not wish nuclear war but rather to expand their influence under the threat of superiority, Nitze provides a much more specific portrayal of the details of the CPD's geopolitical scenarios than the earlier papers which were all short on specifics. It involves a series of outflanking manoeuvers thus:

> By achieving dominance over the Middle East, they aim to outflank Europe. They propose to outflank the Middle East by achieving controlling positions in Afghanistan, Iran, and Iraq on one side, South and North Yemen, Eritrea, Ethiopia, and Mozambique on the other, and by achieving the neutrality of Turkey to the north. Concurrently, they are attempting to encircle China by pressure on Pakistan and India, by alliance with Vietnam, and dominance over North Korea. The United States is the only power in a position potentially to frustrate these aims. It is therefore seen as the principal enemy. [CPD, 1984, 160]

The use of the term 'outflank' borrowed from military parlance stretches its meaning to great lengths, calling into question the CPD's understanding either of the term or of the geographical arrangements of the continents.

Rostow (1976) also uses this geographical allusion repeatedly. However, it also suggests the use of the logic of dominos to which O'Sullivan (1982) draws attention. This suggests that an increase in influence by the USSR in one part of the globe is automatically followed by other increases in non-contiguous areas, by mechanisms that are left unexplained. It reduces the complexity of international politics to a spatially homogeneous arena like a chess board where pieces act in purely geometric terms. Local considerations are simply ignored. The moves are military, any economic influences are solely in terms of the denial of minerals or oil to Europe and Japan.

The discussion then goes on to argue, as before, that Soviet nuclear supremacy at each level of escalation in a potential conflict in these zones confers on them unsurpassable diplomatic leverage, thus ensuring that they can continue to expand their influence because if the USA interferes it can be forced to back down. Strategic superiority, the level of ultimate force, helps at all lesser levels. Thus, strategic superiority is seen again in its relationship to geopolitical expansion.

The geopolitical themes remain constant through the CPD papers in the late 1970s, although the degree of specificity and the relative emphasis shifts from paper to paper. The danger from the USSR is ultimately seen in terms of their expansion or political domination into Western Europe primarily. Their most likely avenue of approach is through the 'outflanking' of the Middle East via bases in Africa. Thus they can gain control of large areas of the Euro-Asian landmass and, hence, by threats and the decline in US influence remove Japan and other nations from their friendships with the USA, thereby gaining hegemony which will leave the USA powerless and isolated. Behind all this lies the buildup of military force which provides the ability to intervene in areas beyond their traditional sphere and behind that the buildup of nuclear weaponry which the CPD is so concerned will deny the USA the possibility to stand up to the Russians in a crisis. These ideas of nuclear superiority are the key to understanding the CPD's consistent vehement opposition to SALT II, the subject of Chapter eight's analysis. What is crucial, however, is the CPD's understanding of nuclear superiority as being essential to extended deterrence, necessary to stop the Soviet geopolitical momentum.

Realism as geopolitics

Historical analogy is important to the CPD position. Thus they rely on the argument that the USA is appeasing the USSR. They argue this by conflating the totalitarian foreign policy tactics of the USSR with those of Nazi Germany in the 1930s. The parallels include the use of threat by the USSR to accomplish expansion. Military intimidation is a key tactic. All this assumes that the USA is really militarily unprepared, beset by Podhoretz's 'culture of appeasement', the inevitable result of which would be retreat and the USSR gaining global domination. In contrast to this, other commentators (Kahler, 1979) have pointed to the historical analogy of 1914 as more appropriate. This analogy points to a situation of complex alliance structures with numerous foreign entanglements and interests facing each other; accidents waiting to happen to drag them into a war that neither side wants but which the logic of events compels them to fight. The consequences of adopting this historical analogy are fundamentally different, pointing to the need to negotiate a series of agreements that limit the possibilities of entanglement and escalation, and also limit the overall number of nuclear weapons. This is a conclusion that the CPD cannot accept because of their axiological specification of the Other as evil and threatening, and the USA as purely defensive. With this specification the only possible source of war, accidental or deliberate, is ultimately traceable to the actions of that Other. This is because in realist terms the USSR is a revisionist power, one attempting to change the international order to its benefit. The alternative is the CPD solution: build such a formidable force of weapons that the USSR could not think of contemplating war. Faced with such military power, its geopolitical campaign would be stalled.

The geopolitical perspective of the CPD is conflated with their realism. Politics is understood as power politics, which relates to military control over territory. The point needs to be made that this is a very crude form of realism indeed. The tradition of realism associated with Morgenthau, Carr, Kennan as well as writers like Bull and Wight, is open to much more subtle readings of power in international affairs. Ideas of international community and the respect for the perceived national interests of all actors are essential to this tradition. Balancing power and maintaining international order are delicate matters in which diplomacy and politics is important; not everything is reduced to the crude calculus of overkill capabilities.

But what is essential here in the CPD formulation of the international situation is the specification of the USSR as evil and crucially expansionist. The whole specification of the USSR as evil on the axiological dimension of Otherness denies the applicability of the classical concerns of realism with international order and stability. Because the USSR is expansionist, and because the CPD 'knows' its true nature by the application of its superior 'historical method', the 'interests' of the USSR can be dismissed as illegitimate. Thus Kennan can denounce the militarist policies of the 1980s while remaining entirely consistent with the original realist formulation of his position in the 1940s when he clearly advocated a firm policy towards the USSR, but one which recognized that it had legitimate security interests in Eastern Europe (Kennan, 1947, 1983; Mayers, 1986). Likewise, Morgenthau can remonstrate against the 'pathologies of American power' (1977), criticizing the failure of many policy-makers to take seriously the importance of nuclear weapons.

The CPD's geopolitical perspective can be critiqued on theoretical grounds, in terms of its conceptions about the relations of space and power, and in empirical terms, by assessing the relative increase or decrease in relative influence of the superpowers in terms of their control of global resources, and in terms of its failure to deal with the particular circumstances in the Third World where the geopolitical contest is played out. The theoretical critique will be dealt with later, this section outlines the empirical limitations of the CPD's geopolitical discourse.

In simple empirical terms, the CPD arguments are vulnerable on two grounds. First is simple arithmetic; the CPD litany of Soviet takeovers in the 1970s considers only those cases that can be interpreted in terms of a unilateral advantage. Thus the ambivalent changes in their position in the Horn of Africa are ignored, in strategic terms the changing of sides in the Ethiopian–Somali conflict lost them bases on the Indian Ocean in Somalia which are important to their monitoring of the US Polaris SLBM carriers operating in the North West Indian Ocean. The Centre for Defence Information (1979) attempted a summary although crude assessment of the global balance of forces which argues that far from a Soviet geopolitical momentum in the 1970s the Russians had in fact lost influence globally from the late 1950s. (Walter Laquer's (1980) response in the pages of *Commentary* to the Centre for Defence Information's (1979) assessment shows clearly that the neo-conservatives reduced influence and power solely to matters of military power. Thus he argues that Cuba has been able to project power in the Third World where the USA has been unable to. Economic influence or political and cultural domination in more complex patterns are simply excluded in these formulations.)

The major decline in influence in the Middle East, in part as a result of the Egyptian disenchantment with the USSR and the efforts of Kissinger's diplomacy and subsequently the Carter administration's 'Camp David' process, was overlooked by the CPD. Rostow (1976) even went so far a to try to argue that the US diplomatic initiatives after the Yom Kippur War resulted in a decline in US influence in the Middle East and was to the USSR's advantage. More sophisticated evaluations of the geopolitical developments of relevance to the USSR (Dibb, 1988; Kaplan, 1981; Mccgwire, 1987a, 1987b; Steele, 1985) show the USSR as a major military power but one constrained internally and externally, certainly not one with a grand design for global domination on any time scale.

The second empirical problem with the CPD position is the reduction of all developments in the Third World to matters of superpower conflict. Thus the indigenous developments are overlooked, all causes of political and economic change are reduced to the machinations of the adversary or the benign assistance of the USA. This gross oversimplification is clear in the Middle East and the so called 'Arc of Crisis' (Halliday, 1982). It operates to heighten concern over foreign developments because everything not immediately identifiable as a benefit to 'our' side is portrayed as a potential opportunity for the USSR to gain influence. The result enhances the paranoid style of foreign policy. Its premises deny indigenous factors and are hence insensitive to the geographical diversity of political developments. Paranoia in the context of military definitions of national security encourages further militarism which in turn feeds the dynamics of the security dilemma.

Coupled to this is the key ethnocentric ideological assumption that 'we', being moral and upholding the universal aspirations of the human race for freedom and so on, are justified in involving ourselves in the affairs of the world whether invited or not. As was pointed out long ago (Franck and Weisband, 1972), the verbal strategies used to justify this kind of action by both superpowers are effectively identical. They function by axiologically identifying 'us' as good and the Other as evil. The merits of the individual case are of secondary importance to the overall imputation of evil intention to the other side. Once that has been established, then the details can be placed aside; intervention is justified when you are on the side of the angels.

In the case of the CPD, geopolitics was grafted onto existing ICBM vulnerability concerns within the intelligence community. The technical arcana of ICBM vulnerabilities and the possibilities of first strikes given the unknowns of missile accuracy were in some cases for public consumption reduced to a comparison of the relative sizes of nuclear missiles in the superpower arsenals. While ideological mobilization around these kinds of issues was possible, it was even more so around the theme of the geopolitical expansion of the USSR. This was because the expansionist theme, coupled to the critique of the appeasers of *détente* rendered complex international developments coherent around a simple axis of explanation: it was all part of the Soviet quest for global domination. Thus, US setbacks were blamed on the machinations of the Other. The KGB, if not the Cubans, could always be blamed for adverse developments in the global arena even if their direct hand was not visible. Threatening developments, particularly in the Middle East, were implied to be the work of the USSR; their increased military buildup and, in particular, the development of the naval forces which gained a global presence in the 1970s fit simply into an overall image of Soviet expansion first given concrete expression in the 1947 *Life* graphics of a red amoeba-like growth spreading its tentacles across the globe (O'Sullivan, 1986).

Here the CPD forged a link between the two themes: the Soviet expansionist theme; and the strategic theme that the Soviets were developing a nuclear supremacy and a strategic doctrine of fighting a nuclear war. The two come together in the coercion thesis, where the USSR could supposedly compel the USA not to intervene in a crisis in the Third World because of its potential ability to win any confrontation. Thus extended, deterrence is brought into the picture. The USA has an obligation to defend any and all countries from the predations of the USSR; to do so requires deterring the USSR in any field in the Third World. Thus a nuclear war-fighting capacity is needed that can 'project power' anywhere on the globe. The USA is justified in being there because of its interests in saving the world from communism, but it has to have a nuclear force capable of compelling the USSR to back down in a crisis. Only then will it be able to contain the Russians.

If it fails to contain the USSR, then gradually the USSR will encroach on Africa and elsewhere, and the USA will decline in global influence. What worries the CPD about this is not really the fate of various countries in the Third World, but that its influence will decline in Europe, Japan and China. In these circumstances Europe might allow itself to be Finlandized and Japan would drift beyond US dominance. In these circumstances the USA would lose its global hegemony and cease to be the dominant power on the planet. To maintain its dominance the CPD argued that a major military buildup was needed. It is here that the particular controversy over new missiles in Europe comes into focus (Johnstone, 1984). The so called Euro-Missile controversy is best understood as an attempt to reassert US political control over an increasingly restive Europe with ideas of *détente* and political co-operation.

In all of this the Third World is reduced to a playing field in which the superpowers play out the great game of influence (O'Loughlin, 1986), the prize to the winner is the global influence over Europe and Japan. Thus the traditional Cold War theme of containment as a political device to mobilize European societies in the service of global capitalism is rerun. Here the major conflict is not about political and military control in the Third World for its own sake, but is secondary to maintaining the Europeans in *pax Americana*. This specification of the Third World as a playing field suggests a physical model of the area as a politically empty part of 'absolute space' waiting to be 'filled' by 'projected' power. What matters again in global terms are not local cultures or politics, it is the abstract clashing of military power in spaces that can be used to outflank the West if not filled with Western 'power'. Again, the assumptions of space as the container of political activity is present; security is defined in terms of spatial exclusion and territorial control.

Underlying these themes was the old geopolitical theme of the Heartland land power attempting to wrest total control over the Rimlands from naval powers. The expansion of the USSR into the Rimlands is of serious concern in all of the CPD texts. Although they rarely explicitly use geopolitical language, Soviet domination of the Eurasian landmass is referred to. The most explicit statement of the geopolitical theme and the utility of its overarching conceptualizations of the global political scene is found in Colin Gray's attempt to update the work of Mackinder and Spykman.

Chapter 7

Geopolitics

Containment and geopolitics

Realism came to dominate many discussions of international relations in the post-war period, and the key concept of interest understood in terms of power is important in the post-war political discourse. Interests are intimately related to security, understood in the sense of preventing the potential adversary invading one's (territorially understood) space, which in turn relates to physical protection and political alignments at, in the US case, the global scale. And at the global scale this involves considerations of matters of classical geopolitics.

In 1950 NSC68 put the threat to US national security in classical geopolitical terms:

> On the one hand, the people of the world yearn for relief from the anxiety arising from the risk of atomic war. On the other hand, any substantial further extension of the area under the domination of the Kremlin would raise the possibility that no coalition adequate to confront the Kremlin with greater strength could be assembled. It is in this context that this republic and its citizens stand in their deepest peril. [NSC68 as quoted in Etzold and Gaddis eds, 1978, 368]

This theme is a reiteration of Spykman and Mackinder which was to recur repeatedly. Thus in a major statement on the post-war role of the USA, Walt Rostow (1960) defined the term of national interest in an explicit statement of geopolitics, although the term as such never appears in the relevant passage. In it Rostow argues that the USA has been in danger since the late eighteenth century because of

> the simple geographic fact that the combined resources of Eurasia, including its military potential, have been and remain superior to those of the United States – Eurasia being here defined to include Asia, the Middle East, and Africa as well as Europe. The United States must be viewed essentially as a continental island off the greater land mass of Eurasia. [Rostow, 1960, 543]

There are two threats that Rostow identifies as stemming from these facts of global geography. First:

> Since the combined resources of Eurasia could pose a serious threat of military defeat to the United States, it is the American interest that no single power or group of powers hostile or potentially hostile to the United States dominate that

area or a sufficient portion of it to threaten the United States and any coalition the United States can build and sustain. [Rostow, 1960, 544]

Second, because of modern communication technologies:

> Whatever the military situation might be, a Eurasia coalesced under totalitarian dictatorships would threaten the survival of democracy both elsewhere and in the United States. It is, therefore, equally the American interest that the societies of Eurasia develop along lines broadly consistent with the nation's own ideology; for under modern conditions it is difficult to envisage the survival of a democratic American society as an island in a totalitarian sea. [Rostow, 1960, 544]

This statement reflects the classic geopolitical concerns of Spykman with global domination based on the supposedly inaccessible Heartland of Eurasia in Sibera, updated to include the opposition to 'totalitarian' communism. On the basis of this there follows a detailed discussion of the US 'ideological interest' in working to prevent the accession to power of 'totalitarian' regimes in Eurasia.

In the 1970s these arguments were often disregarded, Kissinger's geopolitics had blurred the formulation of containment into a US role as a power balancer in a more complex global power scheme (Sloan, 1988). The SALT process in particular, and arms control in general, focused political attention on the technical arcana of nuclear weapons systems rather than the geopolitical contexts of their potential usage in global confrontation. Precisely because of these shifts in the nuclear discourse, Colin Gray (1977a) set about reinterpreting the geopolitical context for US military policy.

Colin Gray is unique among his fellow members of the CPD in the extensive and the comprehensive nature of his writings. The overarching components of his conception is a consciously articulated geopolitical vision; he makes explicit what is often implicit in the CPD materials. In particular, he rewrites Spykman and Mackinder to present an argument that their ideas of geopolitics are not only still relevant to the understanding of international politics, but that they are *the* essential basis to any adequate understanding of global affairs. He draws from the discourses of realism, strategy and sovietology to construct a global perspective of world affairs structured explicity in the terms of geopolitics. His arguments provide the theoretical framework for the CPD's geopolitical concerns outlined in the last chapter and lead into his conception of the USSR as an expansionist Empire; the key political assumption in his subsequent nuclear 'theory of victory'.

The conflation of realism and its concerns with the 'national interest' with the military concerns for forward defence against the USSR immediately after the Second World War, subsumed security into a hegemonic geopolitical framework. Power was equated with the military domination of territory; containment was a geopolitical strategy. The *détente* and arms control approaches to international affairs challenged this hegemony because they emphasized other concerns. Gray's rationale for reassessing the literature on geopolitics is clearly to attempt to rearticulate these themes precisely because the geopolitical premises of foreign policy were no longer accepted by the *détente* advocates and the arms controllers. 'The primary intention is to outline an appropriate framework of assumptions for the analysis of East–West relations' (Gray, 1977a, 2). Thus his document is an attempt to reconstruct the premises of containment militarism as an attempt to redirect the concerns of security discourse to matters of military domination by territory. Enough of *détente* and economic issues, security is to be once more understood in terms of space and power.

Geopolitics and superpower rivalry

Colin Gray's intellectual debt to the writings of Nicholas Spykman is clear. Recently in an article in the *Washington Quarterly*, Gray calls him a 'great Geopolitical theorist' (1986a, 64), but references to his writings appear periodically throughout Gray's work. In the *Foreign Policy* article on realism, discussed in the last chapter, Gray terms Spykman's book *America's Strategy in World Politics* (1942) '*the* outstanding work on realpolitik' (1976a, 125). Spykman also wrote *The Geography of the Peace* which was published in 1944. Gray's *The Geopolitics of the Nuclear Era* (1977a) starts with four long quotes from these two works which outline Spykman's credo of power and territorial control as the essence of international politics. In this realist conception sovereign states are in never-ending competition to enhance their relative security, which is defined in terms of power. Power is in the last resort the ability to wage war in a world where the most fundamental factor in foreign policy is geography because it is the most permanent of the factors. This notion of permanency and enduring relations is important in Gray's perspective.

In a reiteration of the realist theme discussed in Chapter six, Gray's monograph opens with an assertion that US foreign policy analysts are operating on the bases of inadequate analyses, having succumbed to 'fashionable shibboleths that do not speak to the vital interests of Western societies (1977a, 2). In particular the 'pseudo-sophistication' of international relations teaching in US universities is criticized, with the principal journals called 'scholarly monuments to irrelevance' (1977a, 3). This is coupled with an expression of regret that Spykman's texts are not on many university book lists. This observation is justified by an assertion that '– for all the admittedly dated details – Spykman directs the student toward the important and the enduring as opposed to the trivial and the transient' (1977a, 2). We are then informed that the only approach to the field of international relations that 'enables the student to appreciate the essence of the field' is the approach best termed 'power politics' (1977a, 2).

Other approaches may be of value but they all tend to lead away from 'what one must call the real world' (1977a, 3). In contrast:

> This study focuses upon the most pressing, dangerous, and potentially fatal fact of the contemporary world – namely, that we are at the mid-stage of a shift in relative power and influence to the Soviet Union that is of historic proportions, and which promises, unless arrested severely, to have enduring significance. This

easily demonstrated fact does not detract from the importance of other processes, sometimes only distantly related, that are eroding familiar structures in international relations. . . . But the rise in Soviet standing in the world, which may be traced almost exclusively to the increase in relative Soviet military capabilities, both dwarfs other concerns in its immediacy and seriousness, and renders other problems far less tractable. [Gray, 1977a, 3]

Thus the argument is not that he deals with the totality of international relations, rather, in keeping with the traditional tenets of realism, he suggests that there are other aspects of international relations, but that the military-diplomatic aspects are the most important. He charges that international relations practitioners have forgotten that the central concern of their craft is with relative influence and physical survival, ultimately a matter of power. In particular, he argues that the central role given to arms control and international diplomacy has caused the pre-eminent importance of constructing a defence policy that can guarantee foreign policy success to be neglected. The rationale for geopolitics as a framework for understanding international relations is reintroduced in the terms 'directing attention to matters of enduring importance' (1977a, 5).

More specifically geopolitics is defined in Saul Cohen's (1963) terms as 'the relation of international political power to the geographical setting' ('Gray, 1977a, 5). Denying any deterministic implications we are assured that the 'Geopolitical factors – that is to say, both the operational environment (the world as it really is) and the psychological environment (the world as seen by conditioned and fallible human beings) – do not *require* that certain policies be adopted' (1977a, 6). Governments may or may not pursue the policy options presented by their geopolitical situation. But a clear understanding of geopolitical matters, in Gray's estimation, will lead to better foreign policy. This monograph is his contribution to the cultivation of a geopolitical sensitivity, motivated by a fear that the 'historical bid for world hegemony on the part of the Soviet Union is not appreciated for what it is by Western publics' (1977a, 6–7).

This bid for hegemony (understood in the realist sense of domination) is central to his concern, and it underlies the central fact of political life on the global scene. Thus the East–West rivalry is a permanent feature of the international scene. 'In the very long term, Soviet–American rivalry may wither away after the fashion of the Christian–Muslim competition, but such a prospect can play no sensible part in the policy making of the late 1970s' (1977a, 8). Soviet ideology is very important in Colin Gray's conception of things; the Soviet system defines all non-socialist countries as 'enemies' and hence he argues there is no distinction between the USSR as a unit of power and as a bearer of ideology ('a church') (1977a, 8).

In Gray's analysis the central tenets of communism involve a long-term struggle between communism and the West so there is no possibility of any genuine endeavour to stabilize East–West relations. The rest of the argument in this section is predictable from CPD material discussed in the last three chapters. Thus all views to the contrary are myths; the ideas of *détente* and common interest are not valid. The myths of *détente* are as a result of psychological projection of Western humane views on an alien culture. Time is not on the West's side as the USSR remains a command society, ultimately prepared to use the threat of military force to pursue its foreign policy objectives. To understand all these factors and their implications the only adequate framework is that of geopolitics. He continues, in a manner consistent with Mackinder's understanding of geopolitics:

> geopolitics is not simply one set of ideas among many competing sets that help to illuminate the structure of policy problems. Rather it is a meta- or master framework that, without predetermining policy choice, suggests long term factors and trends in the security objectives of particular territorially organized security communities. [Gray, 1977a, 11]

The leitmotiv of geopolitics, we are informed, is the struggle of land power against sea power. Nuclear weapons and their methods of delivery have, Gray argues, led to the abandonment of geopolitical thinking. Thus a major war between the superpowers is now conceived as a matter of immediate massive nuclear attack by nuclear missiles. Gray argues that much international history is also forgotten but that the major geographical features of the planet continue to pose unresolved problems of nuclear strategy for Western officials. In another article published the same year Gray elaborated on the theme of lessons of strategy from the pre-war era being forgotten in the nuclear age (1977b). The realist/geopolitical perspective relies on these continuities. He argues that the global situation is best seen as a long-term struggle between the 'insular imperium' of the USA and the 'heartland imperium' of the USSR (1977a, 14). In this Mackinderian conception, Eurasia and Africa comprise the World Island and the USA and Australia comprise the outer crescent of islands. 'As of the mid-1970s, in geopolitical terms, superpower conflict may be characterised as a struggle between a substantially landlocked Heartland superpower, and a substantially maritime dependent (in security perspective) insular superpower for control/denial of control of the Eurasian–African 'Rimlands' (Gray, 1977a, 14).

More specifically, in an argument consistent with Nitze's concerns with Soviet 'outflanking' of the Middle East and Europe discussed in the last chapter, we are offered the following essential credo:

> 1. Control of the World Island of Eurasia–Africa by a single power would, over the long term, mean control of the world.
> 2. Land power and sea power meet/clash in the Eurasian–African Rimlands and marginal seas. Control of those Rimlands and marginal seas by an insular power is *not* synonymous with control of the World Island, but it does mean the denial of eventual global hegemony to the Heartland power (that is, the Soviet Union). [Gray, 1977a, 15]

Again in line with the CPD position, we are informed that the 'proximate stake' in this conflict is the control of Europe which the USSR might gain by military conquest, 'Finlandization', or by control over the oil production areas of the Middle East. Gray argues that the second option would be difficult and risky as a result of the 'ideological infection' that would result within the Soviet sphere. The whole key to the long-run Soviet foreign policy is thus one of 'hemispheric denial' (see Atkeson, 1976) in keeping the USA from access to the Rimlands of Eurasia. In particular, echoing the CPD concerns discussed in the last chapter, the Soviet interventions and 'proxy wars' in Africa are viewed with alarm as their gains there supposedly provide them with future bases of military action and undermine US credibility in the support of regimes opposed to the USSR.

But Europe remains the key to limiting Soviet expansion. Gray further argues that it is unlikely in the foreseeable future that a European defence arrangement will be forthcoming. Thus there will be, in his geopolitical scheme, a continued need for the USA to maintain forces there to defend *its* interests. Gray notes that no president of the USA has ever spelt this out for the US people. He argues that a familiarity with geopolitical ways of thinking would remove the difficulties in seeing this. In other words, it will be rendered acceptable, common sense and hence, to some degree at least, hegemonic. Once this geopolitical scheme is familiar, all else will follow. Hence the necessity to review and update the theoretical literature of geopolitics.

Mackinder updated

Having laid this argument about growing Soviet military and geopolitical power before the reader, only then does Gray turn to review in detail the writings of the earlier geopoliticians. He carefully distances himself from the *geopolitik* of Haushofer vintage and the too enthusiastic emulations of it in wartime USA. Gray argues that Halford Mackinder is the most influential of the geopoliticians; the key idea of the land-based invulnerable 'pivot area' on the World Island is reviewed, along with the Outer Crescent, of Japan, Britain and North America, being invulnerable to land power. Mackinder's argument that railroads had rendered the premises of sea power's supremacy outdated, and that there was a possibility that an alliance of Germany and the USSR could take over the World Island is reviewed and Gray is careful to note the changes in his arguments over time as he rethought his theories.

The term Heartland was borrowed by Mackinder from Fairgrieve (1915) for his 1919 book *Democratic Ideals and Reality*, and Gray emphasizes that Mackinder never argued that the Heartland takeover of the World Island was inevitable. Thus it is possible for a combination of Inner and Outer Crescent powers to stop its expansion. Mackinder's later writings argued that there was a possible counter-weight to the expansion of Soviet power in the formation of a Midland Ocean basin power grouping in the North Atlantic. In Gray's estimation Spykman's modifications of Mackinder's scheme overestimated the power of the Rimlands to resist Heartland power. However:

> looking at the world of the late 1970s the theories of Mackinder and Spykman yield a common logic for policy. The United States cannot afford to tolerate the

effective control of Eurasia–Africa by the Soviet Union. It must serve, in its own vital interests, as the functional successor to Great Britain as an active balancer of power on, and bearing upon, the Rimlands of Eurasia. Such a geopolitical task is as essential as it should – given steadiness of purpose and an appropriate popular understanding of that purpose – be successful. [Gray, 1977a, 28]

Gray argues that the case against geopolitical thinking, in the sense that the presence of long-range nuclear-armed bombers and ballistic missiles deny the invulnerability thesis of the pivot area, is countered by the presence of the growing Soviet counter-deterrent which would easily neutralize the use of the US nuclear arsenal against this territory by promising a devastating riposte. Thus with the strategic arsenals effectively neutralizing each other, the matter of controlling territory and resources again takes on primary importance. Hence the need for the focus on geopolitical thinking. Gray argues that the USSR is very far from gaining 'real-time control over the policies of all states in Eurasia–Africa' but it does not need to accomplish such a task 'in order to secure for itself predominance over the World Island, and the ability to deny American access' (1977a, 32).

The third chapter of this monograph outlines in some detail Gray's views of Russian history drawn significantly from Richard Pipes's writings in particular. This takes the position that there is a historical continuity through the events of 1917; the non-liberal 'patrimonial' social system merely acquired a new controlling apparatus which faced the same political and social problems as the Tsars, and crucially, the same geopolitical situation.

There follows a discussion of the Soviet increase in military forces in the late 1960s and through the 1970s, and an alarmed account of the Soviet presence in Africa, seen as significant because it allows Soviet naval activity to outflank 'the Eurasian–African Rimlands' (1977a, 52). Again, this CPD theme is reiterated, now the logic of it is more clearly spelt out. Gray points to the compartmentalization of military expertise in the USA as a major problem in understanding this buildup and its implications. Specifically he argues that overly technical analyses have failed to place the specific elements of the buildup in overall (geopolitical) perspective. Thus:

Much defence analysis suffers from a seeming inability to appreciate that geography imposes different tasks upon the armed forces of the rival alliances. Many Americans appear to have difficulty understanding that if they wish to deny hegemony over the Eurasian Rimlands to the Soviet Union, either the maritime alliance must sustain a very robust local denial capability, or the United States must invest in a significant margin of strategic superiority. To recap in question form, how are the Eurasian–African Rimlands to be defended against the Heartland power, if strategic parity (or, more likely, parity-plus) is conceded to that power? If superiority in the European theatre is conceded? [Gray, 1977a, 53]

Here the geopolitical theme is directly linked to the matter of strategic superiority, a precursor to Gray's later arguments about the 'theory of victory'. Gray argues that the West may become aware of the danger too late to make the appropriate military response.

The fourth chapter of this monograph deals with the US containment policy following the Second World War in terms of defending the Rimlands against the Heartland power. In these terms the USA is seen as taking on the defensive role formerly undertaken by the Germans and the Japanese before their defeat in the war. 'The compelling logic of geopolitics has indicated to any American capable of reading a map and drawing fairly elementary policy lessons from recent history that Heartland and Rimlands on the World Island must never be organized by a single political will' (Gray, 1977a, 54). As argued above, containment is understood in geopolitical terms.

Despite this, and what he terms the 'Mackinderesque writings' of George Kennan, Gray argues that the post-war policy was far more the result of reacting to events than the outcome of an overarching conceptualization of a geopolitical plan. The overall policy objective of the USA must in this conceptualization remain the containment of the USSR well short of a hegemony over the World Island. While the USA might survive this hegemony, it could do so only as an isolated fortress, not as a global power. The assumption that the communist bloc is not monolithic is also contested. Specifically, Gray argues that the Sino–Soviet split might not outlast a decline in US power as he argues the Chinese would probably be unable to continue an independent foreign policy without a US counter-weight to the Soviet nuclear arsenal.

Gray is concerned that the US political culture is not suitable to the long-term containment role forced on it by geopolitical circumstances. The 'neo-Mahanian' analytical perspective (see Collins, 1981; Wohlstetter, 1968) argues that transportation economics make it easier for the USA to project power onto the Rimlands than it is for the USSR to do so; oceans connect rather than divide because of the cheapness of sea transport and the relative ease of navigation. But Gray argues that geopolitics is more than a matter of transportation economics and that in the case of the USA the psychological dimension of distance is important but overlooked by analysts like Wohlstetter. The example given is Neville Chamberlain's dismissal of Czechoslovakia as a 'faraway country' at the time of the Munich agreement (Gray, 1977a, 58).

The next assertion is logical in Gray's scheme; if they had read their Mackinder the British would have known that 'Who rules East Europe commands the Heartland' and consequently recognized that a strong tier of Eastern European states was essential to limit German ambition. Further, however, is the argument that if geopolitics were only a matter of transport-ation economics then the USA would have quickly won in Vietnam. 'Our minds carry psychological maps, not ton-mile cost analysis maps' (Gray, 1977a, 59). These psychological maps often promote isolationist sentiments because of the oceanic distances between the USA and other major powers. The standard version of this is in terms of the 'credibility' of the US guarantee to defend Europe in the event of Soviet attack.

Here Gray introduces a repeated theme in his writings that specifically links the notions of style that relate to psychological factors and geopolitics.

His argument is the standard realist one, used by the other CPD writers distinguishing between revisionist and status quo powers. The USA is the latter or a 'satisfied' power, assuming that the stable world order is viewed as a desideratum by all other powers also and that peace is the normal order of things. Thus, he argues, that the SALT process of the 1970s has allowed the USSR to acquire a nuclear supremacy by building up all the weapons systems that it was allowed and fudging at the margins of arms control agreement compliance. Here the crucial link in the whole nuclear superiority argument is directly related to the geopolitical vision that underlies Gray's and indeed the whole CPD position. Thus the argument follows that parity, let alone inferiority, puts the USA in a position where it has 'no margin of nuclear strength which could be invoked on behalf of endangered friends and allies in Eurasia' (Gray, 1977a, 62). A further complication of the neo-Mahanian scheme is the widespread presence of the Soviet navy in many oceans, a navy whose function is obviously to buy time for the conquest of parts of the Rimland by Soviet ground forces operating in a 'blitzkrieg' mode. To do this all it must do is seriously to hinder transatlantic resupply or sink a sizeable portion of the world's supertankers plying from the Middle East to Europe and Japan.

Thus the whole Soviet arms buildup (and Gray assumes that it is between 13 per cent and 15 per cent of the Soviet GNP) is interpreted as an attempt to develop a credible military threat to conquer Rimland territory, while its navy interdicts US responses, and its central nuclear forces act as a counter-deterrent to the use of the US strategic arsenal in the event of the escalation of conflict to the level of limited (theatre) nuclear war. In the worst scenario (the 'window of vulnerability' argument) the USSR could launch a counter-force strike against the USA destroying its ICBM force and leaving the USA 'with no sensible strategic options' (Gray, 1977a, 62). Thus we are reminded that in geopolitical terms the forces of the superpowers have very different roles to play and that therefore, because of these roles, the tolerance of the parity principle in SALT is a recipe for disaster.

In summary, Gray argues that a global perspective on political affairs is greatly helped by 'the Mackinder–Spykman view that the world, reduced to its power related essentials, consists of a Heartland superpower that is locked in a permanent struggle with the offshore, insular continental superpower, the United States, for effective control of the Rimlands and the marginal seas of the World Island' (Gray, 1977a, 64). Within this grand scheme the USSR's goal is power and then more power. The widespread deployment of the Soviet fleet indicates a developing strategy for global influence, which, tied into Soviet nuclear superiority and local ground force superiority in the Rimlands, bodes ill for the USA. But:

> If the maritime alliance can deny the Soviet Union hegemony over Western Europe, by whatever means, and if American strategic nuclear power offers some options that are useable *in extremis*, and are not negated by the Soviet strategic counterdeterrent, then Soviet gains in the Rimlands outside Europe are either tolerable or reversible – with the exception of the reforging of a very solid Sino-Soviet alliance. [Gray, 1977a, 66]

Gray concludes his study by arguing once again that there is a lack of geopolitical understanding in the foreign-policy-making circles in the USA. He also restates his contention that the Soviet intentions are indelibly written in the long course of Soviet and Russian imperial history. In a position consistent with Richard Pipes, he argues that these expansionist tendencies can be met only with the credible threat of the use of force to stop them. These expansionist tendencies, drawn in part from Pipes's writings, are key to the geopolitical scheme advocated by Gray. His argument about Soviet attempts to expand and at least to deny the USA access to the World Island are the most explicit working out of the geopolitical theme in the CPD literature. It provides a theoretical clarification of their concern about increased Soviet influence in Africa 'outflanking' Europe.

The geopolitics of Soviet Empire

Empire is Gray's preferred term for the Soviet system; he wrote a number of papers and reviews which expand on this conceptualization of the Soviet system and which build on his earlier ideas of geopolitics in the early 1980s (Gray, 1981a, 1981b, 1982a,; Strode and Gray, 1981). In between these themes are connected by a number of papers that deal explicitly with the questions of crisis management (1978a) and the 'theory of victory' in geopolitical terms (1979a, 1979b, 1980a). The imperial thesis articulates these points into the overall geopolitical framework, hence its importance. Gray goes so far as to state that the USSR is continually misunderstood in the West because it is not appreciated specifically as an empire (Gray, 1981a, 13), and consequently Western policies towards the USSR are inappropriate.

Scholastic sophistry concerning 'social science' definitions is one of Gray's more frequent targets for criticism in his ongoing critique of non-realist academic pursuits in international relations. Hence, on this idea of empire, Gray argues that one has to have recourse to 'common sense' in the definition of an empire. Thus an empire will have the following attributes: rule of one nation over many nations; a sense of duty or mission authorized by some 'mandate of heaven' to exercise authority over ethnically different peoples; and a profound sense of insecurity since the domination of the subject peoples implies that they have other loyalties than to the empire. 'Imperial rule fundamentally implies a relationship of authority founded on the power to coerce' (1982a, 4). The final important point is that often military adventures and the expansion of empires are undertaken with primarily defensive measures in mind. The examples used to support this contention range from the Roman conquest of Britain to the history of the Russian Empire, whose geopolitical problems the Soviet regime has inherited.

Gray's appeal to common sense, in other words to widely prevalent conceptions of empire opens him up to critique. Thus these arguments on what an empire is are simply given, it is unnecessary, precisely because they are designated as common sense, to justify them, although Gray offers some examples in this outline. What Gray thus does is to create a series of factors that are useful to his discussion and use them to define this entity of empire. These factors then conveniently support Gray's analysis.

It is the specifics of the geopolitical predicament facing the Soviet Empire that are of particular importance. These arguments about the dynamics of expansion are central to the argument that both Pipes and subsequently Gray make; Gray explicitly references Pipes (1974) as a source on Russian history. According to Gray (1977a, 34) the geopolitical problems are tied centrally to the Russian tradition of 'patrimonialism' and to Russian, and subsequently, Soviet militarism. 'The conquest of the black earth belt of the steppe, and later of the entire Eurasian Heartland, by a state that had its origins in the northern taiga must be explained in terms of reactions to physical geography, rather than imperialistic impulses' (Gray, 1977a, 34). But this expansion required constant military protection. Gray is careful to note that the subsequent expansion of the Russian Empire and the USSR is not simply attributable to any one factor, but the historical link between physical geography, Russian militarism and imperial conquest is clearly made by drawing on Pipes's 1974 book and from his 1976 article 'Detente: Moscow's View'.

Gray's later arguments expand on the geographical theme, arguing that it is crucial to understanding the structure of the Soviet Empire. In the opening pages of his article 'The most dangerous decade: historic mission, legitimacy, and dynamics of the Soviet Empire in the 1990s' in *Orbis*, Gray (1981a) argues that the key to the Soviet Empire is geographical, in terms of territorial control. 'As with all empires, the Great Russian has a core area (Muscovy, Byelorussia) and succeeding layers, each protecting the others. Time after time since the early 1950s the Soviet Union has shown that it is trapped in the dynamics of empire' (1981a, 14). This dynamic is a situation in which the outermost holdings protect those nearer the centre, a failure to hold on to control over the outer areas in turn calls into question the legitimacy and effectiveness of the central control over inner areas. This requires that for long-term maintenance so that at least the Empire does not shrink. Preferably, to shore up internal legitimacy and support, it should expand – at least in visible influence if not in physical dimensions. Gray argues that outside the central Muscovy–Byelorussia core 'it is improbable that the Soviet state has any popular roots worth mentioning' (1981a, 14).

Further to this point is the increased internal control that follows from increased influence outside the imperial boundaries. Thus the domination of Western Europe can, within the imperial logic, be seen in purely defensive terms as a removal of a threat to Eastern Europe. 'The USSR is not merely a country surrounded by potential enemies, it is an empire that virtually by definition can have no settled relations of relative influence with its neighbours' (1981a, 14). Then, in a phrase borrowed indirectly from Haushofer, Gray continues that the geopolitical inheritance of the USSR is to believe that 'boundaries are fighting places', this being the 'natural belief for a country without natural frontiers' (1981a, 14). Gray's elaboration of this theoretical formulation of empire can be read as a clever interpretation of the debate over whether the Russian/Soviet expansion can be explained in terms of acquiring defensive buffers or not. Gray integrates both positions by arguing that there is an internal logic within the empire that requires expansion. Thus the Soviet Empire does not expand only when the opportunity is presented and hope to benefit by increased territory, as the buffer argument sometimes suggests.

The reason why Gray devotes a series of articles to analysing the 'imperial thesis' is that if the thesis is valid, which he attempts to show repeatedly, then it follows in a determinist fashion that the problem in Western policy-making circles of attempting to predict Soviet intentions is answered because they can be inferred from the Empire's own dynamics independent of what the Soviet leaders might wish. 'The imperial thesis is vital because it settles, persuasively, arguments about Soviet intentions' (Gray, 1981a, 14–15). It relates to the composition of the leaders of the Soviet society and particularly to this history of the Soviet Communist Party. He paints a very unflattering picture of the Soviet experience, the following not being untypical:

> The legitimacy of the Soviet State has nothing to do with a social contract of any kind; it rests instead upon the bizarre facts that a handful of adventurers, having turned some nineteenth century political economic theorizing on its head, seized a historic opportunity to acquire a country as the vehicle for their Historic Mission. Their right to rule rests on the validity of the Historic Mission. If the Historic Mission, to effect socialism worldwide, comes generally to be seen as misconceived, then what right has the CPSU to be obeyed? The domestic authority of the Soviet government, today, depends upon the habit of obedience, fraud, force when needed and, to the extent to which such a dangerous sentiment can be invoked in a severely multinational country, national pride. [Gray, 1981a, 15]

Thus, in an expansion of Pipes's arguments, the Soviet Empire is portrayed as fundamentally insecure, only expansion to gain territories beyond its borders and hence increase the degree of external control offers any increase in security. The whole structure rests on force, usually latent, the leaders know that they cannot rule a universal empire even if they could create one, 'but they are condemned by circumstance to try' (Gray, 1981a, 15). In this scheme they must attempt to reduce other centres of power that abut their borders because as long as any alternative sources of power offer alternative models of society the rule of the Communist Party of the Soviet Union will remain insecure.

Having stated such a blunt position, Gray then counsels caution on the theme of whether the USSR views nuclear war as a usable policy option, to reduce its insecurity. He concludes with the position that the USSR would launch a nuclear war only in circumstances where the integrity of the Empire was seriously imperilled. Under those circumstances the leaders would launch a first strike to attempt to cripple the USA in a pre-emptive strike. In Gray's phrase, they would 'go first in the last resort'. The rest of the *Orbis* paper presents the crucial links between his geopolitical analysis of the dynamics of the Soviet Empire and these matters of nuclear strategy. Thus he argues that the West has allowed the USSR to gain military supremacy through neglect on its part. Supremacy measured not in the 'largely meaningless counts of defence inputs (men under arms, missile launchers, warheads, megatonnage, and so forth) but, rather, to the potential defence *output*: the ability to prevail in arms competition, acute crisis, and even war itself' (Gray, 1981a, 17).

Gray then argues that there will be a decade-long period of intense danger as the military supremacy of the USSR is used to check the power of NATO and the USA and the superiority is used to exploit other areas of the globe where gains are to be had (see also Gray, 1981b, 66; Strode and Gray, 1981). After this the rearmament programme of the Reagan regime and the inevitable increase in NATO defences that Gray expects will reduce the Soviet lead. China is modernizing, a process inevitably challenging as it will have military spin-offs. The Soviet domestic economy is slowing down and is unlikely to expand quickly because of increasing energy costs and demographic factors. Finally, there is the possibility of political paralysis as a result of the anticipated power struggle over succession in the post Brezhnev period, but a period of dangerous instability when an adventurous clique might exploit military power to gain a major foreign policy success to ensure their supremacy in the internal political struggle. Thus a move in the Middle East is seen as a possibility in the wake of the invasion of Afghanistan.

A more drastic scenario might anticipate an invasion of Western Europe and an attack on the Chinese which would set their modernization programme back generations. The latter scenario comes about as an assessment of temporary superiority and long-run pessimism, thus the argument would suggest that the USSR should seize the only chance it was likely to get historically and act to shift drastically matters in its favour, using the military strength built up over two decades. This scenario could work only in Gray's analysis if the USA were unable to launch effective nuclear strikes in response because its forces were effectively 'counter-deterred' by Soviet counter-force capabilities. This is the link between the geopolitical analysis and nuclear strategy which is crucial to the CPD position.

The ideology of geopolitics

Gray's analysis relies on his self-proclaimed realist perspective. In this he draws on Spykman more than any other writer. He effectively conflates geopolitics and realism, and he does so by arguing that the key to both is the focus on the long-term and enduring factors of international affairs. The most enduring of all are those of geography. *Ipso facto* geopolitics and realism are one and the same. This, as was noted in the last chapter, is not necessarily consistent with others of the realist tradition. Morgenthau, one of the founders of the realist tradition in international relations, includes a warning against the use of oversimplified geopolitical notions in assessing the dynamics of power politics in his seminal text *Politics Among Nations* (1978).

But this conflation is a very powerful ideological tool. Added to this is the whole quasi-determinist theme of the cold climate forcing a militarized southward expansion, drawn from Pipes's writings. Here geopolitical arguments are used as a lever against political moves of compromise with the Soviet regime. They rely on their credibility in terms of this long-term trend, a matter which is obviously deep-seated and hence not likely to be fundamentally disturbed by transient political arrangements such as *détente* and the SALT process. In the CPD's geopolitical discourse, the USSR is driven by harsh geographical facts to expand. Against this only a committed military posture can work.

Reading Colin Gray's extensive writings, in particular his later works where he addresses in an academic way the matters of security studies, one detects an unease in the whole operation. Being overly cautious is a necessity in this kind of analysis, but Gray comes very near to demolishing his own case in a number of places, only to fall back on his realist credo in terms of there not being any possible way of operating in the international arena, other than in terms of power understood in military terms. In a number of places he comments that until some other political conditions arise, the game of power politics will continue to be played according to the current rules.

Thus, international politics is an autonomous sphere, one that we are stuck with. Except that where the new political arrangements might come from is not clear. But, apparently they come, if at all, from somewhere beyond the realist world. There are several implications in this position. First, the realist does not need to concern himself with the possibilities for change that might occur. Not being concerned with the possibilities of changing the game, there is no incentive to work to change the game. As Gray makes very clear in his earlier article on realism (1976a), only how one plays the game matters; one has to play to win. But further than this, there is no consideration in Gray's world about how it might be possible to initiate change. Here the contradiction in the whole scheme comes to the surface. Thus the Western world is economically much more capable than the Soviet bloc and consequently it can, with a mobilization of political will, contain the Soviet ambitions in the Rimlands, but it is incapable of taking any initiatives other than passively accepting the necessity of defensively responding to the bully on the block, in the hopes that eventually he will reform himself.

As MccGwire (1984, 1985–6) points out, the doctrine of deterrence is one that eschews any higher political policy or vision of a global order which might guide political action. The decades of acceptance of deterrence as the essential fact of global politics has led to a situation in which US policy-makers do not attempt to develop plans for the reform of international relations by the reduction of the most dangerous military element (Johansen, 1987). Thus the most powerful social system (in terms of the

USA and NATO) is reduced fatalistically to preparing for suicide/genocide, rather than developing a political plan for world order in which priorities other than military technology and strategic planning are available. Thus realism is, as Ashley (1984, 1987) argues, a discourse of power which operates to perpetuate its practitioners in their institutional positions overseeing its rituals. The realist perpetuates the military nature of politics by arguing that there is no choice but more military buildup. Thus the spiral of armaments continues. Thus military buildups operate to maintain the realist credo; they provide the very tokens of the realist competition.

But Gray is also aware of the need to break out of the narrow technical preoccupation of the strategic vision of national security. That is precisely why, in many of his writings (Gray, 1971a, 1971b, 1975a, 1977–8, 1982b, 1982c, 1986b), he looks beyond the technical strategic literature to larger concerns of the formation of political policy. In this he joins critics like Herken (1987) and Kaplan (1983) in his criticism of the formal strategists and the operations research approaches to strategy although he draws different conclusions. He comes back to the fascination with the technical details of nuclear war-fighting strategies because of his reliance on the 'totalitarian thesis' and the geopolitical framework which he constructs. Thus, as will be shown in the next chapter, he constructs a political rationale for defeating the USSR which requires a whole panoply of technical calculations.

He argues in effect that there is no choice; the attempt to get beyond the limits of technocratic strategic planning to some larger political purpose is vetoed because of the nature of the USSR. This is his second crucial move, he takes the critique of the technocratic preoccupations seriously, but evades the consequences because he argues that the USSR is inherently expansionist, and beyond our influence because of its historical experience and rigid internal controls. Because of this, huge arsenals are required and the technical analysis of 'thinking the unthinkable' must proceed. We have no choice because of the nature of the Other.

Gray relies on the realist distinction between status quo powers, those whose interest is in the maintenance of the global order, and revisionist or revolutionary states, whose international policies are designed to change that order. Revolutionary states are thus a threat to peace because their actions in attempting to change the international arrangements are likely to unleash social forces that lead to war. There is thus no way out of these realist rituals. Unless, of course, the whole geopolitical scheme on which he and Pipes rely is fundamentally inaccurate. This is why the geopolitical premises of the CPD foreign policy perspective are so crucial. They provide the ideological keystone to their whole position. If it is possible to construct an alternative analysis of the geopolitical arena, then the rationale on which the whole nuclear war-fighting edifice which imperils us all is built will be removed and the justifications for ever-increasing militarization become untenable.

But Gray is also vulnerable to a critique from within the realist tradition itself. As Carr (1946) made very clear in one of the key texts on international affairs that provided the groundwork for the realist tradition, idealist understanding is also needed at times in international relations to allow change to occur. Gray has carefully constructed an intellectual universe in which change is not possible. The utopian vision is dismissed as fantasy and irrelevant in the ongoing historical game of great powers. Gray suffers a failure of intellectual courage in failing to seek the new political vision that he says is needed; hence, the inevitability of the arms race. This is his crucial failing.

His conflation of realism and geopolitics privileges once again structuralist elements which emphasize historical continuity to the exclusion of change. Historical determinants are given overarching importance. This construction operates as the background to the arguments on nuclear strategy that the CPD repeatedly presented. As an expansionist power, driven by the geopolitical necessities of its position, the possession of large numbers of nuclear weapons would presumably be fitted into the overall scheme of political and military strategy. The nuclear strategy arguments link up with these underlying geopolitical conceptions to present a particular represent-ation of the 'Soviet threat', and crucially to provide a specific rationale for nuclear targeting in Colin Gray's 'theory of victory'.

There is also a theoretical concern with geopolitics linked to the ideological force of the CPD argument. It relates directly to Gray's conceptions of geopolitics in *Geopolitics of the Nuclear Era* and his later conceptualizations of the dynamics of the Soviet Empire. Thus Gray argues in a comment on the old theme of whether geopolitics determines political behaviour or merely operates as one among a number of factors (see Brunn and Mingst, 1985), that

> geopolitics is not simply one set of ideas among many competing sets that help to illuminate the structure of policy problems. Rather it is a meta- or master framework, that, without predetermining policy choice, suggests long term factors and trends in the security objectives of particular territorially-organized security communities. [Gray, 1977a, 11]

This appears to run counter to his assertions in the imperial thesis argument that the Soviet leadership is compelled to attempt to expand their Empire and gain a global hegemony because of the internal political and historical factors which are based in turn on the geographical determinist view of Soviet history that Gray takes on board from Pipes. 'Many Western commentators have yet to understand that "the Soviet Threat" in the 1980s flows from the dynamics of empire, from geopolitics – and fundamentally from weakness' (Gray, 1981a, 14). Here, as also in Pipes (1984), geopolitics is used in its determining sense, not simply as a meta-framework for policy.

This is an extension of the determinist framework to encompass the whole globe. Geopolitics is defined clearly here as the only legitimate perspective from which to view the matter of the USSR. It operates to delegitimize other perspectives because it claims to be the only perspective that can accommodate all the factors that are essential to understanding the global situation. The geopolitical view is the view of the long-term, permanent operating factors in international politics, and hence is the only legitimate perspective upon which to base policy decisions. Gray implies that the USSR is compelled by the geopolitics of its Empire to expand; the West has policy choices. Except, of course, the argument is thus phrased in terms of a choice to acquiesce to the Soviet expansion or to resist it. This restores consistency to his argument in that there is nothing determined about whether the Soviet expansionist drive will succeed, all that is determined is that it will occur. Thus the Western leaders must understand geopolitics to understand the Soviet threat. Geopolitics does not determine the West's response, just the Soviet challenge. Gray has it all ways: geopolitics determines when it is convenient for his scheme for it to do so; it is a framework for understanding the long-run development of events when it relates to the West. Thus the term covers multiple meanings articulated to lead to one particular policy response, that of military buildup and military containment of the Heartland power.

Sustained over a long period, geopolitical containment can break the momentum of Soviet expansion and then, and only then, will real change come to the Heartland. Here is the essential link of the classic geopolitical texts to the CPD scheme. The USSR is destined by geography to expand, the oceanic alliance, if it is to survive, has to intervene in the Rimlands to prevent this expansion. This intervention is understood as military containment, a spatial exercise in limiting the spread of influence; power is spatially understood. To contain militarily requires a plethora of nuclear weapons and other military hardware to make the threat of intervention militarily credible. This requires sufficient numbers of weapons to ensure that the USA will not be self-deterred in a crisis, and it also requires a worked-out plan for the deployment and, if necessary, the use of nuclear weapons; it requires a nuclear strategy.

Chapter 8

Nuclear Strategy

Strategy and deterrence

The term 'strategy' is widely used to mean a number of different things. Classical strategy as discussed by Clausewitz basically meant the use of military forces in battles designed to promote the aims of the war being fought (Clausewitz, 1968). The political goals were considered paramount; strategy was the organization of military force to pursue these aims. In a militarized world situation obviously military forces play a role in international diplomacy and international relations even if they are not engaged in active hostilities. Thus the definition of strategy needs to be expanded to include the role of military force in non-combat roles. Liddell-Hart's (1968, 338) definition of strategy as 'the art of distributing and applying military means to fulfil ends of policy' covers this additional use. Thus strategy in the Clauswitzian sense encompasses more than just the battlefield skills of generals, it refers crucially also to the domestic mobilization of populations and economic resources in the service of the state (Klein, 1987).

The term strategy is also used in a number of other senses. In common parlance it can simply refer to a plan for accomplishing some specified goal. In international affairs it is sometimes used to refer to a combination of military, economic and political policy, becoming a term synonymous with broadly defined foreign policy. In nuclear parlance 'strategic' has taken on a specific meaning of nuclear weapons capable of reaching the territory of the adversary. Thus a weapon becomes 'strategic' solely because of its range or location. Further confusion enters the picture when distinctions are drawn between 'declaratory policy', that is the official publicly declared policy on the use of weapons, and the actual operational planning assumptions used in organizing nuclear forces (Aldridge, 1983; Kaku and Axelrod, 1986; Pringle and Arkin, 1983). The term 'nuclear strategy' encompasses all the above, and the confusions are reflected in the debates about 'nuclear strategy'. The debates over *détente* and strategy repeatedly confused these distinctions, sometimes deliberately for political effect (Leitenberg, 1981; MacNamara 1983).

As nuclear weapons became more powerful and more numerous in the years after the Second World War, new concepts were devised to discuss their use and their role. Given their enormous destructive power, serious doubts have been expressed since 1945 about whether they are 'usable' in military terms.

The question has been whether any useful purpose could be served by the employment of devices which invited discussion using words such as 'holocaust', 'doomsday' and 'armageddon', and whether any employment could be sufficiently deliberate and controlled to ensure that political objectives were met. Which means at issue has been whether a 'nuclear strategy' is a contradiction in terms. [Freedman, 1983, xviii]

The answers given to this question determine the approaches to foreign policy advocated by the academics and 'experts' in defence and foreign policy. The answers to this question have shaped US policy for four decades. But the question is not posed in isolation, it is posed in conjunction with the 'what about the Russians?' question. The fear of Soviet geopolitical advance is viewed by some as a greater threat than nuclear war. For many the awesome power of nuclear weapons has made the avoidance of all out war the primary consideration of policy (Beres, 1980). The contrasting policy recommendations flowing from the relative importance of each of these perspectives underlie the debates about nuclear strategy (Jervis, 1984; Snow, 1983).

Those who argue that nuclear war has made avoidance essential sometimes turn to international arms control agreements as a way forward. Others, agreeing with the sentiment that it is essential to avoid it, turn to deterrence and argue in classical realist style that the only way to deter is to be strong. Without strength, measured in nuclear weapons, war will inevitably come, because the Russians will come unless deterred by nuclear weapons. This stance, in MccGwire's (1985–6) terms 'the dogma of deterrence', the priority given to the necessity of deterrence above all other considerations, is the essential discursive move of the US discourse of nuclear strategy.

The nuclear strategy discussions of the 1950s that followed Brodie's initial formulation of deterrence theory (1946, 1965) are particularly important because they laid the groundwork on which just about all subsequent thinking on these topics has operated. The discourse of deterrence has dominated discussions of foreign policy in the USA since the original formulations of containment militarism. It has also shaped the conduct of international relations in areas where nuclear weapons were not clearly present. This discourse has constructed a series of rituals of discussion, the assumptions of which were raised to unquestionable aprioria. It has a clear institutional expression in the thinktanks, of which RAND is just the most famous (Kaplan, 1983). The language is distinct, often obscure, operating to reinforce the premises of the discourse, it has moved to monopolize discussion of military matters in ways that limit what it is possible to discuss (Cohn, 1987). The basic formulation of its texts, and its self-stated *raison d'être*, is the clear designation of the Other in the totalitarian USSR, which had to be deterred from carrying out its expansionist programme.

The study of strategy in the 1950s was preoccupied with the problems of nuclear weapons, deterrence doctrine and theories of limited nuclear war (Halperin, 1962; Kaufman, 1956; Kissinger, 1957; Nitze, 1956). The

traditional sources of strategic thinking in the disciplines of political science
and military history were soon replaced by people from the 'axiomatic
disciplines like mathematics, physics and economics' (MccGwire, 1985–6,
56). These strategists took for granted the assumption that the USSR had a
relentless drive for territorial conquest. The concept of the communist bloc
being monolithic went unquestioned. They were convinced that it was
determined to seize Europe.

> This assumption provided the basis for most strategic theorizing. The field
> developed a new breed of self-styled 'tough-minded' strategic analysts, who liked
> to think through problems abstractly and in a political vacuum. To this new
> breed, the opponent was not 'Sovietman', not even 'political man', but an
> abstract 'strategic man', who thought, as they did, in game-theoretical terms.
> [MccGwire, 1985–6, 56]

'Flexible response' in an era of ICBMs and instant global communications is
very much the field of the 'nuclear strategist' where military considerations
are overtaken by the arcane rituals of systems analysis derived for operations
research and applied to political situations. The language of operations
research, complete with its reduction of policy matters to questions of 'the
efficient management of resources' was applied to nuclear matters in
particular by the 'whiz kids' McNamara brought with him from the RAND
corporation when he became Secretary of Defense in 1961.

The preoccupation of the axiomatic thinkers was with rigorous analysis
of quantifiable data drawn from a situation reduced to manageable proportions by simplifying assumptions. The tendency in the analyses was towards
worst-case situations. In particular the focus on surprise attacks encouraged
a policy of over-insurance. This dovetailed nicely with the bureaucratic
power struggles between the missile advocates, the manned bomber service
and the nuclear navy, all of whom were happy to have analyses that justified
larger arsenals (Herken, 1987). These operations research approaches are
sometimes distinguished from the 'formal strategists' (Freedman, 1983,
181) who attempted to rethink the whole nuclear situation from first
principles. They drew on developments in game theory to elaborate theories
of superpower behaviour. In particular they ran repeated games of 'chicken'
and 'prisoners dilemma', attempting to elucidate the psychological dynamics
of binary competition. These simplifying assumptions squeezed out many of
the political factors and reduced international politics to a technological
zero-sum situation where what counted was what could be counted; in
other words nuclear weapons and their delivery systems. Thus the world
was reduced to two sides engaged in a complex series of games. Tied to this
was a series of assumptions about how the actions of one side sent 'signals'
to the other side.

Underlying these game theory models was the assumption that both sides
evaluated the rewards of certain outcomes equally, an ethnocentric assumption which is rarely accurate (Plous, 1985). A more serious ethnocentric
assumption was that the USSR saw itself as the USA portrayed them;
namely as an expansionist aggressor. Thus the logic assumed that the USSR

would understand the force postures of the USA as defensive, because it supposedly could do strategic analysis. At times during the arms control talks in the 1970s the USA argued that the Soviet positions showed that they were 'behind' in the development of their thinking because they operated on different assumptions. The assumption was that there was only one way of developing nuclear strategic thinking – the US way (Booth, 1979).

The assumption of the superiority of theoretical modes of reasoning was again present. The strategic discourse 'certainly did appeal to the American habit of seeing the world in black and white, and the tendency to believe that problems should (and can) be solved – rather than managed or even avoided' (MccGwire, 1985–6, 59). Added to this is the prestige of a 'scientific' approach complete with computerized models of conflict situations. Coupled with this is the focus on the enemy's military capabilities and assumption of hostile intentions.

Three features of this 'deterrence dogma', as MccGwire terms it, are crucial in understanding its role. First, is the abstract style of reasoning, favouring definitions of rational behaviour conjured up from investigations of 'the prisoners dilemma' rather than investigations of political psychology. Second, was a remarkable absence of sovietologists from the debates, although one notable exception from the RAND social science department was Leites's (1950) study *The Operational Code of the Politburo*. Soviet expansionist and malign intentions and reactions were simply taken as a given. These two factors led to analyses focusing on worst-case scenarios and hence to ensuring that there were enough weapons to ensure that whatever happened the US arsenal would always be big enough to carry out its mission of destroying the USSR. Third, deterrence was formulated in punitive terms, the USSR was evil by definition and would be punished if it refused to comply with the rules of international behaviour established by the USA. The language of the USA as global magistrate and enforcement agency inherent here is very important in the ideological structuring of the post-war global situation (Chilton, 1985). These intellectual practices have become so entrenched that it proves difficult to talk of strategic matters in innovative ways. The modes of strategic thinking thus exclude practices which would fundamentally challenge their presuppositions, reproducing the world of the 1950s in the 1980s.

The CPD against SALT

The CPD argued that the Soviet negotiating posture in SALT was merely an attempt to negotiate unilateral advantages in crucial weapons systems, in particular 'heavy' ICBMs with their potential to carry numerous warheads on a single missile. The geopolitical perspective discussed in the last two chapters is linked here to the strategic discourse; in particular to the debates over Soviet strategic doctrine (Lebow, 1988–9), which supposedly revealed the intentions behind their SALT negotiating positions. Thus military supremacy is seen, in particular by Pipes, as the key to Soviet geopolitical expansion; their military doctrine focuses on the use of military threat to achieve political gains, if necessary they are prepared to fight a nuclear war to achieve their goal of global domination.

The CPD based a considerable amount of its campaign on detailed criticism of the SALT process and, in particular, the Vladivostok accords and the subsequent SALT II agreement negotiated by the Carter administration. In July 1977 they released the first in a series of statements that dealt directly with the SALT negotiating process. 'Where We Stand on SALT' argues that the USA and the USSR have differing objectives in the SALT process, the US position being to use the SALT process to 'reduce the weight of nuclear weapons in the relationship between the US and the Soviet Union' (CPD, 1984, 16). The CPD argues that agreements were designed to assure that both sides have 'essential equivalence in nuclear capabilities' and that neither side could hope to gain more than it would lose by striking first. 'The US hoped to slow down the brutal momentum of the massive Soviet strategic arms buildup – a buildup without precedent in history' (CPD, 1984, 17). (As Gervasi [1986] makes quite clear, the precedent that is an appropriate analogy in numerical terms is the US buildup of strategic weapons a decade earlier.) Thus we are told that the USA has restrained its research, development and deployment of weapons, a move not matched by the USSR. Thus the USSR is using SALT as a means of 'impeding the adversary's momentum while maintaining its own' (CPD, 1984, 17).

In addition, the USSR is charged with trying 'to use public opinion and Congressional pressure to induce Washington to agree to unequal compromises unfavourable to the United States' (CPD, 1984, 17). Horror of horrors, the Russians are trying to pressure Congress into usurping the powers of the National Security managers! Thus an additional factor 'of some value to the Soviet Union is the unrealistic level of expectations stirred by the optimistic statements of successive US administrations. Inevitably, SALT has become enmeshed in domestic politics and popular hopes for detente, and "progress" has seemed a political imperative' (CPD, 1984, 17). They argue that the USSR was under no time pressure to come to any agreement because it was using SALT to limit US developments while it continued to develop and deploy its new missiles. Also, 'the Soviet side ignored the US interpretation of their ambiguities and stretched the agreed language to its full limits or beyond' (CPD, 1984, 17). Finally, 'The Soviet view is that the best deterrent is the capability to fight and win a nuclear war – and survive in the process. It is our task to deny them that capability' (CPD, 1984, 21).

Three broad themes are interrelated here. First, is the basic denial that the USSR was taking arms control and *détente* seriously; the buildup of their strategic rocket forces is repeatedly brought to the forefront of discussion. Evidence of this comes from the period of the Team B process when the CIA revised its estimates of Soviet defence expenditure sharply upwards. During this period concern grew that the USSR was also building a large and effective civil defence system (Goure, 1976). This was of particular concern to Paul Nitze, whose assistant, T.K. Jones, specialized in the area. The second theme is the non-acceptance in the USSR of US concepts of war deterrence; specifically the argument is made that the USSR believes in the possibility of fighting and winning a nuclear war. The key article that triggered a wide public debate in the strategic and policy communities is Richard Pipes's 'Why the Soviet Union Thinks it Could Fight and Win a Nuclear War', published in *Commentary* in 1977. In this article Pipes argues that nuclear war-fighting is part of the Soviet global strategy for world domination. Third, both these themes require a US response in terms of nuclear strategy.

The rest of this chapter outlines Pipes's concerns over Soviet nuclear strategy; the questions raised by Nitze in terms of how the USA should respond; and Colin Gray's working out of a 'theory of victory'. The key to Gray's theory lies with his conceptions of geopolitics and the 'imperial thesis' derived from his geopolitical writings and Pipes's theory of the patrimonial nature of the Soviet system. Here Gray pulls together the themes of each of the security discourses. The nuclear strategy arguments are very important because they were subsequently used to provide the rationales for the Reagan administration's massive strategic weapons procurement policy (Knelman, 1985; Lebow, 1988–9) and contribute to explaining the complete lack of progress in arms control negotiations in its first term of office (Talbott, 1985).

Soviet war-fighting strategy

The theme of the importance of understanding Soviet military doctrine is present in many places in the CPD literature. In 'Is America Becoming Number 2?' (released 5 October 1978) the CPD argues that an understanding of 'Soviet Military Doctrine' is essential to the wider appreciation of the military balance. 'The Soviet literature – not propaganda written for the West but Russians talking to Russians – tells us that the Soviets do *not* agree with the Americans that nuclear war is unthinkable and unwinnable and that the only objective of strategic doctrine must be mutual deterrence' (CPD, 1984, 42). It goes on to argue that they see that 'war is an extension of diplomacy; that nuclear superiority is politically usable and that the Soviets must prepare for war fighting, war surviving and war winning' (CPD, 1984, 42).

Soviet strategy, the CPD argues, calls for a pre-emptive nuclear strike in the event of the preparation of a nuclear attack by the 'imperialists' in the West, followed up immediately by a land offensive by conventional forces, presumably principally in Europe, although this is not specified. 'They believe the best deterrent is the capability to win and survive were deterrence to fail' (CPD, 1984, 42). The CPD goes on to argue that the Soviets recognize that nuclear war would be awfully destructive, but using nuclear weapons is not 'unthinkable' to them.

> Nevertheless, the doctrine described above is that of a nation that does not rely solely upon the theory of deterrence. The crucial difference from a common US

approach lies in the Soviet recognition that deterrence might not succeed and that the Soviet Union must be prepared to fight, survive and win, even in a nuclear conflict. [CPD, 1984, 42]

Further, the CPD argues that Soviet doctrine affirms the importance of defence in a nuclear war, in contrast to Americans who see it as destabilizing. Thus we are assured that the USSR signed the ABM treaty in 1972 only because the USA had a long technological lead, not because the USSR had been converted 'to the concept of Mutual Assured Destruction (MAD), the mutual hostage theory' (CPD, 1984, 42). We are told that the USSR has maintained its research and development programme in the field of ballistic missile defence 'with apparent emphasis on systems that would be rapidly deployable should they, or we, decide to abrogate the ABM treaty' (CPD, 1984, 43).

Their strategic nuclear weapons complement these developments by 'moving toward a counterforce damage limiting capability' which involves improving the accuracy on their large ICBMs to 'permit high confidence in "hard target kills" against US ICBM silos' (CPD, 1984, 43). In other words, they are developing the technology to inflict a first strike on the US ICBM force. Richard Pipes's article 'Why the Soviet Union Thinks it Could Fight and Win a Nuclear War' (Pipes, 1977), where these themes were most explicitly stated, was crucial to the public debate about SALT II and the emergence of the Nuclear Utilization Theories (NUTS) debate. Pipes is important because he clearly states the 'Clausewitzian' position on Soviet military doctrine. He argues that nuclear war is the continuation of the USSR's policy of global domination by nuclear means. His strategic arguments are thus a continuation of his earlier papers on the essential expansionist and militarist tendencies in the USSR, and the essential inter-linkage between the two.

In the long tradition of the 'worst-case' analyses of US strategic thinking (MccGwire, 1985–6; Lebow, 1988–9), Pipes's estimates that the USSR is aiming at achieving a nuclear superiority which will effectively paralyse US political actions in the 1980s. Pipes begins, following the pattern of his earlier articles, with an analysis of the differences between the US and Soviet doctrines.

> The prevalent US doctrine holds that an all-out war between countries in possession of sizeable nuclear arsenals would be so destructive as to leave no winner; thus resort to arms has ceased to represent a rational policy option for the leaders of such countries *vis-à-vis* one another. The classic dictum of Clausewitz, that war is politics pursued by other means, is widely believed in the United States to have lost its validity after Hiroshima and Nagasaki. Soviet doctrine, by contrast, emphatically asserts that while an all out nuclear war would indeed prove extremely destructive to both parties, its outcome would not be mutual suicide: the country better prepared for it and in possession of a superior strategy could win and emerge a viable society. [Pipes, 1981, 136]

As Pipes puts it, Clausewitz is ignored in the USA while he is revered in the USSR.

The differences between the superpower positions are traceable once again to the commercial culture in the USA. Here, mistrust of the military professional is combined with 'a pervasive conviction . . . that human conflicts are at bottom caused by misunderstanding and ought to be resolved by negotiations rather than by force' (Pipes, 1981, 137). This, Pipes asserts, has militated against a serious strategic tradition in the USA. The historic experience of war has been of quick wars with relatively small loss of life. Once involved in a war, the USA mobilizes its vast industrial resources and wins by the application of tremendous technological capabilities, which inflict tremendous suffering on the enemy. This 'American Way of War' (Weighley, 1973), coupled with the rapid demobilization of the US forces immediately after the Second World War, is crucial to understanding the acceptance of the atomic bomb as a potential war-winning weapon immediately after the war. In the 1950s fiscal measures in the USA more or less guaranteed its role; it provided the means for a massive retaliation strategy at little cost relative to the alternative of conventional forces. This changed in 1957 with Sputnik, which led the way to the acceptance in the USA of the doctrine of mutual deterrence, first argued by Bernard Brodie in 1946. This doctrine was worked out by civilian practitioners, not military thinkers. 'Current US strategic theory was thus born of a marriage between the scientist and the accountant. The professional soldier was jilted' (Pipes, 1981, 142).

Pipes argues that by absolutizing the atomic bomb, this doctrine argued that all earlier military theory was outmoded. Nuclear wars could not be fought; they had to be avoided. These arguments remain in the literature of nuclear strategy and influence the US declaratory doctrine, although not in its operational planning, a crucial point on which Pipes is not clear. Declaratory doctrine is not concerned with the nuts and bolts of operational planning. The policy of assured destruction was, in part, introduced in the 1960s by McNamara to attempt to restrict the huge expansion plans of the US strategic forces. As Gray makes clear, the US operational planning to strike economic ('counter-value') targets is based partly on these premises, but Pipes's argument is a gross oversimplification. Pipes argues, as Gray was repeatedly to do also, that it is doubtful that this is a strategy in any sense. It fails at precisely the moment when strategy is most needed, at the outbreak of hostilities. All it supposedly offers is the possibility of lashing out blindly in the event of war.

Here is the assumption that US thinking about nuclear war involves beliefs that it is unthinkable and unwinnable. Much of the history of US nuclear strategic thinking is concerned about using nuclear weapons in various limited scenarios (Freeman, 1983), and much of the crucial operational planning, as opposed to declaratory policy, is based on counter-force considerations Kaku and Axelrod, 1986). There are also plans for first-strike scenarios (Aldridge, 1983; Gervasi, 1986); the USA has always asserted that should war start in Europe it will use nuclear weapons to prevent Soviet conventional attacks succeeding. This continues to be the basis of the NATO reliance on the US nuclear 'umbrella'. Pipes has effectively ignored the operational planning of US strategic forces by conflating political discussions of MAD with operational planning.

For Pipes, the sources of the differences in thinking are deeper, related to the differing conceptions of the nature of conflict in both societies and the different functions that the military performs in both societies. This returns us to the argument (see Chapter five) about the peasant background of the Soviet leadership, and the marriage between Marxism and Clausewitz, in comparison to the commercial middle-class approach in the USA. The Soviet view regards violence and conflict as 'natural regulators of all human affairs: wars between nations, in its view, represent only a variant of wars between the classes, recourse to the one or the other being dependent on circumstances' (Pipes, 1981, 147).

In Pipes's reconstruction of Soviet strategic thought, the initial Soviet reaction to the atomic bomb was that it had not significantly altered the science of warfare or rendered obsolete the principles that the USSR used to defeat the *Wehrmacht*.

These basic laws, known as the five 'constant principles' that win wars, had been formulated by Stalin in 1942. They were, in declining order of importance: 'stability of the home front', followed by morale of the armed forces, quantity and quality of the divisions, military equipment, and finally, ability of the commanders. There was no such thing as an 'absolute weapon' – weapons altogether occupied a subordinate place in warfare; defence against atomic bombs was entirely possible. [Pipes, 1981, 152]

He asserts that the strategic guidelines that were formulated late in the 1950s following a brief interregnum in the post-Stalin years remain the overall framework for Soviet strategic planning. Pipes takes Sokolovsky's (1963) edited volume, titled in translation *Military Strategy*, to be the key Soviet strategic text. Pipes argues that Western strategists have ignored this work and others because of the presumed superiority of US strategy.

Pipes thinks that the military is the one winning weapon in the Soviet system. In addition, Pipes points out that a strong military force offers the possibility of expansion and also ensures domestic tranquility. If the omnipotence of the Red Army were ever called into serious question, then the whole legitimacy of the regime would be open to challenge. Thus there are compelling political reasons for the USSR to maintain and expand its military forces. Along with this must go a credible doctrine which offers the Red Army a role in any potential conflict other than as a target for nuclear annihilation. Its social role requires this and hence some theory of nuclear war-fighting is essential. The novelty of nuclear weapons is in the speed with which they can accomplish what previously took sustained sequential tactical and operational actions. Nuclear weapons can now obtain strategic results immediately. Their destructiveness is not a matter of great concern in Pipes's view.

In one of his statements on this theme which was to subsequently cause outrage (Scheer, 1983), he summarizes the argument thus:

The novelty of nuclear weapons consists not in their destructiveness – that is, after all, a matter of degree, and a country like the Soviet Union which, as Soviet generals proudly boast, suffered in World War II the loss of over 20 million casualties, as well as the destruction of 1,710 towns, over 70,000 villages, and some 32,000 industrial establishments to win the war and emerge as a global power, is not to be intimidated by the prospect of destruction. [Pipes, 1981, 156]

In case there is any doubt, Pipes quotes the following 'Clausewitzian' argument from Sokolovsky; 'It is well known that the essential nature of war as a continuation of politics does not change with changing technology and armament' (Pipes, 1981, 156). Thus nuclear war is not suicidal, it can be fought and won, the exact opposite, he argues, of the current doctrinal position in the USA.

Pipes comments, as does the CPD (1984, 42), that what literature comes from the USSR on the impossibility of winning a nuclear war is intended solely for Western consumption, it does not reflect official thinking. This distinction relates to Pipes's totalitarian assumptions of complete control of information by a centralized elite. The distinction between what the Russians write for themselves and for foreigners is a clever move to exclude all counter-arguments. Again, the totalitarian move excludes all contradiction. All Soviet statements that do not agree with Pipes's position are dismissed from consideration by relegating them to propaganda.

Pipes continues from here, arguing that the Soviet doctrine calls not only for the defeat of the enemy but his destruction. Their nuclear doctrine calls for prompt and massive nuclear attack at the beginning of a war. 'Limited nuclear war, flexible response, escalation, damage limiting, and all the other numerous refinements of US strategic doctrine find no place in its Soviet counterpart' (Pipes, 1981, 158). Specifically, their doctrine consists of five key elements.

1. Pre-emption

The USSR learned the costs of passive defence by its losses in 1941 when attacked in an unmobilized state by the Nazis. The importance of surprise is not lost on them. In nuclear terms with ICBM flight times of thirty minutes, pre-emption means firing first to prevent the other side using its weapons. The USSR claims it would never attack first, but would attack pre-emptively if it concluded that an attack against it was imminent. All this requires a high state of combat readiness; there is no possibility of mobilization in a nuclear war, forces will fight where they are, with what equipment they have at hand.

2. Quantitative superiority

The more the better seems to be the Soviet approach to nuclear weapons. This is based on the premise in their planning that despite the speed at which the initial strikes are likely to occur, a major war would take months to conclude. A large supply of weapons would be useful in these conditions of prolonged conflict. It also provides a useful counter to the technical instabilities introduced by equipping ICBMs with multiple independently targeted re-entry vehicles. Their large ICBMs with many warheads are also useful for a potential anti-silo counter-force strike.

3. Counterforce targeting

The Soviet doctrine has in part, Pipes argues, as a result of close study of the post-war strategic bombing studies in Japan and Germany which US strategists have ignored, never given much emphasis to counter-value targeting, preferring to emphasize the destruction of the enemy's military forces: its ability to wage war. This is in contrast to the US declatory policy of retaliatory counter-value targeting.

4. Combined-arms operations

The long-war view of superpower conflict requires that the USSR have non-nuclear naval, air and ground forces to follow up the initial nuclear attack, to take control of areas including Western Europe in the aftermath of the initial nuclear exchange, and to destroy the remains of the navies and merchant fleets of the USA and other adversaries, to prevent their use against the USSR.

5. Defence

In contrast to the US notion that no meaningful civil defence is possible, the USSR has developed a sophisticated air defence system and civil defence preparations are taken seriously. The Anti-Ballistic Missile treaty was agreed to only because the Russians were having serious technical problems and they were afraid that the USA would gain a tremendous lead in the necessary technology. Pipes reiterates his assumptions that the USSR would be prepared to risk millions of casualties, on the basis of its historical experience.

In conclusion, Pipes argues that the differences in doctrine are significant, but that 'The point lies not in our ability to wreak total destruction: it lies in intent. And in so far as military doctrine is indicative of intent, what the Russians think to do with their nuclear arsenal is a matter of utmost importance that calls for close scrutiny' (Pipes, 1981, 167). Pipes's scrutiny of these matters, from his totalitarian perspective, has led him to conclude that the USSR is not likely to forgo the chance to achieve global pre-eminence by nuclear war if it is presented. The implication of his position is the CPD concern that without a US awareness of Soviet doctrine, the USA will underestimate the threat. In this circumstance it will find itself at best, intimidated in a series crisis confrontations with the USSR; at worst, defeated by a surprise counter-force nuclear attack.

Sovietology and strategy

The totalitarian sovietological discourse is essential to Pipes's approach to strategic matters; it provides the key discursive move to his whole position. Here we see how Pipes's sovietology leads him and the CPD to their position on Soviet war-fighting strategies. In the patrimonial interpretation, the USSR is expansionist, militarist and totalitarian in the sense that all aspects of society are regulated by the central government. Because the USSR is defined as a monolith, it follows that learned military journals will produce the central line of official policy. Hence, when officers discuss military operations in their journals this can be interpreted as a statement of political intention. Because of the monolithic assumption there is no distinction here between the institutional requirements that the Soviet officer corps discuss military eventualities and the actual intentions of political leaders.

In the subsequent 'Garthoff–Pipes debate' in *Strategic Review*, Garhoff (1982a) has charged Pipes with repeated misuse of evidence, selective quotation and failure to consider material in its historical context. These arguments, although directed at Pipes's later (1982) criticism of Garthoff's (1978, 1982b) position, are apposite here, too (see Weeks, 1983). But rather than rehearse these empirical inaccuracies in detail, what is important to emphasize here is how Pipes's overall conception of the Soviet system, as patrimonial and totalitarian, leads to the interpretation of Soviet strategy as deliberately developing the capabilities to intimidate the West. Alternative interpretations, relying on more complex political analyses, are delegitimized by the discursive practices of sovietology and Pipes's 'historical method'. The totalitarian interpretation of sovietology thus provides Pipes with the Soviet theory of nuclear war-fighting.

The critics of these simplistic interpretations rely on a more complex sociological understanding of the USSR. As Holloway (1983) and MccGwire (1987a) make clear, there are major institutional differences within the armed services, and the relative importance of the various tasks assigned to different services has varied considerably in the last few decades. Serious political debates have occurred in the military press and scholarly journals on these issues, with each service staking out its respective position. An analysis of selected writings which neglects either these debates or the historical evolution of the overall strategic discussions about nuclear war is inadequate.

In particular, the assumption that a major war would inevitably escalate to a nuclear exchange was, MccGwire (1987a) argues, no longer held in Moscow. However, Pipes (1977) and Douglas and Hoeber (1979) show no recognition of this change in doctrine which MccGwire dates to the mid-

1960s, although more sophisticated contemporaneous analyses were aware of nuances and changes in Soviet positions (Ermath, 1978; Garthoff, 1978). Pipes, as well as Douglas and Hoeber (1979), rely on documents from the 1960s and assume a continuity ever since. Pipes (1981, 153) argues that the 'war-winning doctrine' which was in force in the 1970s was developed in the 1955–7 period. In a totalitarian system the assumption is of very long-term planning and little change therefore is a fair assumption. Pipes argues that statements that nuclear war would be suicidal were intended only for export to the West but not taken seriously in the USSR (1981, 158).

In a continuation of this line of argument, the obvious silences and changes in the materials published in the USSR in the 1970s from the 1960s line are subsequently attributed by Lee and Staar (1986) to a Soviet disinformation effort to confuse Western scholars and military analysts as to the facts that their war-winning strategy remained intact. While this may 'flout common sense' (MccGwire, 1987a, 359), it is entirely consistent with the CPD 'common sense' totalitarian interpretation of the USSR as a society where everything is controlled and manipulated by the ruling Politburo. Thus, the USSR could supposedly orchestrate all military publications to lull the West into complacency and an acceptance of SALT, a move which would ultimately constrain US weapons in ways that guaranteed Soviet nuclear supremacy. Thus, internal bureaucratic dynamics and audiences can be ignored in the analysis of the Soviet texts. Subsequently, the Russians admitted that Sokolovsky (1963), in particular, is outdated (MccGwire, 1987a, 358).

The patrimonial/totalitarian assumptions of Pipes's analysis also lead to the assumption of an aggressive use of military power to promote Soviet expansion, nuclear weapons are just another tool of totalitarian empire-building. What is important here is the assumption by Pipes that being Russian is more important than being Marxist. The implications of this are fundamental to the analysis of Soviet military positions; Pipes is led to his position by the assertion of long-term continuity in Russian history.

The alternative position is one that argues that the Russians are convinced that capitalism as a social system is doomed to be transcended by a socialist system. Thus, so long as the USSR maintains a strong defence, so that imperialist capitalism in its death throes does not attempt to eradicate socialism in a war in a last attempt to save itself, then socialism will triumph. In such circumstances, the USSR will play a leading role in the new global political arrangements, ones that will occur without the use of nuclear war-fighting strategies by the Red Army's strategic rocket forces. The implications of this understanding are diametrically opposite to Pipes's views. What is of crucial importance to the argument here is the consequences of Pipes's patri-monial 'historical' analysis that leads to a position that the USSR has to expand; the risks of nuclear war are merely another obstacle in its historical bid for domination.

But Pipes does not argue that the USSR intends to fight a nuclear war. This bid for domination involves the building of a massive ICBM force and in the CPD literature this is interpreted unambiguously as an attempt to gain such a nuclear supremacy that any US consideration of the use of nuclear weapons in a contest over the Rimlands would be self-deterred in the face of Soviet supremacy. This connection between geopolitics and strategy is the focus of many of the CPD texts and in particular the writings of Paul Nitze.

SALT, geopolitics and strategy

Paul Nitze (1974–5, 1975, 1976, 1976–7, 1977, 1987a, 1987b, 1980a) was not alone among the CPD authors to criticize the SALT process, but having been intimately involved in the process for years under the Nixon administration, his voice carried authority. Rostow (1979) wrote against SALT II and Gray produced a stream of critical articles on the process (1973, 1975a, 1975b, 1976b, 1976c, 1977c, 1977d, 1979c, 1979d, 1980b). Nitze presented the kernel of his arguments at a CPD panel at the Foreign Policy Association meeting in March 1978.

Here he outlined the problems of SALT and argued that the Russians were gaining a tremendous superiority in strategic nuclear potential measured in terms of prompt counter-military potential and megatonnage, seen as 'the best index of population vulnerability to fallout' (CPD, 1984, 27). He went on to argue that nuclear superiority was crucial in international confrontations with the USSR, contrary to many arguments that it was irrelevant. Here the link between geopolitics and nuclear strategy is restated bluntly.

> To those who lived through the Berlin crisis in 1961, the Cuban crisis in 1962, or the Middle East crisis in 1973, the last and key judgement in this chain of reasoning – that an adverse shift in the strategic nuclear balance will have no political or diplomatic consequences – comes as quite a shock. In the Berlin crisis of 1961 our tactical theatre position was clearly unfavourable; we relied entirely on our strategic nuclear superiority to face down Chairman Khruschev's ultimatum. In the Cuban crisis the Soviet Union faced a position of both theatre inferiority and strategic inferiority; they withdrew the missiles they were deploying. In the 1973 Middle East crisis, the theatre and the strategic nuclear balances were roughly equal; both sides compromised. [CPD, 1984, 28]

In the following paragraph we see these roots of the CPD strategic view once again as Nitze argues that it 'is hard to see what factors in the future are apt to disconnect international politics and diplomacy from a consideration of the underlying balance of the real factors of power. The nuclear balance is, of course, only one element in the overall power balance 'but, in the Soviet view, it is the fulcrum upon which all other levers of influence – military, economic, or political – rest. Can we be confident that there is not at least a measure of validity to that viewpoint?' (CPD, 1984, 28). Nitze has made it abundantly clear that he does subscribe wholeheartedly to this viewpoint. Nitze believes the Soviet view, or rather his creation of the Soviet viewpoint. The contradiction is obvious. They are evil, but we had better share their understanding of interests and power as ultimately sought by any methods. Such are the canons of realism coupled to geopolitical thinking and this logic is where it leads. We had better arm ourselves to counter this threat, and start seeing the world as ultimately being about means. Once again, the contradictions between the axiological and praxaeological definitions of Otherness appear.

These ideas are clearly laid out in greater detail in Nitze's published articles. In *Foreign Affairs* in 1976 he contended that the SALT process was failing to accomplish its avowed goals, at least from the US perspective. Specifically, it failed to assure strategic stability:

> On the contrary, there is every prospect that under the terms of the SALT agreements the Soviet Union will continue to pursue a nuclear superiority that is not merely quantitative but designed to produce a theoretical war-winning capability. Further, there is a major risk that, if such a condition were achieved, the Soviet Union would adjust its policies and actions in ways that would undermine the present detente situation, with results that could only resurrect the danger of nuclear confrontation or, alternatively, increase the prospect of Soviet expansion through other means of pressure. [Nitze, 1976, 207]

This theme, as seen above, was to become a familiar refrain in following years.

Nitze (1976) traces the origins of *détente* to the Chinese fears of the Soviet military buildup in the period of the late 1960s and their consequent approaches to the USA in search of a counter-weight to the Soviet buildup. In response to all this the USSR moved to a policy of '*détente*' to limit the US support for China, and which involved a series of agreements including the 1972 SALT I, Anti-Ballistic Missile and interim agreements and the 1973 'Basic Principles of Relations Between the United States and the Soviet Union' and subsequent documents. In parallel with Rostow (1976), Nitze argues that these agreements had no effect on restraining Soviet involvement in the Middle East, where they encouraged the initiation of hostilities and then threatened to intervene in the Yom Kippur War when the Egyptians were losing, and in South-East Asia, where the USSR helped the Vietnamese violate the Paris accords. All this assumes very considerable control by the USSR over its 'proxies' in the Third World.

In addition, he cites a number of Soviet writers who boasted of the favourable shifts in the correlation of forces in the early 1970s made possible by the policies of *détente* and the arrival of nuclear parity. Nitze concludes that *détente* is no different from peaceful coexistence; in other words there has been no shift in basic Soviet intentions. He further argues that a clear indication of their seriousness should be visible in the negotiation process on strategic weapons; if they are serious then they will move towards a stabilizing posture, if not they will follow other strategies in the negotiations.

He argues that the USSR spends up to a billion dollars per annum in civil defence planning, showing a serious appreciation of the possibility of nuclear war. Like most other analysts Nitze argues that, after the Cuban Crisis in 1962, the Russians probably concluded that strategic superiority was a crucial factor in superpower confrontation, and commenced a concerted military development programme in its aftermath. Thus, he concludes, in a slightly less alarmist position than Pipes's, that the USSR is striving for a war-winning capability as the ultimate deterrent, and having acquired it they would probably use its influence, in a crisis, to promote the global advance of socialism.

Nitze presents two graphs which portray a growing Soviet strategic advantage, and he concludes that after 1977 the USSR will increasingly improve its relative position after a counter-force strike against the US forces. This theoretical calculation is the basis for subsequent 'window of vulnerability' concerns which were so important in the 1980 election campaign. It also relates to the matter of self-deterrence (Nitze, 1976–7), in which the Russians could threaten a pre-emptive strike against the US ICBM force which would leave them with a tremendous preponderance of strategic forces after their first strike, and also after a retaliatory US second strike, leaving the US president with few options but capitulation.

The results of this analysis required, according to Nitze, a policy to increase the survivability of the US forces and compensate for the Soviet civil defence programme. These include accuracy improvements to compensate for the lack of 'throwweight' in the US arsenal. But he argues that it is necessary to go much further than this and construct a multiple basing mode mobile ICBM, a position that was the rationale for the MX missile the development of which the Carter regime debated at length. This would remove the potential instability of the current Soviet throwweight advantage by offering too many targets for a possible counter-force strike. With this system in place, the argument went, there is no possible advantage to be gained by firing first and consequently stability is restored. In conclusion, Nitze suggests that the Russians have shown no inclination towards unilateral restraint in their weapons procurement policies nor have they shown any inclination to abandon a view that strategic superiority is useful in a crisis situation. The implication is simple; if they think that strategic superiority is essential in a crisis, then the USA had better make sure they do not get it.

The necessary force structures for fighting a nuclear war are clear: they include a counter-force capability that can reduce the enemy's forces by a greater number of weapons than it takes one to accomplish the task; dispersed and protected forces which makes them a difficult counterforce target; reserve forces to threaten the enemy's population and industry; active and passive defensive measures to minimize damage should the enemy respond with a counter-value strike; and, finally, the means to pre-empt if necessary. Nitze argues that the USSR nuclear weapons buildup initiated in the early 1960s seemed designed to fulfil these criteria. Assessing the force capabilities of the superpower arsenals, Nitze (1976), argues that all indicators are moving against the USA and towards Soviet superiority. More seriously he argues that the arrangement is becoming more unstable, in that the relative advantage to the USSR of a first strike is growing. In other words, their relative advantage in forces is greater after a first strike against US forces than before a strike. This encourages the USSR to pre-empt in a crisis, because they would be better off after initiating a counter-force first strike and hence could further intimidate the USA into acquiescing to their demands.

Nitze then asks if any of its matters, a position that would seem to be the logic of MAD. Thus, if the USA is still capable of doing 'unacceptable damage' to the USSR, principally with its invulnerable submarine-based weapons, then no matter how much the relative advantage swings to the USSR's favour they will still not be tempted. But Nitze argues that the USSR's leaders may not assume that the damage will be unacceptable, principally because they have a comprehensive civil defence programme which should be capable of limiting the casualties to a few percent of their population. In this they are helped, Nitze argues, by the changes in the US arsenal towards smaller more accurate warheads. Thus, these weapons in counter-value mode are designed to be airburst for maximum blast damage effects. But this reduces the fallout to the level of relative insignificance (groundbursts produce most fallout) in a situation where civil defence shelters are planned for a large percentage of the population. 'The usual assumption that the US possesses a vast population overkill is in essence, without foundation' (Nitze, 1976–7, 206).

Crucially, all of these considerations are related to the different defence requirements of the superpowers due to their differing geopolitical positions. Here the notion of extended deterrence is raised, although not in those specific terms.

> The defence problems of the United States and the Soviet Union are quite different. The United States must be able to project its power over many thousands of miles to support allied defence structures on lines close to the concentrations of Soviet power. The Soviet basic defensive task is much simpler; that is, to maintain military preponderance on the exterior lines of its relatively compact land mass. [Nitze, 1976–7, 206]

This also links the possession of the strategic superiority by the USSR to geopolitics in the Third World where traditionally the USA was able to intervene with conventional forces knowing that if it came to a showdown with the USSR its nuclear superiority would ensure that the USSR would back down. He argues that in the context of the USSR building a series of weapons and developing forces capable of 'projecting power' that the loss of US strategic superiority implied the removal of the USA's ability to intervene in the Third World in a direct military way with impunity. Indeed, he argues that the situation was moving to a position where the USSR would be able to do so. The implication of this is that the USA can no longer effectively intervene to support 'allied defence structures'. This reveals the essential role of nuclear superiority in the whole geopolitical scheme, it provides the assurance that US forces can intervene in the Third World.

But in the strategic logic a decline in nuclear capability would also lead to a position in which the USSR could militarily defeat the USA. Thus the military position has, or shortly will, even under SALT II, deteriorate to the situation in which the President, in a major crisis in which the USSR launches a counter-force strike, in the absence of a survivable counter-value, much less counter-force cabable arsenal, has to make a decision whether to fire the US ICBM force in a few minutes in a launch under attack situation, or else surrender immediately, without any other option of being able to mount a credible threat to destroy the USSR. In this crucial sense the USSR was in the process of gaining strategic superiority.

This being the case, Nitze argues for an immediate introduction of the B-1 bomber programme, an emergency programme to build road mobile transporter/launch vehicles for the Minuteman III missiles and the develop-ment of the MX in a multiple basing mode. This programme could ensure that the Russians could not pre-empt in a way that would allow them to survive a counter-value retaliatory strike. Hence the Presidency would have a variety of options available to it, and the USSR would once again be deterred from launching a first strike because it could not gain a military advantage by doing so. This massive buildup would prevent the President from being self-deterred in a crisis, and in the event of a Soviet first strike would leave numerous weapons intact to allow a variety of strategic responses.

This is effectively a strategy of 'victory denial', which in various forms became central to the war-fighting strategy debates under the acryonm 'NUTS' which Gray elaborated in greatest detail. The conclusion of Nitze's argument was that only in terms where the USA could credibly guarantee to deny a plausible victory to the USSR would the USSR come to the arms negotiating table with a willingness to make the drastic mutual cuts in the nuclear arsenals that were the ostensible rationale of the arms negotiation process. All this assumes a remarkable faith in the technological capabilities of the weapons systems on both sides. While Kaplan (1983, 379) may be only partly correct in his assertion that Nitze has taken the strategic analysis to yet new levels of abstraction, he is assuming that the whole nuclear counter-force strike is a technically feasible operation because one can rationally develop a hypothetical scenario for such an eventuality. In Tonelson's (1979) terms, Nitze's world is one of 'clarity and crusades'; it is not one in which the complex compromises of politics sit comfortably. In the chaos of a wartime situation, it is highly unlikely that strikes could be cleanly distinguished between counter-force and counter-value. Whether first strikes could be cleanly executed in a short time span is extremely doubtful, and unknowable in the absence of the possibility of testing the whole procedure.

But the core of the CPD case against SALT II rests on precisely these abstract strategic calculations. This is particularly clear in the CPD's major statement 'Is America Becoming Number 2?' which was released in October 1978. Here the CPD considers a scenario of a Soviet nuclear attack in which their putative superiority in counter-force weapons is used to attack the US ICBM's and airforce bases in a first strike. This leaves the USSR with a larger number of warheads surviving than are present in the remaining US submarines and aircraft. The argument then proceeds, as with Nitze's analysis, to suggest that the US President would be forced either to negotiate or to retaliate with an attack on Soviet cities, in the knowledge that the Russians could respond in even greater force on US cities. This is a situation of a Soviet third strike superiority which would come about as a result of a large nuclear superiority.

The alternative presented by the CPD is that a US President would have to negotiate in a crisis from a position of weakness and thus gradually be forced to concede to the Russians' demands.

> Under such circumstances, we would be vulnerable to the scenario of a Cuban Missile Crisis in reverse – a confrontation in which we should have to yield in the face of overwhelming force. A clearly superior Soviet third strike capability, under the assumption of clear Soviet strategic nuclear superiority, would undermine the credibility of our second-strike capacity, and could lead us, either to accommodation without fighting or to the acceptance of unmanageable risks. [CPD, 1984, 41]

They go on to argue that the President should have a series of options in a crisis that prevent him being presented with only the options of 'retreat or a nuclear war under grossly unfavourable circumstances.

Thus the 'United States must be able to deter military aggression throughout the spectrum of armed conflict with forces appropriate to the threat' (CPD, 1984, 41). Thus extended deterrence and some form of escalation dominance is called for, in which the USA can outmatch the USSR in all spheres and levels of possible military confrontation; strategic superiority is directly tied into matters of geopolitical confrontation; strategic superiority is needed to guarantee that the USSR cannot use nuclear weapons at the local level against US interventions for fear of losing at the theatre or ultimately at the strategic level. Strategy and geopolitics are mutually interconnected in the CPD's argument.

To undertake the strategic force posture that the CPD advocated to deal simultaneously with the strategic and geopolitical concerns of extended deterrence requires a massive buildup of weapons and forces right across the spectrum. Thus not only must the buildup be sufficient to avoid the supposed predicament of self-deterrence in a central nuclear war; it must also provide the necessary weapons to enable the USA to intervene anywhere in the Third World to challenge and effectively militarily defeat either Soviet forces or 'proxy' Soviet forces attempting to expand the area of Soviet geopolitical control. These in turn require the ability to deter the Russians from escalating the conflict to larger levels of destruction in the event of their losing on a local level. This requires nuclear superiority at tactical (battlefield or local) and theatre (regional), in addition to the strategic (global) level.

Hence what is required is a massive weapons buildup and the creation of forces capable of intervention globally at short notice. This is precisely what the CPD repeatedly advocated. They were particularly concerned with the SALT process because they thought that it would hamstring the development of new strategic weapons and with that ensure a Soviet 'superiority' which would be used to force political concessions from the USA and lead to its gradual isolation in world affairs. In particular, this lack of US superiority would ensure that the USA would have to back down in conflicts over the Middle East and elsewhere where resources essential to the US economy are located.

As Pipes makes clear, the CPD did not accept that the USSR was serious in its assertions of the existence of a state of mutual deterrence. Consequently its military objectives were pieced together by analysing Soviet military writings and assuming that the totalitarian regime that dominated the Soviet military was bent on global domination, if necessary by the use of nuclear weapons, preferably by the use of proxy forces to expand its geopolitical influence under the shadow of a nuclear superiority. Hence the need for US weapons to counter the perceived Soviet buildup; weapons that supposedly will remove dangers of the US being self-deterred. Here the strategic, sovietological and geopolitical discourses are linked together in a manner that each supports the case made by the others.

But the strategic arguments do not stop there. Assuming that these weapons are built, there is a further requirement for worked-out strategies for their use in conflict, and, so the argument goes, the co-ordination of these to bring about political defeat of the USSR in a nuclear war. If this can be accomplished, in a way that the Russians believe to be a credible, then the argument suggests (in a direct rerun of the early 1950s case made by NSC 68) that they will believe themselves to be ultimately deterred, and hence incapable of continuing their geopolitical campaign of expansion. The final step in the argument is that only then will they come to the bargaining table in good faith and negotiate drastic reductions in nuclear arms.

This theme of nuclear strategy brings us to the 'theory of victory' associated with Colin Gray. His arguments link the strategic concerns with US self-deterrence with the concern with Soviet geopolitical expansion, and Pipes's reading of Soviet strategic doctrine. In linking all these themes together, we come to the final articulation of the security discourses: the Nuclear Utilization Theories and Strategies (NUTS), and specifically to Colin Gray's 'theory of victory'.

The theory of victory

The key papers in which the 'theory of victory' is outlined are in *International Security* (Gray, 1979a) and in a more polemically phrased argument co-authored with Keith Payne in *Foreign Policy* (Gray and Payne, 1980). Rarely does Gray actually argue that nuclear war should be initiated, rather he argues that should deterrence fail and a major conflict occur then there need to be plans on how to conduct that conflict, and the force structures of the US forces should be organized in such a way that they are usable and that escalation does not run into the problem of self-deterrence. Effectively, what Gray has done is take Pipes's and Nitze's concerns and combine them with his own ideas to elaborate a theory of victory. Gray's own concerns are threefold: first, his geopolitical writing discussed in Chapter seven; second, his long series of studies on the various parts of the US nuclear arsenal and their roles in strategic doctrine (Gray, 1974a, 1975c, 1976d, 1976e, 1977e, 1977f, 1978a, 1978b, 1978c, 1979e, 1980c, 1980d); and third, his extensive writings on arms races, strategy and related matters of policy-making (Gray 1971a, 1971b, 1971c, 1974b, 1975d, 1977–8, 1978c). Gray argues that US debates over specific weapons systems and the need for civil defence etc. are reflections over a fundamental disagreement as to what nuclear strategic posture should be for. The thrust of his seminal 'theory of victory' paper (1979a) is to develop a clear argument of what this posture should be and consequently how it should be structured.

First, he argues that the only effective deterrent which will guarantee Western security is one which denies any possible plausible theory of victory to the other side. Thus, in a moment of crisis within the USSR, he argues, the US military posture should be such that there is no way a group of Soviet generals could brief the Politburo on a possible plan of attack that could disarm the US in a pre-emptive strike. The denial of the possibility of a plausible theory of victory to the Soviet military is thus the key in Gray's argument. The second point is that even if one buys the MAD position, which argues that the mere prospect of a nuclear war is enough to deter any leader from initiating it, one still needs a more detailed series of guidelines for force acquisition around the question of how much destruction is enough. Gray's third point in the argument for a coherent strategic position is that nuclear war may occur. In that event, a leader would require that the military planners have a workable war plan ready. In parallel with Pipes he argues that the doctrine of MAD works only before the outbreak of hostilities. Once hostilities commence simply killing people and destroying buildings is not a strategy. 'Unless one is willing to endorse the proposition that nuclear deterrence is all bluff, there can be no evading the requirement that the defence community has to design nuclear employment options that a reasonable political leader would not be self-deterred from ever executing, however reluctantly' (Gray, 1979a, 57).

Much of his argument is a criticism of existing US strategic thinking which he contends fails to think strategy through fully. Gray divides the schools of strategy into the MAD school and the revisionists. The latter argue that the MAD preoccupation has caused the serious failure of strategic thinking that plagues US reasoning on matters of international politics. This he traces to the abandonment of the notions of damage limitation (counter-force) in favour of the notion of strategic stability providing a strategic stalemate. In this situation security was defined in terms of mutual vulnerability and consequently systems of Ballistic Missile Defence (BMD) were seen as a destabilizing threat of that putative security. Gray, in contrast to Pipes, is careful to point out that operational planning has never reflected the MAD reasoning. Thus, Gray's target here is arms controllers who argue on the basis of MAD positions and advocate reduced nuclear weapons acquisitions programmes, not the operational planners in the Pentagon who develop targeting plans (Pringle and Arkin, 1983; Kaku and Axelrod, 1986).

The revisionist school, of which Gray is a self-declared member, argues that the USSR does not appear to accept the logic of the MAD and that the technical posture position on which it was argued has significantly changed. 'US official thinking and planning does not embrace the idea that it is necessary to try to effect the *defeat* of the Soviet Union. First and foremost the Soviet leadership fears *defeat*, not the suffering of damage – and defeat ... has to entail the forcible demise of the Soviet State' (Gray, 1979a, 61). Gray then argues once again that the lingering effects of the deterrence through MAD school by focusing on pre-war deterrence have prevented the analysis and preparation of workable operational strategies.

> Incredible though it may seem, it has taken the United States' defense community nearly twenty five years to ask the two most basic questions of all pertaining to nuclear deterrence issues: these are, first, what kinds of threats should have the most deterring effect upon the leadership of the Soviet State? – and, second should pre-war deterrence fail, what nuclear employment strategy would it be in the United States' interest actually to implement? [Gray, 1979a, 62]

The logic to all this is that it is impossible to plan for a war if one has no conception of war aims, without which there can be no guidelines as to what criteria would determine a successful termination of hostilities. Gray argues that this has historically been a problem in the US conduct of war, Vietnam being the classic case of a failure to develop a theory of war conclusion. Relying on strategic assumptions of escalation in response to threat, and without a clear theory of victory the USA found itself in a position where defeat was inevitable eventually. Without a conception of ultimate war aims, planning cannot take place for operational strategy, without which force acquisition procedures remain incoherent and inefficient. The MAD position avoids all this by arguing that given the extraordinary destructive power of nuclear weapons and their likely modes of use, it is impossible to plan rationally for the fighting of a nuclear war. Gray argues that that assumption is questionable, in that limited use of forces could be rational and that one may happen anyway, and if so some targeting planning will have to be done in advance, and should be so done that it incorporates a specific strategic conception of winning the war.

The Nixon administration flexible response position, and Schlesinger's pronouncement of flexible targeting options (see Richelson, 1983) as operational doctrine is not sufficient for Gray. This, he argues, is obvious given the inadequacy of the weapons systems for counter-military attacks, and the lack of an overall framework which makes the limited strikes sensible in terms of a theory of war-winning which the USSR's leaders would believe as a credible strategy to inflict a defeat on them. The counter-value war recovery targeting policies in place are not adequate either, he argues, simply because there is inadequate knowledge as to how the Soviet economy actually works, and consequently it is difficult to devise a credible series of attack scenarios. Thus, he argues that it is impossible to talk convincingly of a counter-recovery strategy in the absence of an overall conception of war aims which would determine how much damage was necessary. A counter-recovery strategy that was aimed at setting the economy back a decade is obviously very different from one that aims at setting the economy back a couple of generations. But causing extensive economic damage may lead only to retaliation against Western economic targets, and further it may well not succeed in ending the war on terms favourable to the West.

Gray argues that this might well be the case because

> The Soviet Union, like Czarist Russia, knows that it can absorb an enormous amount of punishment (loss of life, industry, productive agricultural land, and even territory), and recover, and endure until final victory – provided the *essential assets of the state* [original emphasis] remain intact. The principal assets are the political control structure of the highly centralised CPSU and government bureaucracy; the transmission belts of communication from the centre to the regions; the instruments of central official coercion (the KGB and the armed forces); and the reputation of the Soviet state in the eyes of its citizens. Counter-economic targeting should have a place in intelligent US war planning, but only to the extent to which such targeting would impair the functioning of the Soviet State. [Gray, 1979a, 67–8]

While Gray admits that the problems of dividing the state apparatus from the rest of the society and the economy would be formidable, none the less targeting the USSR with the avowed aim of destroying the political apparatus and control mechanisms would at least provide a coherent war aim which would provide a potentially desirable state of affairs in the post-war world.

While not easy to make operational, at least a theory of this sort offers some guidelines as to how to plan to fight a war in a way that the Soviet leadership would consider credible, and such a risk to their survival that they would be deterred from initiating a war.

> Stated directly, the Soviets should know that if they prosecute a major war against the West they stand to *lose (in their own terms).* [original emphasis] In a conflict over the most important political stakes, our principal war aim should be to effect the demise of the Soviet state: It should not be to kill Soviet postwar economic recovery. [Gray, 1979b, 10]

This raises the question of precisely what targets would be essential to the strategy of destroying the Soviet state. Gray argues that five key facts are crucial to devising this kind of strategy. These are drawn from Richard Pipes's work on Russian history, specifically from *Russia Under the Old Regime* (1974) and 'Detente: Moscow's View' (1976) which was reviewed in detail above. Specifically, the imperial thesis is crucial.

Thus we are told first that the Soviet peoples have no affection for their political system; second, the colonial peoples within the Empire have no love for the USSR; third, the state is very careful with its domestic respect and reputation because it is so fragile; fourth, the over-centralization of the system suggests that it can be paralysed if the lower levels of political command are severed from the central 'brain'; and fifth, the peoples of Eastern Europe are likely to maintain respect for the USSR only so long as its armed forces are not defeated or tied down in a long or interminable war. Thus Gray argues that the war-fighting strategy of targeting the Soviet apparatus would, in the context of conflict that could not easily be defined as self-defence of 'Mother Russia', seriously undermine the legitimacy of the system. It would also work to undermine the legitimacy of the regime if it were fighting a war in distant parts, and the domestic devastation were limited to clearly identifiable political targets.

Precisely because the USSR is an Empire, without legitimacy in the peripheral areas, it would be vulnerable to this kind of strategy. Because the imperial structure is essential to the survival of the state, the highest value in the Soviet leadership's calculation being the self-preservation of the regime, upon which the *nomenklatura* depends for its power and privilege, then a declaratory policy of attacking the Soviet imperial administrative apparatus, backed by a clear technical ability to do so, offers the USA a potentially war-winning strategy. Faced with this, the Russians will realize that they face an impossible situation. If they initiate a war, they know that their system will not survive it. Hence they will be effectively deterred from initiating hostilities. Further, faced with the long-term impossibility of winning a nuclear confrontation with the USA they will finally come to the bargaining table and negotiate a SALT regime that reduces the nuclear threat.

What is crucial to all of this is Gray's amalgamation of the imperial thesis, drawn from Pipes's writing, with the strategic considerations of the 1950s concerning counter-force and nuclear war doctrines. Critics of the NUTS positions have not so far, in any detail, incorporated the links between the geopolitical and specifically the 'imperial thesis' formulation of the geo-political situation in the Soviet system. This book argues that this inter-connection is precisely what is the linchpin of the whole CPD discourse on the Soviet threat.

While it might be objected that the imperial thesis, although present in 'the case for a theory of victory' (1979a) was elaborated only subsequently in Gray's writing, the crucial passage in the 1979 paper does refer to Pipes's analysis of Russian imperialism. The five key factors that Gray draws on are taken directly from Pipes's formulations, the relevant footnote (1979a, 68), refers to these writings as 'the imperial thesis'. Here the totalitarian thesis, taken for granted as the backdrop of nuclear strategizing in the past, is directly inserted into nuclear planning. The key to Gray's theory of victory thus resides on Pipes's interpretation of Russian history. If this view is fundamentally flawed and oversimplistic, as argued above, then the theoretical basis for the nuclear strategy that Gray argues is likewise flawed.

Gray also specifically critiques the MAD counter-value position in the 'theory of victory'. If the US strategic forces are poised to strike at Soviet cities in the event of a nuclear war, then the only option facing a US President is the initiation of genocide. Reliance on some version of this deterrence through punishment line, or alternatively the reduction of strategy to numerical interactions between isolated missile fields considered in the abstract, is partly responsible, in Gray's estimation, for the focus on essential equivalence as the cornerstone of the SALT II negotiating position.

In Gray's line of argument, following Nitze's analysis, MAD self-deters because if a conflict did develop, there would be no way in which the USA could initiate the use of nuclear weapons if the logical consequence was the certain destruction of US cities. Thus the MAD posture, and also an only partly thought-through revisionist position focusing on targeting the Soviet command structure, leaves huge holes in the logic of a war-fighting strategy.

The key villian in the piece is, according to Gray, the concept of stability (see also Gray, 1980b), which, he argues, was premised on a serious misreading of the Soviet system and its goals. This refers to the criticism of the US policy-makers of *détente* in assuming that the Russians are serious in their pursuit of *détente*. Thus the policies of the USA in the late 1960s and 1970s have provided a situation in which the USSR will have a strategic superiority in the 1980s. This, in part, was premised on the concern that, in developing a large arsenal of counter-force capable weapons that would threaten the other side's retaliatory capabilities, one would increase the incentives to go first in a crisis, to prevent being caught on the ground and disabled by the other side's forces. But Gray argues that because of unilateral US restraint, the USA is now vulnerable to just this danger.

This discussion of counter-military strategies brings Gray back to his earlier arguments about the fragility of the Soviet Empire and here he offers a clear statement of how the strategic targeting suggested above might fit into the larger political and military scheme of a global conflict.

> A theory of victory over the Soviet Union can be only partially military in character – the more important part is political. The United States and its allies probably should not aim at achieving the military defeat of the Soviet Union, considered as a unified whole; instead, it should seek to impose such military stalemate and defeat as is needed to persuade disaffected Warsaw Pact allies and ethnic minorities inside the Soviet Union that they can assert their own values in very active political ways. [Gray, 1979a, 80]

The implications of this are directly linked to the assumptions of a limited nuclear war being possible and to the assumption that in these circumstances the USSR could not escalate to a full-scale nuclear war. But also if the USA escalated there might be no possibility of political victory. 'It is possible that a heavily counter-military focused Single Integrated Operational Plan might have the same insensitivity to Soviet domestic fragilities as may be found in the counter-economic recovery orientation of the 1970s (Gray, 1979a, 80). But, and here again there is a notion of limited warfare in the background, 'With a clear war aim – to encourage the dissolution of the Soviet state – much of the military war might not need to be fought at all' (Gray, 1979a, 80). Gray's repeated criticism of the failure of the US strategic community to think things through in political, as opposed to purely military terms, is again operating here.

The final section of the 'theory of victory' points to the need for defence as a means of reducing the dangers of self-deterrence. Gray concludes that the USA has done itself a disservice in failing to protect its societal assets in terms of a Ballistic Missile Defence system and civil defence preparations, which, he argues, the USSR has developed. The USA's greatest asset is its ability to mobilize its industrial potential to defeat the USSR, but without a BMD system such possibilities are likely to be denied. Anticipating the subsequent debate about the Strategic Defence Initiative (SDI) and the so called 'defence transition' (Gray, 1985a, 1986a; Payne and Gray, 1984), he argues that the balance between strategic defence and offence has to be rectified because 'If escalation discipline is to be imposed upon the Soviet Union, even in the direst of situations, potential damage to North America has to be limited' (Gray, 1979a, 84). This damage limitation has to be due both to passive defence and counter-force action.

Gray argues that with defence the strategic forces are credibly usable in that the self-deterrence limitations are partly removed. On the question of civil defence, which would improve this situation further, Gray includes two sentences on the disparities between the superpowers that can be read as being self-contradictory. Thus:

> among the more pertinent asymmetries that separate the US from the Soviet political system is the acute sensitivity of the former to the *personal* [original emphasis] well being of its human charges. It is little short of bizarre to discover that it is the Soviet Union and not the United States, that has a serious civil defence program. [Gray, 1979a, 84]

By definition, of course, it has to be bizarre given the a priori definitions of the natures of the two regimes in question. It is simply not possible for an insecure empire of the sort Gray, following Pipes, depicts to have any concern for the welfare of its population, despite the evidence that Gray musters that suggests that this is the case.

Gray concludes his 'Case for a Theory of Victory' with a call for a reinstatement of strategic superiority as a desirable criterion in strategic planning. This assurance would deny the USSR any plausible theory of victory and hence ensure that no adventurist policies were likely to be forthcoming from Moscow. Given (in the language of realism) that it is a revisionist state which has little vested interest in the status quo and hence it is a danger to the principal status quo power, namely the USA (Gray 1981c), then the only way to produce with certainty a position where in a crisis one could face down the Russians and 'win' the crisis without a shot being fired is to be in a position of strategic superiority. But the possession of enough weapons is not enough on its own, it requires a plausible theory of victory to be completely convincing. Providing this has been Gray's self-appointed task.

Nuclear war-fighting strategies: NUTS to DEAD

There was a whole string of strategic counter-arguments to the nuclear war-fighting strategies of the Reagan administration, and to Gray's ideas of a theory of victory in particular (Hanson, 1982–3; Howard, 1981; Lambeth, 1982). Here they are simple enumerated briefly. The point for this book is that the NUTS position is tied to a particular geopolitical formulation; detailed strategic analysis belongs elsewhere (Ball and Richelson eds, 1986), although for completeness a few crucial points on it need to be discussed here. In a number of places Gray's critics have missed the point of his argument precisely because they have not taken the crucial geopolitical dimension, and in particular his 'imperial thesis' argument drawn from Pipes, into account.

Gray is concerned to emphasize the political differences between the superpowers, and the consequences that these may have for strategy. This point relates to his consideration of limited war, either entirely non-nuclear or limited to very selective strikes on both sides. 'It should not be forgotten that damage wrought against the Soviet military machine translates, in Soviet perspective, into threats to the political integrity of the Soviet Union. This is one of the very healthy assymetries in the Soviet-American compet-ition, and its importance should not be undervalued' (Gray, 1980d, 16). This argument suggests that a limited conflict could militarily defeat the USSR to a degree sufficient to cause internal disintegration without causing a major nuclear exchange. The problem of how, in these circumstances, the Soviet leadership would be deterred from gambling on a massive use of nuclear forces remains. Even if this limited scenario did not hold, Gray is still concerned to develop scenarios and strategies for fighting a long, partly nuclear, war.

Gray and Nitze notwithstanding, there remain serious doubts that it is possible to fight a nuclear war in any rational way. The argument relates to the problems of survivability of communications systems; both in terms of whether it is possible to protect them from the disruptive effects of nuclear weapons and, crucially, whether it is humanly and technically possible, amid the chaos of war and reaction times of minutes, to assess the situation, the damage caused by enemy action and the effectiveness of your side's actions in a way that allows militarily useful decisions to be taken and a decision forced in military terms. The doubtfulness of this is central to the arguments against nuclear war-fighting (Ball, 1981; Blair, 1985 Bracken, 1983). The only logical way out of this is to do a first strike against the other side while your communications system is still intact. The pressures to pre-empt in a crisis are indeed great.

Developing the counter-force capable weapons systems that could pre-empt adds tremendously to these pressures. In the terms of international relations, these developments aggravate the security dilemma (Buzan, 1983). In the search for absolute security, here in the terms of Gray's theory of victory, they render other countries less secure. Except in the CPD's universe the argument is inappropriate. Knowing the nature of the USSR to be what it is, 'we' know that it threatens us. The counter-argument that we are making it more insecure is taken as a bonus, ensuring that its behaviour will be curtailed. All this is premised on the realist assumption of revisionist powers' 'interests' being illegitimate, coupled with the particular version of totalitarianism that Pipes applies to the USSR. That external threats might make the USSR more dangerous thus cannot be a consideration, given the 'facts' that it endeavours to take advantage of all opportunities to weaken the West already.

The whole notion of controlled escalation present in the NUTS extended deterrence arguments also relies on there being Soviet interpretations of the US use of nuclear weapons in a manner that the USA predicts in advance. The Soviet strategy, as interpreted by the CPD school of strategists, suggests that the USSR rejects notions of limited nuclear war, precisely what they need to accept to operate in the escalation dominance pattern. While more recent work suggests that the Russians may indeed accept notions of limited superpower warfare that does not escalate to strategic interchanges (MccGwire, 1987a), the analysis offered by Douglas and Hoeber (1979) in particular argues that they do not accept this position. Thus the logic of extended deterrence once again becomes inconsistent with the strategic position advocated by the CPD.

Colin Gray's theory of nuclear targeting aimed at destroying the CPSU is also vulnerable, as he admits in places (1980d, 1984a, 1984b), in that in the chaos of war it would be improbable that the inhabitants of a Soviet town could distinguish the subtlety of a nuclear explosion on a Communist Party headquarters in the centre of the town from an attack on the town itself. But even more important than all this is the assumption that they could make the distinction, and then form some sort of political organization that could emerge to challenge the CPSU, overthrow it and make peace by contacting the US leadership. If the CPSU, and its repressive apparatus, the KGB, is as efficient as the totalitarian model requires, then the possibility that alternative political organizations would suddenly appear, gain local popular legitimacy and communicate with the USA is implausible (Richelson, 1980). Amid the chaos of nuclear war the scenario is at best far-fetched.

It is, however, premised on the assumption that the CPSU is a reviled organization somehow separate from the people. Gray repeatedly asserts that the CPSU has few genuine roots in the population outside the Moscow region. The state–society separation, central to the patrimonial/totalitarian viewpoint and to the imperial thesis is again operating here to influence Gray's strategic vision. In particular, Gray is anxious to promote the dissolution of the Soviet state by targeting the CPSU presence in an unambiguous manner which will force ethnic divisions to the surface. Thus the targeting could undo the imperial structure by geographically splitting up the Empire along its fringes. Once the imperial structure unravels, all else follows. This point is crucial to Gray's whole scheme.

Freedman (1983, 393) argues that in advocating a targeting policy directed against the Soviet political structure, Gray and Payne (1980) have come full circle, back to the crude political science of the early air power theorists. Douhet (1942) and Fuller argued, before the Second World War, that a massive aerial bombardment would detach the societal elite from the population and force a termination of hostilities due to social breakdown. By attributing Gray and Payne's (1980) argument to the discredited air power theories, Freedman (1983) misses the specific history of their argument drawn from the 'imperial thesis'. In a similar vein, Herken (1987, 310), without providing a citation, attributes Gray's interpretation of the Soviet political structure as fragile to the early RAND study *The Operational Code of the Politburo* (Leites, 1950). But in 'The Theory of Victory' Gray cites Pipes in the crucial passage; Leites is never mentioned. Herken apparently has also missed the importance of Pipes's formulations for Gray's strategy. Howard (1981, 14), in particular, charges that Gray fails to clarify the political object of his strategy of victory; the imperial thesis provides just this missing link.

Thus the USSR is not viewed as a homogeneous political society in which most of the politically capable people are somehow incorporated within the CPSU structure, but as an Empire that can be dismantled by judicious targeting triggering the internal political forces of dissolution which are present precisely because the CPSU presides over an Empire, rather than any other form of political organization. Thus, Gray is consistent in his claim to seek a political end for his strategy. Whether this is operationally feasible is another question of importance which requires a detailed empirical assessment that is beyond the scope of this study, but there are arguments that ethnic nationalism may be an overestimated threat to the Soviet state (Colton, 1986; Motyl, 1987; Smith, 1985). In wartime a policy of preventive detention or military conscription of nationalist leaders or dissidents could seriously hamper any attempts to establish local political organizations capable of effective local control.

If one takes the other interpretation of Gray's targeting policies, effectively a decapitation strategy (as Hanson, 1982–3 does) in which one targets the Soviet leadership, then there remains the old problem in nuclear war planning of not having any political leadership left on the other side to negotiate a cessation of hostilities. Reconstituted in these terms, the theory might be made to make some sense in terms of selective nuclear targeting promoting factionalism in the CPSU itself. Its dissolution would present the possibility of parts of its being able to organize to present a political alternative capable of negotiating a peace. But how US military decision-makers are supposed to be able to know all these possible developments in the midst of nuclear warfare is unclear (Richelson, 1980).

A further critique of the whole war-fighting argument is the lack of specificity of the scenarios in which the USA could win, or 'prevail' (Hanson, 1982–3). This is a variation of the 'chaos' argument against nuclear war-fighting theories presented above. Thus Gray argues that it should be possible to limit US casualties to a mere 20 million in a major nuclear war by a combination of passive defence (civil defence and crisis relocation etc.) and damage limitation counter-force strikes. There are two aspects of this that are important.

First, one needs to show how such a counter-force strike can be accomplished; presumably it has to be a first strike. There will always remain crucial technical imponderables on that score, including missile reliability, doubts about accuracy, the impact of fratricide, the electronic disruption of communications problem, damage assessment and follow-up targeting, etc. which render the whole exercise extremely dubious on technical grounds. The only way to test the system is to fight a nuclear war.

Second is the crucial matter of the scale of damage involved in 20 million casualties to the USA. As has been pointed out repeatedly, the possibilities of accurately predicting what even the immediate consequences of a nuclear attack would be like are extremely difficult. But the long-term and indirect consequences in economic and social terms (Peterson, 1983) let alone the ecological factors (Turco et al., 1983, 1984) are likely to be at least as severe as the short-term impacts which are partially calculable. There remains tremendous uncertainty about the whole enterprise of a theory of victory in that the essential parameters for advocating it remain effectively unknowable. Thus it fails where all other nuclear strategies fail: it constructs formal logical scenarios, surrounds them with terminologically dense defences, but ultimately fails to convince.

Despite all these objectives Gray persists. He does so because he has to by the logic of his own realist position. Political solutions to international conflict are not plausible except in the very long term. He has nowhere to go in the interim except to dreaming up war-winning strategies that are increasingly implausible as each assumption is worked in and the logic developed. The dogma of deterrence leads inevitably to these positions.

Because of the CPD portrayal of the USSR as expansionist, driven by its geopolitical logic to try to expand, it follows that mutually agreed arms control can never work because the USSR will never use it as a means genuinely to stop military buildups, merely as a device to make a first-strike temptation irresistible. Thus Gray, Rostow, Pipes and Nitze all argue against the dangers of 'mirror imaging', and yet end up perpetrating these types of ethnocentric fallacies. These fallacies are based on the articulation of axiological difference between the moral defensive USA and the machinations of an evil empire. But it is coupled to with the presumed epistemological superiority of their specification of Otherness.

Thus they go the next step in the argument. The Russians really do understand their activity in our terms; denial of it is mere propaganda. If 'we' hang tough they they will be forced to admit that 'we' are right. They have been peddling propaganda, the political crisis engendered by this admission will force reform on the CPSU. A less-threatening regime will result in the long term. The possibility that forcing the USSR to the wall might produce a really aggressive military state determined to resist and fight rather than undergo internal reform is taken seriously, at least by Gray. The whole point of the theory of victory is to prevent the possibility of their being able to fight in such circumstances, particularly in the circumstances of 'the most dangerous decade' of the 1980s. Unable to export the crisis the USSR will be compelled to reform, is the final rationale of this position. This is nothing less than military coercion on a grand scale.

A final critique can be made in terms of the whole NUTS argument as being a massive case of psychological projection (Lambeth, 1982). Thus Pipes and the other analysts of Soviet nuclear strategy point to the Soviet possession of a nuclear war-winning strategy and in turn advocate a US policy that mirror images the Soviet one. This is the result of the specification of the Other in ways that ensure an adoption of precisely its methods to counter its activity, i.e to build up a nuclear arsenal and adopt a nuclear war-winning strategy, precisely what the evil Other is imputed to be doing.

But it is a theory of military power that fits into a broader scheme for reasserting US hegemony in world affairs and hence is useful in a blind assertion of US power, derived from an attempt to deny the Russians the ability to do precisely that (Halliday, 1983; McMahan, 1985). Here the dynamics of the superpower arms race really do lead to the 'Logic of Exterminism' (Newlett Review, 1982). Thus the two superpowers are locked in a spiral of technological 'progress' from which there is no escape. The USA has led in nearly every stage of this process, the Strategic Defence Initiative (SDI) being the latest manifestation. But it is a manifestation based on the definition of 'security' in terms of the spatial exclusion of Otherness, an exclusion relying on ever-more expensive and sophisticated military technologies (Connell, 1986).

This technological competition may well lead to our destruction automatically if the NUTS ideas and the new generation of counter-force weapons contribute to further technological competition. A possible response to a wartime crisis is to place one's ICBMs on a 'launch on warning' posture to ensure that they are fired before a nuclear strike by the other side can destroy them in their silos. This is a logical response to perceived vulnerability in a crisis situation. A version of this argument was the case against the Pershing II deployment in Europe. This, it was argued, would likely lead to the Russian adoption of a high-alert 'launch on warning' posture as the only possible way of avoiding the decapitating counter-force capabilities of this very fast and accurate weapon. Thus, Soviet missiles would be launched as soon as radar detection (correct or not) of the incoming Pershings was made.

The final twist on this move from NUTS to DEAD (Destruction Entrusted Automatic Devices, to use Deudney's [1983] apt acronymn) is the US Strategic Defence Initiative programme. Reaction times for the proposed technologies require that they be fired automatically in the event that the sensors detect an attack. Politics is finally completely removed from the decision to initiate hostilities. This is the ultimate rationale of technological development and the deterrence dogma. Politics is denied in the beginning by the totalitarian assumptions about the USSR; it is denied in the ultimate end by DEAD, weapons fired automatically without human intervention.

Part Three
Contra-text

Introduction

In summary, the second part of this book has focused on the discourses of realism, geopolitics, strategy and sovietology, and has elucidated their operations as discourses which support the policies of containment militarism. Each of them operates to define their object of study by excluding other approaches and by defining as legitimate a particular ensemble of practices. These in turn are deeply conservative operations reproducing the past of the Cold War and attempting to defer all other considerations to some future time when the Cold War has been resolved in favour of the USA: a resolution understood by Gray and Pipes to be the internal reform of the USSR to make it more acceptable to the USA, a redefinition of Otherness to more of the same, i.e. more like the USA. Chapter 9 summarizes the critique of the security discourses used by the CPD and suggests possible larger interpretations of the CPD's ideological position in terms of recent international relations literature. It also shows how these discursive themes appeared in the first Reagan administration's foreign policy, and influenced actions both in terms of Third World interventions and in terms of arms control.

The final chapter turns its attention to the question of how security discourse might be reformulated. It questions who the audiences for these reformulations might be and how political space can be understood in terms of contemporary politics which increasingly operates in ways that apparently render the conventional political spaces of states and even 'blocs' questionable. It points to the limitations of Western security discourse, arguing that very different formulations of the security *problematique* are forthcoming from the Third World, and increasingly from critical European and US scholars. Finally, it reiterates the theme of critical geopolitics as a mode of inquiry that operates to challenge conventional certainties and to disrupt hegemony, in the process asking disconcerting questions of power.

Chapter 9

The geopolitics of security discourse

CPD geographs

Realism is traditionally structured in terms of the difference between domestic and international politics. The enlightenment project of progress and community is constrained within the boundaries of domestic politics; the international anarchy is constructed as the realm of power, unmediated by moral concerns (Ashley, 1987). The task of the crude version of the realist foreign policy practitioner preferred in the CPD conception is cast solely in terms of the maximization of power by the state he represents; this is the only moral course in a world of competing states. In the context of the CPD, the realist move is usually constructed at a larger scale, that of the Western system, beyond which is the expanding Soviet imperial threat. Enlightenment and progress are now constrained within the boundaries of the non-Soviet world. Power is all that matters; all political concerns with development, human rights, environmental problems and so on are deferred until after the 'Soviet threat' is removed. It can be removed, according to the CPD, only by massive military confrontation.

But here the CPD steps beyond realism's focus on power and interest. It does so by relying on another device of realist discourse: the distinction between revisionist and status quo powers. The USSR is a revisionist state, challenging the global order, hence it is defined as such as the threat to order which, in the realist lexicon, often equates with peace. Thus change is defined as a threat to peace, understood as the status quo. Once again the difficulties of the encompassing political change within the realist discourse are encountered (Walker, 1987).

This move distances the CPD position from the position of the traditional realists, Carr, Morgenthau and also Kennan. The latter has always argued that a peaceful arrangement between the superpowers is possible provided the West is prepared to take seriously the interests of the Soviet Union in ensuring its security (Kennan, 1983; Wolfe, 1986). But the CPD position, based on Pipes's conception of patrimonialism, excludes the USSR's interests as legitimate political concerns. It does so by discounting their interests, arguing that their only interest is world domination, an interest that history and geopolitics determines, and one that the rest of the world has to face up to and deal with through armed preparedness, which in the nuclear age means nuclear weapons and the dogma of deterrence.

Nuclear strategy is an arcane enterprise that has had inordinate importance in the formulation of US policies since the Second World War.
Premised on the geopolitical view of the USSR as expansionist and
totalitarian, it argued through much of its early development for a policy of
punishment, or deterrence, as the basic strategy. Using abstract reasoning
and 'scientific' methodologies, it acquired an aura of plausibility which
combined potently with the aura of power that the nuclear technology, of
which it spoke, possessed. In the CPD argument against SALT II their case
ultimately rested on a theoretical inferiority because of potential vulnerability
to a third strike. In strategic discourse politics is in many ways reduced to
technologism; all questions have rationally computable solutions. The
whole ethos within which the debates occur is one of the primacy of
technique: all problems are solvable; all matters of concern reducible to
quantitative measures; any which cannot be so reduced are avoided or
ignored. Politics, in the sense of social arrangements in the context of
power, is neatly evaded in preference for a narrow conception of two
monolithic 'rational' actors engaged in a 'struggle' for superiority defined in
mathematical terms. The ultimate, so far, development of this line is the
SDI. All political considerations are removed; the answer to the 'Soviet
threat' is purely technological.

But the CPD position also critiques the failure of strategists, at least those
of the arms control inclination in the USA, to think through the political
dimensions of the deterrence posture. But their reformulation of the USSR
as inherently expanionist and an imperial structure enhances the power of
the strategic logic. As developed by Colin Gray, the strategic task is to
develop a series of weapons systems that could deny the USSR any possible
way of conceiving of a victory in a nuclear war; and simultaneously to
devise a series of nuclear utilization tactics that would focus targeting on the
imperial apparatus of empire, supposedly guaranteeing that in the event of a
war the Soviet apparatus could be destroyed by a series of 'surgical strikes'.
This geopolitical interpretation provides the key to Gray's theory of victory,
a key that most commentators have missed.

All this follows from the a priori assumption of the evil nature of Soviet
society which came to nuclear strategy from the political climate of the Cold
War. The sovietology literature developed around a conceptualization of
the USSR and all other communist societies, conceived as a bloc directed
from Moscow, as a totalitarian society. This suggested that the society was
unchanging, dominated by a small powerful elite whose power rested on the
apparatus of terror that they yielded without restraint. This social machine
was inherently expansionist, resisted only by force; perpetual vigilance was
needed so as never to make a mistake which would undoubtedly be
exploited to the full by the Russians. The CPD added the geographically
determinist theme of the expansion of Russian militarism to the totalitarian
theme reinforcing it by linking Russian history to the communist regime.
In Gray's formulation, this simultaneously provided a rationale for the
targeting options in the theory of victory. The determinism had ideological
force because it relied on assumptions that the long-term trajectories of

history were the only adequate guide to the future; its structuralism precludes change.

The traditional geopolitical texts, Mackinder in particular, have a theme of the fear of the Other as the Asiatic hordes threatening European civilization. The fear of the triumph of land power over the sea power of the British Empire is important, sometimes in terms of the Russian Empire, other times in terms of the alliance of the German with the Russian system as a dominant Heartland alliance which could impose its will over the Rimlands. The CPD arguments update this theme, embellishing the Heartland as the territorial bastion of totalitarianism, a political formation compelled by its internal nature and its geopolitical circumstances to expand to try to exercise global dominion. Its threat lies in this proclivity to expansion; in contrast security is formulated as the spatial containment of that threat.

All these formulations reduce the world into simplistic dualisms which contain powerful constraints on how the world is understood. The nuclear strategy and sovietology prespectives reduce the world to a zero-sum game in which one side always gains at the other's expense. The geopolitical discourse squeezes out of consideration the complexity of international interaction, the 'Third World' is reduced to a playing field on which the superpowers play out their rivalry. Any indigenous interests are removed from consideration on the global space of superpower rivalry, a space filled only by projected power. The object of the geopolitical discourse is the enhancement of security by the spatial limitation of the domain in which the adversary can project power.

The state is privileged by the realist discourse as the only actor in the international arena which is worthy of consideration. International relations – the very term itself defines matters in terms reminiscent of diplomatic procedures. Economic, cultural, historical and political factors are removed from the foreground, unnecessary clutter in the exercise of the rituals of realist power. Any wider considerations of social theory are excluded from the realm of international relations. As far as the CPD is concerned, power is about the ability militarily to confront the USSR. Economic, cultural and political developments are all secondary to the overarching need for nuclear supremacy, the ultimate arbiter of everything else.

The totalitarian conceptualization denies politics and history by creating an Other as perpetual adversary. Key to its understandings of the USSR is the specificiation of it as monolithic and unchanging. This denial of history reduces the possibilities of politics, by erecting the spectre of the permanent adversary, against which perpetual vigilance is needed. It denies the possibility of an alternative vision of the future on either side of the great divide, hence perpetuating the political status quo. The device is simple and in ideological terms hugely effective. The responsibility for all 'our' problems is neatly encapsulated in the creation of the Other. Thus the particular specification of Otherness in terms of a geopolitical expansionist threat is the key element which articulates all the security discourses together. It provides the point of articulation for the CPD version of US hegemony. It reinforces its position in blatently ethnocentric fashion, but an ethnocentrism that reinforces its arguments precisely by how it specifies the Other. Thus the CPD argues that by analysing the USSR in terms of its internal historical and crucially geopolitical make-up we will understand what their society is like and hence we will understand the threat. Having understood the threat, we will act accordingly and move to counter it by developing appropriate nuclear strategies. The crucial ethnocentric move is related to the totalitarian formulation in which all information and writing is designed to further the purposes of the political leaders. All arguments that purport to be conciliatory to the West must be dismissed as disinformation. The additional step is then easy. They really do know that their society is as we now understand it, i.e. it is totalitarian and bent on world domination. The possibility that there might be other thinking in the USSR is excluded by the 'superiority' of the 'historical method' which focuses on the 'real' factors rather than those dreamt up by political scientists concerned with abstract models, or strategists who ignore the societal dynamics of the USSR. Thus the whole matter is a neatly circular argument, any possible bases on which one might construct a critique are disallowed in advance. It is precisely these series of exclusions that gives their arguments their coherence, and hence, when articulated together, their ideological power.

This series of ideological moves, discussed here in terms of the articulation of the security discourses, supports the overall hegemony of US modernity. Within the West the language of politics is inscribed within discussions of modernity, rationality and specific references to time and space. As Said (1979) goes to great length to point out, the process of European imperial expansion was coupled with, and defined in terms of, the expansion of enlightenment, whether in religious terms of salvation of the heathen or in terms of the scientific enlightenment. With this went the incorporation and administration of the primitive (distant in time) and ignorant. The same pattern of domination, exclusion and incorporation is present in the CPD discourse.

Modernity comes with universal space and time, within which the great drama of modernization unfolds (Berman, 1988). There is continuity in the development of progress, a continuity through time that ultimately marginalizes, subsumes, negates or destroys that which is the Other, primitive, different. Progress is identified with the West: rationality, science, the expansion of civilization (Kumar, 1978). The ultimate triumph of reason is equated in the USA in particular with the triumph of that particular policy. The purported reason and rationality of social existence, postulated by the USA in particular, after the Second World War was encapsulated in technocratic approaches to 'solving' 'social problems' using 'scientific' methods – nowhere more so than in nuclear strategy. US manifest destiny combined with operations research and the result was the technologization of politics, coupled with a linear view of societal development in which US reason was bound to triumph.

In the mythic structure of this discourse, the Other is the barbarian, in that he is not enlightened. Not being enlightened justifies our intervention to enlighten 'for their own good', of course. The discourse on communism and the USSR is not the same as that of Orientalism (Said, 1979) where the Other is primitive, to be dominated. True, the Other in this case is partly that, but more seriously is that the Other has false science, technologically capable, but 'possessed' of demonic intentions. In this sense the religous metaphor is tied to a spatial representation of the Other's place as cold, forbidding, alien, tundra. But the Other is also unchanging in its evil nature. Here the USSR is portrayed in Pipes's patrimonial scheme as the inheritor of the primitive Slav nomads of the northern tundra. They are not quite European, not quite part of the Western cultural sphere. The theme of continuity and progress coexists with the manichean theme. The contradictions are only temporary, however, for good will triumph over evil in the end; if good just builds enough nuclear weapons to prevent the Other expanding, the Other will collapse as a result of its own failures. Reason will triumph over superstition; the West, scientific, will triumph over the communist ideological usurper of modernity.

These universalizations of Western modernity, the Newtonian assumptions of uniform space and time, allow the extension of the European culture and politics globally. Development is ultimately understood as more of the same adopted universally. Progress underlies all this as a central theme: new is better; old is intrinsically inferior and hence disposable. In this context the Other in a different space has to be marginalized and ultimately colonized. This theme reinforces the formulation of security as spatial exclusion and limitation. The Other is at the same time a disgrace, a challenge to the supremacy of the Western universalizing culture, one that ultimately undermines the legitimacy of its project. It has to be shut off in a separate space to be kept under observation and controlled. With reference to Foucault's concerns with the discourses of madness, the medical analogy is apt in the link between power, observation and control. Communism is often likened to the spread of a contagion (O'Sullivan, 1982). A geopolitical threat requires a response in territorial terms; security is understood in these terms, a move of spatial exclusion, coupled with perpetual surveillance of that Other.

The CPD discourse is concerned with the maintenance of the US hegemony over Europe and Japan, and the spatial exclusion of Soviet domination from these areas. Conflict in the Third World is seen in these terms. At a very general level the discourse suggests that the Third World is really only a playing field for the superpowers, but it also suggests that our interventions there are justified as legitimate, in the name of enlightment and economic development. The implicit assumption that it really is 'our' space was the rationale of Truman and Carter doctrines.

Combining this geopolitical concern with nuclear weapons and with the denial of politics in realism, and also with the totalitarian approach to the USSR, provides a powerful inhibiting framework for the evolution of broader conceptions of security and international relations. In the USA the hegemonic understanding of the global geopolitical arena involves an acceptance of the necessity of extended deterrence and Third World intervention.

If one examines, for example, the terms of the current debate, liberals argue for the preservation of the SALT arms control regime; conservatives argue that the regime is basically immoral and has been a failure, and advocate instead a transition to defenses. In fact, beneath the rhetoric, many in both camps seem to assume that first use and extended deterrence are both necessary and legitimate. [Arbess and Sahaydachny, 1987, 98]

Underlying the many debates on nuclear weapons within the USA is the overall assumption of the geopolitical divide of the globe into 'them' and 'us', requiring that we must always be prepared to intervene in distant lands, and in order to do so must be prepared to use nuclear weapons to ensure a local victory. To do this requires a constant edge in nuclear technology, and the ability to develop a damage limitation capability that allows extended deterrence to be credible. But '. . . in an era of parity, the attempt to develop the degree of damage limitation required to restore credibility to extended deterrence will invariably subvert not only the SALT process, but arms control in general' (Arbess and Sahaydachny, 1987, 97).

This 'overall assumption' was no longer hegemonic after the Vietnam War, *détente*, the Nixon doctrine and the global managerialist approaches to international affairs promoted by the Tri-Lateral Commission (Gill, 1986). The CPD led the ideological assault in an attempt to ensure that the security discourses were reasserted such that the consensus on the basic necessity of extended deterrence is no longer seriously open to political debate. The technical details of NUTS are the logic of this reassertion, but the geopolitical dimension is ultimately more important because it underlies the technical arguments, and it is ultimately more important in that it sets the terms of political debate.

But it is a political debate that excludes politics by reducing the possibilities of discourse to a number of intellectual specializations, the discourses of security, which monopolize that which may be discussed. The expert, equipped with the theoretical knowledge derived from intellectual work, versed in its techniques and competent in the rituals of the discourses, is the only competent participant in the process. Wider political participation is denied or co-opted within the strategic discourses (Walker, 1983/4). Learning the specialized languages is not unduly difficult, but having learnt them they in turn delimit what it is possible to discuss (Cohn, 1987). Thus the security discourses act in a profoundly conservative political manner, delimiting the possibilities of discourse by the categorizations they impose and the rituals and methodologies they legitimate. These discursive practices reproduce the Cold War in a series of categorizations which limit the possibilities of political intervention precisely by how they categorize.

The CPD and the Reagan administration

As of 1984 the CPD claimed that over sixty of its members had served at some time in the Reagan administration in a senior capacity. The focus on military buildup and aggressive anti-communist rhetoric, including the dubbing of the USSR as 'the Evil Empire' fit with the CPD agenda (Booth and Williams, 1985). So does the focus on 'dominoes' in the Caribbean and Central America, the Reagan doctrine of active measures against 'communist' regimes and, more generally, the administration's plans for global warfare against 'terrorism' (Herman, 1982; Kaldor and Anderson eds, 1986).

Richard Pipes served as the director of soviet affairs at the National Security Council in 1981 and 1982, issuing a statement early in his tenure to the effect that the USSR had to choose between changing its internal political arrangements or fighting a nuclear war (Sanders, 1983, 324). Subsequently he has continued to write articles about his opinions and in 1984 published *Survival Is Not Enough*, which updates and elaborates his articles from the 1970s. Gene Rostow was appointed head of the Arms Control and Disarmament Agency in 1981 and had a stormy career of bureaucratic infighting in the administration before finally being fired early in 1983, apparently because his abrasive style angered Reagan (Talbott, 1985, 168). His colleague and nominal subordinate, Paul Nitze, undertook the task of negotiating in Geneva with the Russians on so called 'Theatre Nuclear Forces' in Europe. Subsequently he remained a member of the administration as a special representative for arms control, while Max Kampleman took over some of the negotiation tasks in Geneva.

Colin Gray formally joined the administration in an advisory capacity in 1982. Since the formulation of the ideas of the theory of victory and the imperial thesis, Gray has continued to write a stream of papers and books on strategic matters (1980c, 1981c, 1981d, 1981e, 1982b, 1982c, 1984c; Gray and Payne, 1983), on Star Wars (1981f, 1982d, 1983, 1985a; Payne and Gray, 1984), on nuclear winter (1985b), and has weighed in to defend the administration in its assertion that the Russians are cheating on arms control (1984d). In 1986 he published *Nuclear Strategy and National Style* (1986b) and updated his ideas on geopolitics as they relate to the theme of the maritime strategy (1986c). He also contributed to the debate on whether the USA had underfunded military programmes in the 1970s, an argument repeatedly made to legitimize the Reagan military budget (Gray and Barlow, 1985; for a rejoinder see Komer, 1985). In 1988 he published *The Geopolitics of Superpower*, a book-length treatment of the requirements of US foreign policy explicitly working from the classical treatments of Spykman and Mackinder.

The adoption by the Reagan administration of strategies influenced by the ideas of nuclear war-fighting, ultimately led to a massive buildup in nuclear weapons: 17 000 new warheads were central to the Reagan arms buildup initiated in 1982 (Knelman, 1985). Since then the SDI and the 'maritime strategy' have come to the forefront of US nuclear thinking, both 'high-tech' solutions to render the Soviet nuclear weapons vulnerable; the latter returning to the traditional geopolitical theme of land and sea power rivalry. In 1985 and 1986 the USA continued its nuclear arms testing programme despite the unilateral Soviet test ban.

Some variants of the 'maritime strategy' (Brooks, 1986; Gray, 1986c; Mearsheimer, 1986) are an attempt to project US power into the coastal waters of the USSR to destroy their submarine launched ballistic missile (SLBM) launchers and so render all of the Soviet strategic arsenal vulnerable in a wartime situation. This is a logical extension of the earlier concerns with a theory of victory, the invulnerable SLBM forces of both superpowers have traditionally rendered nuclear war-fighting strategies implausible. If, however, through advances in anti-submarine warfare (ASW) technologies, the Soviet fleet of missile submarines could be made theoretically vulnerable, then that objection could be removed. This has inevitably increased fears of the accidental outbreak of a nuclear war; a Soviet strategic posture of pre-emption in a crisis only becomes more dangerous as the US strives towards a technical capability to launch a counter-force or decapitation first strike. The US lead in ASW technologies and its development of very accurate decapitation capable weapons like the Pershing II and Trident D-5, countered in part by the forward basing of Soviet SLBMs, has rendered the strategic competition between the superpowers more dangerous.

In Europe the 'pipeline debate' of the early 1980s, an attempt ostensibly to wean Europe away from reliance on Soviet fuel, is understandable in terms of Pipes's interpretation of *détente* strategies as Soviet attempts to undermine the independence of Europe by supposedly gaining an economic stranglehold over its fuel supplies. The failure of the USA to prevent the building of the pipeline and the crisis engendered by the 'Euro-missile' debate in the early 1980s presented difficulties in what Richard Burt termed 'alliance management' (Talbott, 1985, 62). The presence of Cruise and Pershing II missiles in Europe was undoubtedly an attempt to exert political influence over Europe (McMahan, 1985; Johnstone, 1984). The subsequent acceptance in 1987 by the USSR of the original Reagan administration 'zero-option' on 'Euro-missiles' has further complicated matters. Having endured the political difficulties of ensuring deployment of the missiles, they are now being withdrawn, without the original problem of US nuclear credibility in a European war apparently being addressed.

In the Third World the Reagan administration initiated a series of military interventions in Nicaragua, Libya and Grenada on the basis of a broadly conceived 'Reagan doctrine' where the USA reserves the right to intervene to destroy regimes it deems hostile (McMahan, 1985). This is also a logical outgrowth of the CPD geopolitical perspective, as is the revamped CIA and the support for increased covert activity around the world, where proxy forces are the preferred weapons for rolling back the Soviet presence in whatever form it supposedly presents itself (Klare and Kornluh eds, 1988).

The Reagan administration was not able to carry out its programme without restrictions and curtailments from congressional opposition and, in the military sphere, without vehement opposition to its militarist preoccu-pations from the European peace movements and the short-lived 'freeze' movement in the USA, an issue on which Colin Gray had his say, too (Gray, 1982d, 1982e; Payne and Gray eds, 1984). The MX was not placed in a multiple protective shelter arrangement, principally due to intense domestic political pressure against the development of such a scheme on economic and environmental grounds, coupled with determined local opposition in the states where the 'race tracks' were to have been located. The Scowcroft Commission finally fudged the vulnerability arguments used by Gray and others to advocate the building of the MX, and some of them are being placed in superhardened Minutemen silos. The B-1 bomber programme has been plagued with technical shortcomings; the B-2 stealth bomber did not fly until after Reagan had left the White House.

Elsewhere, the Contras have failed repeatedly to destroy the Sandinista regime, although their presence has severely disrupted economic development in both Nicaragua and, to a lesser extent, Honduras. The USA was forced to withdraw, amid much confusion, from its attempts to shape Lebanese politics by military force. The focus on military spending in the US economy has caused economic disruptions (Markusen, 1986). The budget deficit used to finance the military buildup has also caused international alarm, as have the economic repercussions in terms of interest rates and international exchange rate fluctuations. Critics have pointed to the mismatch of the available conventional forces with the ambitious strategic tasks called for by the Reagan administration's geopolitical containment strategies for worldwide warfare (Record, 1983–4).

Arms control was effectively on hold for most of the Reagan administration's period in office despite furtive attempts to negotiate Theatre Nuclear Forces in Europe, about which the administration was never serious (Talbott, 1985). Political developments in Reagan's second term, both in the USSR with the accession of President Gorbachov and the reformist tendencies in the Kremlin, which have resulted in major new departures in Soviet security policy (Evangelista, 1986; MccGwire, 1987b; Meiskins, 1987), and in Washington in the aftermath of the Iran–Contra affair, moved the arms negotiation process forward, changing the political landscape increasingly in directions distant from CPD concerns.

All of these developments point to the limits of the Reagan administration's attempts to reassert US global dominance, and simultaneously to the impossibility of the CPD's programme as a blueprint for US hegemony (Gill, 1986). In Sanders's (1983) terms, the CPD programme 'foundered on the shoals of reality', as the limits of US power, and the limits of military policy, were revealed. The Reagan administration, despite much talk of 'supply side economics', did not provide any clear or coherent economic policies that would enable the USA to reassert its global hegemony in economic terms (Moffitt, 1987). As this book argues, the CPD agenda interpreted US global supremacy as being primarily a matter of military power and the spatial containment of Soviet influence as the *sine qua non* for all other political programmes.

Space, security, hegemony

Apart from the current revival of classical geopolitics, the significance of this persistence of security discourse understood in spatial terms can be seen in the central concerns of contemporary literature both in US foreign policy discussions and in the discipline of international relations, in terms of the relations of security, hegemony, empire and territorial control. In particular, it is clear in discussions of possible emergent global orders in the wake of the declining US hegemony (Calleo, 1987; M. Cox, 1984; Gill, 1986; Goldstein, 1988; Kennedy, 1987; Keohane, 1984; Oye, 1983). Of particular concern to this theme is the focus on the factors involved in the decline of a hegemon's control and the role that the increasing costs of empire play when a hegemon attempts to maintain control over the global system by using territorial strategies. In Gill's (1986) terms, the attempt is to define and then enforce hegemony in realist terms of military power and direct political control over specific areas.

This argument suggests that attempts by a declining hegemonic power to ensure its continued dominance in global affairs will be made by imposing direct political and military control over colonies or territories. Thompson and Zuk (1986) show how this is the case in terms of the relative decline of British hegemony in the nineteenth century. While the problems of leadership in a world where economic innovation may be occurring faster outside the hegemon's domestic economy than internally are more than simply matters of imperial costs, none the less these costs are important. In the late twentieth century security understood in territorial terms involves the application of advanced technologies to 'defend' that territory. Drawing on advances in scientific exploitation of nature, high-tech weapons are exhorbitantly expensive, which aggravates these tendencies.

In terms of the inevitable US decline from its hegemonic position in the post-Second World War world following European and Japanese reconstruction, this is of some significance. It is possible to interpret the US fixation on territorial matters and the current reinterpretation of geopolitics (Gray, 1988; Brzezinski, 1986) as an ideological statement of the attempt to reinstate the US hegemony by the classic imperial device of imposing political control over territorial units, and doing so by means of a military buildup. It is possible to interpret the debate over nuclear modernization and theatre nuclear missiles in Europe in precisely these terms (Johnstone, 1984). Further, it can be argued that one of the key political challenges to the Green movement in Europe, and particularly in Germany, has been to unravel the ideological assumptions of Western European complicity in a US world (Hulsberg, 1988).

However, the economic costs of military buildup, particularly when it involves large expenditures on technologically sophisticated military hardware, aggravates the long-term economic difficulties facing the hegemon (Kaldor, 1982). Thus, the US buildup in armed forces advocated by the Reagan administration, which is draining the US economy and probably reducing its long-run economic competitiveness by diverting capital into military expenditure, is in fact aggravating the long-term security of the USA not to mention inflicting serious economic hardship on the Third World (Kaldor, 1986; Markusen, 1986). Thus, the attempt to reassert a realist hegemony in military terms is, in the long run, counter-productive in that it exhausts the economic resources of the power attempting to maintain a military hegemony (Kennedy, 1987). None the less the first Reagan administration attempted to reassert US domination in precisely these terms, and repeatedly provided ideological rationales for doing so in geopolitical terms. This recurrence of explicitly geopolitical thinking may be a harbinger of attempts to present the increasingly severe US economic crisis in terms of the other traditional geopolitical theme of access by European powers to colonial resources (Haglund, 1986). Updated in the context of renewed emphasis on interventionist conventional military forces, the expansion of the US navy with new theories of a maritime strategy, the emphasis on low-intensity warfare (Klare and Kornbluh eds, 1988) and 'discriminate deterrence', this may lead to geopolitical theorizing as rationale for military action in the Third World. Activities by the US navy in the Persian Gulf in the late 1980s suggest this tendency, although the dramatic shifts in international politics in Europe, and in particular in NATO, coupled with the growing US debt situation may act to ensure the end of the attempt to reassert hegemony by military means.

In the early 1980s the USSR also seemed to be trapped in a cycle of expanding imperial costs which were aggravating its internal economic difficulties (Wolf, 1985) as it attempted to ensure its security through perpetual high military expenditures. The Soviet preoccupation with military security as spatial exclusion has shifted in the era of *glasnost* and *perestroika* where serious rethinking of security policies are underway (Evangelista, 1986). But in Rosecrance's (1986) terms, the superpowers are still territorial states in a world of trading states. The relationship between territory and power is thus not one in which more territory means more power, as the spatial preoccupation might suggest (see also O'Sullivan, 1986).

This argument also suggests the possibility of understanding the geopolitical perspective as an ideological representation of imperial drives in a period of declining hegemony. The spatial representation reflecting, in addition to the desire for territorial control, an attempt in psychological terms to corral the usurper, and in so doing to lessen the external threat and reassert hegemony. As noted above, Gray (1977a) was explicit in stating that his reiteration of the classical geopolitical themes was necessary precisely because this perspective was no longer widely accepted as the essential basis of US security thinking.

In the nuclear period the technologization of political control has accelerated the technical means for asserting centralized state control and developed technologies of information-gathering with tremendous power (Virilio, 1986; Virilio and Lotringer, 1983). But simultaneously with this 'transparency revolution' in Deudney's (1983) phrase, nuclear weapons have shifted the geopolitical situation to a position where the ultimate levels of this technological force are not utilizable in combat situations; this is the point of nuclear weapons as deterrence to their own use. The whole recent enterprise of nuclear war-fighting strategies is an attempt to circumvent these restrictions (Kaku and Axelrod, 1987). But what is often overlooked in the discussions of new nuclear weapons systems is that they are designed for particular geopolitical roles in nuclear war-fighting and deterrence. Gray's (1981d) lengthy argument of the case for the MX missile in a multiple protective shelter basing arrangement is linked into his discussions of the need for nuclear superiority to ensure escalation dominance at tactical and theatre levels of nuclear confrontation. This is necessary, he argues, to allow for US regional interventions in potential Third World conflicts.

The most recent addition to the panoply of military technology, and the linchpin in Reagan's ideological argument for securing US hegemony, is the discussion concerning space-based anti-ballistic missile systems and the SDI. The formulation of security in terms of spatial exclusion is here once again linked to the technological solution to political problems. Nowhere is the spatial exclusion formulation of security clearer than in its formulation of the SDI as a 'peace shield' that would keep out incoming Soviet missiles. This time the aggressor is kept out by high-tech weapons of mind-boggling complexity, but the premise is once again of spatial demarcation as the key to security. In Star Wars power is once again technologically divorced from practical politics. In Visvanathan's (1987) terms, the Hobbesian project of subordinating both sovereign and state to the dictates of scientific rationality takes one more fateful step towards completion in the inevitable development of automatic technological warfare and DEAD (Destruction Entrusted Automatic Devices (Deudney, 1983)). The rationality of these technological developments is premised on the specification of the Other as dangerous, as in this case, the 'Evil Empire'.

Thus the metaphysical structuring of the world into 'them' and 'us', with us as superior, functions to ensure that militarization continues. Given the technological innovations in military equipment capabilities, security understood as force breeds more insecurity for both the possessor of the technology of violence and more directly for its intended victims. These geopolitical formulations simultaneously act ideologically to incorporate disparate elements in a common 'us' versus an excluded Other. They do so by using a series of geopolitical discursive practices, representing security in terms of absolute technological control over territorially demarcated sections of territorial space. Others are spatially excluded, to be feared, ostracized and ultimately reduced to extensions of an imposed identity.

Security is identified as identity, unity and an imposed order. Difference is a threat. Otherness has to be spatially coralled, contained, changed and ultimately reduced to an extension of sameness. Security implies a reduction of difference, making 'their' space like 'ours'. These are powerful ideological moves sustaining the power of modernity and Atlanticism. They raise the questions of how one might reformulate the concept of security in ways that shift the emphasis from force, exclusion and geopolitical boundaries. They also raise questions about how critical geopolitics might counter these discursive practices. In other words, they raise questions of 'the geopolitics of geopolitical space' (Ashley, 1987); how the discourses limit the way in which it is possible to speak, write and act concerning issues of war, peace and security.

Chapter 10

Critical geopolitics

Discourses of war and peace

To talk of peace at all suggests to many a commitment to work for alternatives to the contemporary crisis and the perpetuation of processes of militarization. For others like the CPD, however, to talk of peace is to maintain that precisely these military preparations are necessary because peace is maintained through the readiness to go to war against external 'Others'. It is this latter understanding which has dominated much of the official discourse on security policy since the Second World War in Western states, the enmity of different nations or social structures is seen as the cause of war and conflict. For more critical approaches, the pressing concerns are the investigation of how the political systems that threaten war came to be constructed in the first place, rather than simply taking them for granted. Critical approaches also investigate the structural consequences of global militarization that inhibit development, heighten injustice, endanger numerous populations with instant destruction and render other problems more intractable precisely by raising the stakes of all attempts to initiate social change in the face of militarized oppression (Walker, 1988b).

To enter the debate on matters of war and peace then involves establishing a position from which to speak and selecting from the numerous possible ways of speaking a particular mode of discourse which has intended audiences and some form of political stance regarding suggested courses of action. Those who argue that academic research is some sort of neutral position from which to study matters in an 'objective' manner are not immune from this requirement, whatever claims are made. Simply claiming that it is possible to stand outside, above or beyond the contemporary political situation is in itself a political claim to a privileged form of knowledge, a mode of discourse and to an audience that is socially structured by the common acceptance of a series of academic practices designed to assign 'credibility' to its practitioners, be they researchers, policy advisers, politicians or some combination thereof. Thus, how one speaks relates to one's audience, how one practices a critical geopolitics that challenges the conventional modes of discourse has political consequences. The postmodern insistence on leaving power nowhere to hide in discursive disguise implies a commitment to attempt to make the politics in writing explicit and reflexive.

This section briefly examines the various discourses of peace and war, and contemporary understandings of how these discourses restrict what it is possible to say and the positions from which one can speak to these issues. In particular, it focuses on the positions that dissent from the conventional formulations of security discourse in terms of the various themes of deterrence and containment that have dominated Western and particularly US policy for four decades. These themes are connected to particular understandings of the terms of security, development, national interest, sovereignty and the like, which have come to present semantic obstacles to discussing matters of global politics (Bay, 1983). Postmodern approaches analyse these obstacles to 'rational' debate in terms of the limitations imposed on debate by the discourse available. They focus on their contested histories, in which those in social situations that enabled their voices and arguments to gain some acceptance have shaped the meanings of terms and the accepted ways of linking these terms together. The results of the historical constructions of security discourse are to render dissenting political arguments difficult to maintain; the conventional approaches have achieved a hegemonic position either disallowing arguments and marginalizing them, or co-opting them within the dominant discursive structures.

Particularily apposite is Klein's (1988) analysis of approaches to the strategic enterprise. Klein collapses the strategists and political realists into a single category of discourse whose practitioners practice what he terms the 'celebratory' mode of discourse. The key practices include the analysis of relative military strengths, the analysis of the practices of state diplomacy, concerns with the 'balance of power' and the finer points of military strategy. They also draw on strategic studies, with its own vernacular and series of modes of reasoning. Accepting as immutable the realists' construction of the world as a constant anarchy of competing nation-state powers, the military interpretation of national security has become the highest value of the state apparatus. Tied to this is the implicit and powerful assumption that the existing state system is 'the preferred norm for world order'. Researchers operating in this mode see their task as providing 'advice to the prince'. This book has argued that this 'celebratory' mode encompasses more than realism and strategy, requiring the addition of geopolitics and sovietology to be a comprehensive account of US security discourse.

In Klein's (1988) formulation these rituals and practices of 'the celebratory' have been challenged by the 'ironic' approach which, while accepting many of the basic premises of the celebratory approach, challenge the technological presumptions of 'technostrategy', and point to the need to improve strategy by eradicating the problems of ethnocentrism and misperception present in the thinking of strategic policy-makers. Walker's (1983–4) discussion of the 'strategic-geopolitical' mode of dissent discourse is analogous to Klein's 'ironic approach' and addresses itself to these 'strategic-geopolitical' arguments and their flaws and inconsistencies within the established state system. Precisely because these critiques deal with technical arcana and expert knowledge they simultaneously reduce the audience to which they can appeal and run into the persistent dangers of co-optation within the policy process that they ostensibly challenge.

More provocative are the arguments of those who would reform national policies in terms of alternative defence. Rejecting the premises of deterrence and the technostrategic logic of nuclear weapons, they argue for various combinations of civilian opposition, civil disobedience and various forms of 'non-provocative' defence technologies that can provide so many difficulties for any potential aggressor that it removes any incentive for aggression (Sharp, 1985). This version of the strategic-geopolitical critique can develop in the direction of drastic social reform, involving calls for citizen empowerment and the reduction of centralized high-tech state decision-making in the realm of military planning. Often, however, these 'ironic' approaches hold these challenges to state power in abeyance, merely replicating the acceptance of the power relations of the world, offering a rather different form of advice to any prince with a curious ear. The more critical versions of the 'ironic' approach can raise the crucial questions of how it might be possible to rethink the essential political lexicon of peace and security; a task requiring a re-incorporation of both ethical and structural concerns with justice and development within the ambit of a reformulated consideration of both peace and security.

Loosely related to this theme there is also the socio-economic challenge to militarism, emphasizing that the permanent militarization of society constrains democracy, producing a society at war in most senses of the term short of actual combat casualties. Klein also points to this 'condemnatory' approach, those critiques of contemporary militarism derived from some form of political economy approach which challenge strategic discourse as a form of class interest and ideology. It reveals the links between economic activity and the imperatives of state action in technological innovation and defence procurement policies that support a particular form of economy and the lucrative business of arms trading (Gervasi, 1984; Kaldor, 1982; Melman, 1988). The links between these themes and social and economic underdevelopment of society are clearly made, with technological overdevelopment in the military sector coexisting in glaring contradiction to mass poverty especially in the Third World states. The overall patterns of maintaining alliance cohesion within the blocs are apposite here as well; the Other providing the external threat which requires a continuation of these political economic priorities. Klein points to the difficulties of this approach in terms of its tendency to provide too simple structural explanations concerning the hegemonic dynamics of contemporary militarism.

This condemnatory mode is analagous to Walker's (1983–4) formulation of the discourse of dissent in terms of critiques of the political economy of militarism, often appearing in some form of the 'guns or butter' argument suggesting that the money and research resources spent on building weaponry and devising new and ever-more sophisticated technological ways of destroying people could be much better spent on addressing global crises of poverty, malnutrition, medical care and development in general. This form of critique, while powerful for many, and including a persuasive call to social justice in some forms, may reduce its appeal precisely because its analyses cannot help but challenge the fundamental structures of the modern system which has produced such inequities.

Walker (1983–4) also suggests that there is a mode of dissent discourse drawing on universalist moral arguments of the kind that argue that war is bad, mainly simply because killing people is morally unacceptable. Hence, everyone has a moral obligation to be 'against' war, and hence in this understanding at least, in favour of the supposed opposite of war, namely peace. The problem with this position is that it can mobilize widespread support but it fails to convert a moral revulsion of war into any effective strategy to change matters in practical ways. It is also extremely vulnerable to co-optation: advocates of deterrence claim that they, too, are building weapons precisely to maintain 'peace'.

Klein's final 'diremptive' 'postmodern' approach is somewhat analagous to the approach taken in this book, forcing open the supposed unities of strategic discourse, showing how the CPD's geo-graphs were constituted and how their discourses of security and modernity act to resist counter-hegemonic challenges. Postmodern critiques are powerful in revealing the operations of discursive politics; enabling critics to penetrate the ideological logjams of conventional political discourse. They, too, can suffer from the difficulties which Walker argues the strategic-geopolitical dissent mode suffers; the limited audience that its modes of analysis reach due to its intellectual specialization and at times difficult jargon.

There are no easy ways out of these discursive difficulties; a critical geopolitics is not immune either. The postmodern or 'diremptive' approach is not a final answer to these dilemmas, rather it is an active interventionist form of analysis that recognizes the importance of cultural productions in matters of politics; a constant critique that challenges the claims of all discourses, including, of course, its own. By understanding these discursive limitations, critical geopolitics can at least avoid the worst pitfalls of tackling matters of war and peace. It can recognize the necessity of contributing in a way that is conscious of the power of its discursive practices, recognizing that how we describe and discursively construct social reality are inescapably political acts. Discourses are political resources made available for political mobilization. They are implicating in world-making by how they construct their objects and by the rules and practices they construct and legitimize.

Political space and dissent discourse

This book has explored the interconnections of geopolitics and Otherness in terms of a series of 'security discourses', each of which in turn is structured by and structures the understanding of politics in terms of space and difference. Security is identified as identity, unity and an imposed order. Difference is a threat; Otherness has to be spatially coralled, contained, ultimately reduced to an extension of sameness; security implies a reduction of difference, making their space like ours. Inherent in all this are conceptions of absolute space, and the metaphysical construction of a universalist epistemological position where true knowledge triumphs, gradually extending through absolute space. As has been repeatedly shown above, each of these is a powerful ideological move, sustaining the power of the ideology of modernity and Atlanticism.

The geopolitical concerns of the CPD, and later their presence in the Reagan administration, have fed the state centric military domination of discourse about security. The CPD were 'doing geopolitics' in the traditional manner, providing geographical arguments to support the expansion of military forces and the increased militarization of the domestic political sphere of their respective states. The geopolitical writings have addressed themselves to those concerned with enhancing political power of those states, principally for the politically active elements within the ruling classes who align themselves closely with the expansion of state power. The possibilities that there may be other interests within the nation state whose security might be better served in other ways is neatly excluded by the simple ideological operation of universalizing the particular interests of a narrow segment of the population within the ambit of the concept of 'national security' (Buzan, 1983).

To challenge these practices raises the question of alternative discourses of security, discourses which require a re-specification of Otherness, a recognition in Todorov's (1984) terms of the reality of the social existence of Other cultures as legitimate and not as axiologically inferior, a praxaeological indentification that operates in ways other than the coercive. In other words, what is needed is the separation of security from identity, the recognition of a plurality of cultural realities (Connolly, 1989), each requiring its formulation in its own space. This questioning strikes at the heart of the political theory of the state, premised on the state as a spatial entity, within which a state of security is provided. To reformulate security requires a reconceptualization of geopolitics and, hence, a rejection of the model of security in terms of spatial exclusion. The rejection of security as power and exclusion forces a consideration of power as social relations, not as abstract physical considerations of force understood in terms of the interactions of spatial entities.

In terms of geopolitics, it challenges the essential formulation of its terms by pointing to the presupposition of absolute space on which the theory is built. Geopolitics in its modern guise privileges the military power of the superpowers to the exclusion of other political and social groups. It assumes a pre-given territorial space, in Gray's terms (directly taken from Spykman (Gray, 1977a, 1)) the most permanent factor in international relations, and then fills the pre-given arena with superpower rivalry. Thus this language can use the terms of physics, 'balance of power', 'power vacuum', and the latest 'power projection', because of its assumptions of absolute space as inherently empty. The ethnocentric assumptions of this premise are powerful, all that is of concern is the support or denial thereof of other social groups in the great contest of superpower rivalry.

A critical geopolitics can challenge this geo-graphing of space as a pre-given container of politics by focusing on power in terms of social relations rather in terms of physical domination of abstract space. If a critical geopolitics of this sort is to develop, this theme of absolute space will have to be challenged directly. A detailed critique of the spatial presuppositions remains to be worked out. A critical geopolitics can investigate how the categorizations and cultural creations through which we come to understand and write in turn shape our political existence. In particular, a theoretical engagement with the political implications of the reification of space is long overdue; Lefevre (1976), Sack (1980, 1986) and Smith (1984) have pointed the way, but the task remains to reconstruct concepts of space (Walker, 1988c). Also needed is an elaboration of the interrelations of concepts of political and social space, socially produced spaces, ones not grounded in assumptions of absolute space as political container (Bourdieu, 1985; Foucault, 1986). A promising point of departure lies in the literature focusing on the reconceptualization of 'people's space', understood in Esteva's (1987) terms of locality and horizon, in contrast to the modern formulation of absolute space and rigid boundaries. Here security can be linked to the politics of locality, not to the abstract spaces of state administration and rule. Thus security is extricated from the prerogatives of state rule and analysed in terms of people's control over their own social space.

This provides us with the key point to the theoretical critique of security as a practice of spatial exclusion of Otherness. Decoupling the concept of security from state security simultaneously raises the fundamental issues of politics and citizenship (Gallie, 1978; Linklater, 1982; Waltz, 1959), and also provides political and intellectual space for the development of different conceptions of geopolitics and security. Recognising the importance of the politics of discourse also requires a recognition of the importance of the political contexts within which the various discourses operate. Dissenting discourses within the ambit of NATO have taken a number of forms, and an increasingly important theme in the new social movements (formed initially in terms of feminist, ecological, peace, cultural and regional autonomy concerns) is their recognition of the importance and the potential for operating in ways that refuse the construction of political space in terms of insides and outsides; the refusal to accept the boundaries of the state as providing the space for political action (Magnusson and Walker, 1988).

The new social movements have, in the USA as well as elsewhere, drawn inspiration and political argument from all the forms of dissent discourse discussed above, challenging the strategic logic of states, the militarization of the economy and the morality of nuclear war preparations. In doing all these things, they have also taken the crucial political step of refusing to accept the dominant security discourse specifications of politics in terms of the eternal enmity of competing blocs. These direct political challenges are essential to the new social movements' political programme of challenging power and attempting to democratize and change the nature of modern 'national security' preoccupied state structures. The European Nuclear Disarmament campaign explicitly refused to operate within the categories of the blocs, NATO and the Warsaw Pact 'them' and 'us' (Smith and Thompson eds, 1987).

This refusal of the geopolitical specifications of the Cold War system is an important theme for a critical geopolitics. To modify Konrad's (1984) term 'antipolitics', the arguments for dealignment are anti-geopolitical in their refusal of Europe as the 'theater' of the confrontation (Kaldor and Falk eds, 1987). In this sense, while incorporating in various ways the dissent themes that Walker and Klein elaborate, the dealignment arguments, in particular, in Europe provide another form of dissent discourse, one that directly challenges the geopolitics of US hegemony. Dealignment does so precisely because it refuses to discuss security in terms of 'them' and 'us', 'East' and 'West', NATO and the Warsaw Pact.

Challenging hegemony: dealignment

While the focus of this book has been on the CPD and US security discourse, it is appropriate to consider briefly these critiques of US and NATO military policy emerging from Europe in the last decade. The European 'theatre' is after all the prime focus of US security concern in terms of responses to 'the Soviet threat', Europe being the most important part of the 'Rimlands'. Europe is also the location of the greatest geographical concentration of military technology: Germany, East and West, is practically an armed camp. If a superpower war happens Europeans understand that they are the battleground. Consequently, in the period of heightened tension of the second Cold War critical intellectuals as well as the wider peace movement activists have been active in rethinking the conventional terms of geopolitical discourse. The Independent Commission on Disarmament and Security (1982) popularized the theme of common security; the theme of dealignment embraces a more comprehensive political approach to remaking European politics.

The links between these preoccupations and the more traditional concerns of geopolitics are clearly present in the expanding research literature on what can broadly be termed 'alternative security', an outgrowth of, in Klein's (1988) terms, the 'ironic' critique of the strategic enterprise. Here various approaches have been developed recently, in particular in the European context, by researchers interested in examining alternative defensive arrangements which might provide credible defence systems without the inclusion of nuclear weapons or other weapons of massive destruction. These include proposals for political strategies as well as various possible strategies of civilian defence (Alternative Defence Commission, 1983, 1987; Hettne ed., 1988; Kaldor, 1983; Sharp, 1985; Tatchell, 1985) and the possibilities of neutrality (Joenniemi, 1988, 1989). The obvious importance of this research is that it provides practical alternatives to European reliance on NATO nuclear weapons as a method of 'defence' against 'the Russian threat'. Alternative defence provides just one obvious starting point for a critical approach to geopolitics, distancing itself from the state-centric preoccupations of classical geopolitics. It offers this possibility because it inevitably will raise questions of the status of the state. In the process investigations of alternative security policies raise the fundamental political question of 'security for whom?' (Walker, 1988a); and hence also raise the question of the relationships between centralized command structures in the modern state and the possibility for community defences and security policies controlled at the local level. Security is focused on social relations rather than the abstraction of state security understood in spatial terms.

This concern with security as social relations and social space links security with common security, which points to the interconnectedness of the fates of peoples in different places. Thus, in Europe the emerging discourse on dealignment points to the common insecurity of all Europeans due to the presence of the division of the continent between the USSR and the USA and the consequent presence of numerous nuclear weapons on its soil (Kaldor and Falk eds, 1987). The argument is that all Europeans would be more secure if the political division and its weapons technology could be transcended (Smith and Thompson eds, 1987). But it is also clear in this literature that this transcendence will have to occur in terms of new political sensitivities, ones that transcend and avoid the power plays of the state systems on both sides of the divide. This is not to announce once again the imminent demise of the territorial state (Herz, 1957), but the link between new discursive practices and the political practice of social movements is clearly understood here as elsewhere (Mendlowitz and Walker eds, 1987). From both Left (Smith and Thompson, 1987) and Right (May, 1984) as well as from Eastern Europe (Konrad, 1984) there are renewed calls for rethinking Europe's political future in ways that reduce its subjection to both superpowers' military hegemony.

The move for dealignment involves more than a disarmament campaign or a wholesale dismemberment of either of the blocs, but debates how Europeans can best move to increase their own security by reducing the threat posed by the bloc confrontation in that continent. The equation of military (nuclear) weapons with security is no longer accepted as the premise for political discussion. While these approaches critique the realist agenda, however, this is not to underestimate the monopoly of power and decision-making currently held by states. While the possibilities for change outside the state system should not be overestimated (Bull, 1977), the crucial point is that pressure for state change and adaptation will be impossible without the kinds of linking of the local and the global dimensions of the security problem that are outlined here. Diplomacy is not immune to domestic or international opinion; it will be less invulnerable as alternative centres of discourse and empowerment develop, in the process causing shifts in other political agendas, which in turn restructure the political contexts within which states operate. Here the challenge by the peace movements on both sides of the geopolitical divide are particularly interesting because the rethinking of Soviet security in the 1980s, to emphasize the importance of non-offensive defence, has been influenced in part by critical peace research which has, in turn, been inspired by the critical questions raised by the political opponents of militarization.

Dealignment has been summarized by Falk and Kaldor (1987) as consisting of five loose principles, seen as processes rather than final goals, guidelines for political action to open up the possibilities for political diversity 'while diminishing polarisation and conflict' in Europe. Dealignment is concerned with moving 'beyond the blocs' rather than just out of the blocs, hence its distinction from a policy of neutrality. It is concerned simultaneously to move superpower relations towards more co-operative ventures and to increase the sovereign rights of members of the alliances without simply creating a European superpower to replace the military presence of the USA and the USSR.

The first theme of dealignment is denuclearization: reducing the nuclear weapons component of military forces in Europe; challenging the inherent assumptions of deterrence that sovereignty and power are about the possession of the technical means for mass destruction. This theme includes a multiplicity of proposals for a 'no first use' doctrine, 'freeze and withdraw' campaigns and 'nuclear weapons-free zones'. Second is the theme of demilitarization: reducing non-nuclear components of military technology to ensure that denuclearization does not entail a buildup of other weapons to compensate for the reduction of nuclear devices. Alternative defence strategies are relevant here, refusing both offensive conventional weaponry and nuclear weapons.

The third dimension of dealignment is depolarization: understood in terms of reducing the influence of East–West conceptualizations in dealing with political openings to the Third World. It involves both 'official *détente*' and unofficial citizen *détente*. Following from this is the fourth dealignment theme: democratization. Obviously, this theme is important in Eastern Europe, where the expansion of civil society and the evolution of political institutions in this direction is beginning in the era of *Glasnost*. In the West this would involve a direct challenge to the autonomy of the state in fields of security policy, reducing the autonomy and secrecy of the national security state and, hence, expanding the spheres of democracy in Western societies.

Finally, dealignment also involves development; but development formulated in very different ways from the currently dominant Atlanticist forms of multinational capital and high technology. Understood more broadly, development must involve dealing with the social, ecological and cultural problems that have emerged as part of the Atlanticist model of military-technological progress. Obviously, these themes link up with wider global concerns for ecological survival, development and justice, all endangered by the process of global militarization (Mendlowitz and Walker eds, 1987).

These discourses are direct challenges to superpower hegemony, with their representations of security as spatial exclusion. Thus they have an essential geopolitical dimension to which critical geopolitics can make a contribution. But a critical approach to geopolitics requires in addition a sensitivity to the methodological and cultural limitations of such projects, and also a clear identification of the audiences for its work.

Challenging hegemony: security and development

Where peace is defined as the ultimate objective by Western international relations scholars, for those writing from the underdeveloped areas peace and security are often of concern in terms of the reduction of poverty, social justice, development issues and human rights. To poor people in Third World countries security is more likely to mean a regular supply of food and a roof rather than a relaxation in the pace of nuclear arms development, a series of concerns likely to be seen as extremely remote from their daily struggle for survival. In this conception, peace in the narrow sense of avoiding nuclear war is very much a parochial concern of the West. It also points to the inevitable failure of any attempt to reconstruct global hegemony in terms of US economic leadership of a trilateralist sort. The unreconstituted economic arrangements of modernity cannot provide the kinds of security required by numerous Third World societies (George, 1988).

Thus, security as a concept is not universally applicable in terms of military protection. The nuclear arms race and consequent insecurity for all of the human species is only one facet of this larger tendency. A genuinely critical geopolitics would seem to include a requirement to incorporate the larger issues of technological societies' challenge to global ecology as part of its problematic. In the Third World context violence and war are not necessarily viewed as the primary problem of global order and security. Development, justice and human rights in numerous cultural contexts and interpretations loom large and occupy a central place in political discourse. Neither is an uncritical adoption of modernity a foregone conclusion, although aspects of technology may be deemed desirable, and indeed actively promoted by the ruling classes in developing states.

Thus there is a need to avoid the ethnocentric limitations of politics defined in terms of Western progress, of the universals of modernization. The cultural resistances to modernization, and with it the Western socialist preoccupations with technological progress, are an important theme (Nandy, 1987; Visvanathan, 1986, 1987). The incursion of the science and technology of advanced industrialisms into the Third World often bring with them genocidal implications, not any form of salvation; ecological destruction, not development (Shiva, 1988). This critique extends to numerous Marxist and world systems schemes for global transformation, their ecological viability and the human costs of their implementation. A critical approach should be sensitive to the often very destructive impacts of the expansion of unreconstituted modernity (Visvanathan, 1987) as well as alert to the ethnocentric limitations of the Marxist project (Dumont, 1977; Turner, 1978) and the whole question of whether modernity is not premised on a simple will to power that ensures enslavement (Levi, 1979). A specific avenue of inquiry suggests itself in terms of an ecological conception of security, relating matters of local environmental conditions to the vulnerability of populations to political, economic technological, as well as military threats. These are obviously interconnected aspects of the local societal situation. A comprehensive formulation of security in these terms prevents its easy articulation with state power and the traditional Western forms of security discourse.

The political debates over nuclear power and hazardous chemicals have focused attention on the vulnerability of technologically sophisticated societies to technological disruption (Nelkin and Pollak, 1981). The vulnerability of modern centralized energy systems to warfare are particularily noteworthy (Clark and Page, 1981; Lovins and Lovins, 1982). The concerns of the peace movement raise very clearly the dangers to security in the more explicitly political sense of the term which links these concerns with the domestic political implications of nuclear technology in general (Jungk, 1979). It is no accident that the links between the consequences of the Chernobyl reactor accident and the arms race were so often drawn (Mackay and Thompson eds, 1988). The links between the technological mastery of nature and the political institutions of the modern sovereign state are intimate.

These concerns link with concerns within Western countries about the needs for democratization of the technological sphere, both in terms of enhanced workplace democracy and citizen input into siting and techno-logical development decisions, covering the whole gamut of social and environmental agendas. The alternative technology and local initiatives for community economic development offer some interesting points of departure for the challenges to the state that transcend national boundaries. These point to a way forward through the critique of the discourses of the techno-logical state, recognizing the limitations of each discourse to which it brings its attention. Thus, the implicit ideological functions of these discourses of security are the focus, in challenging them the concepts of power and sovereignty are revealed and challenged rather than accepted and used.

At the local level in many Western states in the 1980s there has been an increase in awareness of security issues at a municipal or local government level, most visible in the campaigns to have areas declared nuclear weapons-free zones and in their refusal to participate in war preparations and civil defence exercises in preparation for nuclear war (Barnaby, 1985). In addition, there are numerous initiatives of 'citizen diplomacy' aimed at bypassing the ritualistic exchanges of international diplomacy. The assump-tion here repeatedly is that peace and security are too important to be left to the politicians. These political interventions link local themes to global themes, recognizing that political actions aimed at influencing the nature of the state are often most effective when links between the local and the global are made (Walker, 1988b). These initiatives in 'village politics' challenge the monopoly of the security discourses in terms of security being something provided by states (Loeb, 1987). In the Third World the potential audience may often be concerned with somewhat different although related matters of development and human rights (Mendlowitz and Walker eds, 1987). These 'critical social movements' are none the less challenging the political and the discursive conventions of their situations in interesting ways that articulate loosely with Western concerns (Walker, 1988b).

All these audiences are concerned with the issues of security and survival in ways that bypass and indeed, to certain degrees, challenge the state's monopoly on issues of international affairs (Falk, 1987). These in turn raise the deeper questions of the nature of sovereignty and the state, challenging the very basis of political organization of the modern state in terms of the twin themes of domination of nature and the control over a precisely defined territory. While obviously this challenge is, as yet, often peripheral, it is important for the argument being made here to recognize that it is at these interstices that political debate and empowerment are occurring. Hence, they are sites for contributions that challenge the bases of the modern security dilemma.

Critical geopolitics

The assumption that international relations will be conceptualized in similar terms globally remains a major problem for any attempts to generate a critical geopolitics. It seems essential to bear this ethnocentric assumption in mind; geopolitical matters in the non-Western societies are likely to have other preconceptions (Abdel-Malek, 1977). The traditional concerns of international relations focused predominantly on European peace and balance-of-power questions. This is the principal concern of classical geopolitics, and for that matter its more current versions. Matters of imperialism or the horizontal extension of power were at best a secondary concern. This suggests the need for caution against simplistic appeals to universal subjects and imagined human communities that may not exist to carry out the programmes and correctives advocated by culture-bound geopoliticians. More specifically, we need to treat with care appeals to a universal humanity that easily take off into idealist abstractions. Such universalistic claims are all to often appropriated by one state to justify its agenda in international politics. The traditional US ideological rituals of moral exceptionalism appropriate human universals to a US imperial project with little apparent difficulty; the CPD used this device blatantly in its policy statements.

There is also the related consideration that grand theorizing is inherently authoritarian, imposing roles on 'Others' in a grand scheme of things. Logocentric theorizing of this type is of the kind traditional geopolitics relished and its current re-interpreters also enjoy (Ashley, 1989). It provides legitimation for the worst excesses of militarist policy and authoritarian rule by providing expert knowledge, in some 'scientific' or 'objective' manner, identifying its position as above sectional interest. Resting usually on some quasi-positivist conceptualization of investigator as separate from the investigated, it defines experience as Other to be manipulated, changed and reorganized into patterns which suit the ultimate good of the society with which the investigator identifies.

Traditional geopolitics was just the sort of grand theorizing that provides blueprints and policy advice to foreign policy specialists and strategic thinkers. In contrast, a critical geopolitical consciousness needs to appeal to audiences beyond the narrow confines of state security bureaucracies. Indeed, given their proclivities, it will be unlikely to receive favourable hearing within these boundaries anyway, although the exceptions may prove important if national security policies are to take different courses in the future. A critical geopolitics, as with a critical social theory, has different concerns, with, in some form or other, human emancipation. Thus its focus has to be on exposing the plays of power of grand geopolitical schemes, and in the process, challenging the categorizations of discourses of power.

A critical geopolitics can ask, as this book has done, how the discourses of geopolitics function politically. Discourses limit what it is possible to talk of and about, the agendas of political geography, international relations and peace research will in turn limit what it is we talk of and about, and how we proceed to conduct our research and writing. With discourse comes matters of political power; we researchers face these choices directly in our work, we have to choose whether our efforts will lead – to grandiose schemes with totalitarian consequences or to more critical pluralistic endeavours empowering new political subjects.

This book has argued for the latter approach; focusing on the rituals of power in the discourse of international politics allows their demystification and contributes to the counter-hegemonic projects of critical inquiry (Said, 1985a, 1985b). In Georg Lukacs's (1973) terms, intellectuals are responsible for their products, perhaps even more so than the engineers and physicists who often get much of the blame for the current crisis. To tackle the hegemonic discourses of power politics requires taking seriously the multiplicity of critiques of existing political discourse, 'all of which take for their point of departure the right of formerly un- or misrepresented human groups to speak for and represent themselves in domains defined, politically and intellectually, as normally excluding them, usurping their signifying and representing functions, overriding their historical reality' (Said, 1985a, 4). In doing so it rejects the politics of grand detachment, the illusion of the Archimedean point from which the whole world can be grasped, in favour of critical disputations of the designations of reality specified by hegemonic discourses; hence the argument in this final chapter for a critical engagement with the political discourses of those who resist the dominant state and bloc centric formulations of security. The focus on the processes of 'Othering' in the creation of discourse remains a powerful interrogative procedure to deconstruct hegemonic formulations. However, none of this should suggest an uncritical acceptance of the critical social movements as providing *the* answer. Rather a postmodern approach suggests that their contribution to an emerging global conversation on the fate of the planet is important precisely because they illustrate simultaneously the limitations of received institutional wisdom and suggest possible reformulations that transcend these limitations. In addressing their various concerns, critical inquiry is distanced from the hegemony of security discourse exercised by the security intellectuals.

The nuclear bomb may have changed the realities of political power but it is the practices of geopolitical discourse that have come to terms with the enduring possibility of mass destruction. It is precisely these discourses of security that define and delimit the bounds of political discussion, acting to reproduce the militarization of culture and politics. By starting from a critical recognition of the role of geopolitical discourse, and then exploring the possibilities of alternative formulations of security with a potential for social transformation, a critical geopolitics can offer some useful contributions to the quest for survival, peace and justice.

Bibliography

Abdel-Malek, A., 1977, 'Geopolitics and national movements: an essay on the dialectics of imperialism', in Peet, R. (ed.), *Radical Geography* (London: Methuen), 293–307.

Abercrombie, N., 1980, *Class, Structure and Knowledge: Problems in the Sociology of Knowledge* (Oxford: Basil Blackwell).

——, S. Hill and B.S. Turner, 1980, *The Dominant Ideology Thesis* (London: Allen & Unwin).

Acheson, D., 1969, *Present at the Creation: My Years at the State Department* (New York: Norton).

Adams, G. 1982, *The Politics of Defence Contracting: the Iron Triangle* (London: Transaction Books).

Agnew, J.A., 1983, 'An excess of "National Exceptionalism": towards a new political geography of American foreign policy', *Political Geography Quarterly*, 2(2), 151–66.

——, 1987, *Place and Politics: the Geographical Mediation of State and Society* (London: Allen & Unwin).

——, and G. O'Tuathail, 1987, 'The historiography of American geopolitics', paper presented to the International Studies Association annual convention, Washington, April.

Ajami, F., 1978, 'The global logic of the neo-conservatives', *World Politics*, 30, 450–68.

Aldridge, R.C., 1981, *The Counterforce Syndrome: a Guide to US Nuclear Weapons and Strategic Doctrine* (Washington: Institute for Policy Studies).

——, 1983, *First Strike: the Pentagon's Strategy for Nuclear War* (Boston: South End).

——, 1989, *Nuclear Empire* (Vancouver: New Star Books).

Alperovitz, G., 1985, *Atomic Diplomacy: Hiroshima and Potsdam, the Use of the Atomic Bomb and the American Confrontation with Soviet Power* (New York: Penguin) (original edition Simon & Schuster, 1965).

Alterman, E.R., 1985, 'Central Europe: misperceived threats and unforeseen dangers', *World Policy Journal*, 2(4), 681–709.

Alternative Defence Commission, 1983, *Defence without the Bomb* (New York: Taylor and Francis).

——, 1987, *The Politics of Alternative Defence* (London: Paladin).

Ambrose, S.E., 1985, *Rise to Globalism* (Harmondsworth: Penguin).

Amin, S., G. Arrighi, A.G. Frank and I. Wallerstein, 1982, *Dynamics of Global Crisis* (New York: Monthly Review Press).

Anderson, B.R., 1983, *Imagined Communities: Reflections on the Origin and Spread of Nationalism* (London: Verso).

Anderson, P., 1974, *Lineages of the Absolutist State* (London: New Left Books).

——, 1976–7, 'The antimonies of Antonio Gramsci', *New Left Review*, 100, 5–80.

Anschel, E., ed., 1974, *The American Image of Russia 1775–1917* (New York: Ungar).

Arbess, D.J. and S.A. Sahaydachny, 1987, 'Nuclear deterrence and international law: some steps toward observance', *Alternatives*, 12(1), 83–111.

Aron, R., 1966, *Peace and War: a Theory of International Relations* (New York: Doubleday).

Art, R.J., 1980, 'To what ends military power?', *International Security*, 4(4), 3–35.

Asad, T., 1979, 'Anthropology and the analysis of ideology', *Man*, 14(4), 607–27.

Ashley, R.K., 1980, *The Political Economy of War and Peace* (London: Pinter).

——, 1983, 'Three modes of economism', *International Studies Quarterly*, 27(4), 463–96.

——, 1984, 'The poverty of neo-realism, *International Organisation*, 38(2), 225–86.

——, 1987, 'The geopolitics of geopolitical space: toward a critical social theory of international politics', *Alternatives*, 12(4), 403–34.

——, 1988, 'Untying the sovereign state: a double reading of the anarchy problematique', *Millennium: Journal of International Studies*, 17(2), 227–62.

——, 1989, 'Living on borderlines: man post-structuralism and war', in Der Derian J., and M.J. Shapiro (eds), *International/Intertextual Relations: Postmodern Readings of World Politics* (Lexington, Mass.: Lexington), 259–321.

Aspin, L., 1978, 'What are the Russians up to?', *International Security*, 3(1), 30–54.

Atkeson, E.B., 1976, 'Hemispheric denial: geopolitical imperatives and Soviet strategy', *Strategic Review*, 4(2), 26–36.

Ball, D., 1981, *Can Nuclear War be Controlled?* (London: IISS, Adelphi Paper 169).

——, and J. Richelson (eds), 1986, *Strategic Nuclear Targeting* (Ithaca: Cornell University Press).

Barnaby, F., 1985, 'Nuclear weapons free zones', in D. Pepper and A. Jenkins (eds), *The Geography of Peace and War* (Oxford: Blackwell. 165–77).

Barnet, R., 1971, *The Roots of War* (Harmondsworth: Penguin).

——, 1972, *Intervention and Revolution* (London: Paladin).

——, 1981, *Real Security* (New York: Simon & Schuster).

——, 1983, *The Alliance* (New York: Simon & Schuster).

Barnett, F.R., 1981, 'Reclaiming the initiative from the Soviet Heartland: the case for a Tri Oceanic Alliance of the Imperiled Rimlands', in *Towards a Grand Strategy for Global Freedom* (London: Foreign Affairs Research Institute) 9–24.

Barthes, R., 1973, *Mythologies* (St Alban's: Paladin).

Bassin, M., 1987, 'Race Contra Space: The Conflict Between German Geopolitik and National Socialism', *Political Geography Quarterly*, 6(2), 115–34.

Bay, C., 1983, 'Hazards of Goliath in the nuclear age: need for rational priorities in American peace and defence policies', *Alternatives*, 8(4), 501–42.

Beres, L.R., 1980, *Apocalypse: Nuclear Catastrophe in World Politics* (Chicago: University of Chicago Press).

——, 1983, *Mimicking Sisyphus: America's Countervailing Strategy* (Lexington, Mass.: Heath).

Berki, R.N., 1984, 'On Marxian thought and the problem of international relations', in Walker, R.B.J. (ed.), *Culture Ideology and World Order* (Boulder: Westview), 217–42.

Berman, M., 1984, *The Reenchantment of the World* (New York: Bantam).

——, 1988, *All That is Solid Melts into Air: the Experience of Modernity* (Harmondsworth: Penguin).

Black, J.L., 1986, *Origins/Evolution and Nature of the Cold War: an Annotated*

Bibliographic Guide (Santa Barbara, Calif.: ADC-CLIO, War/Peace Bibliography Series No. 19).

Blair, B.G., 1985, *Strategic Command and Control: Redefining the Nuclear Threat* (Washington: Brookings Institution).

Blechman, B.M. and S.S. Kaplan, 1978, *Force Without War: US Armed Forces as a Political Instrument* (Washington: Brookings Institution).

Blouet, B.W., 1987, 'Mackinder, Spykman and containment', paper presented to the annual meeting of the Association of American Geographers, Portland, April.

Booth, K., 1979, *Strategy and Ethnocentrism* (London: Croom Helm).

—— and P. Williams, 1985, 'Reagan's myths about detente', *World Policy Journal*, 2(3), 501–32.

Boulding, K.E., 1969, 'National images and international systems', in J.N.Rosenau (ed.), *International Politics and Foreign Policy*, 422–31.

Bourdieu, P., 1977, *Outline of a Theory of Practice* (Cambridge: Cambridge University Press).

——, 1985, 'The social space and the genesis of groups', *Theory and Society*, 14, 723–44.

Bracken, P., 1983, *The Command and Control of Nuclear Weapons* (New Haven, Conn.: Yale University Press).

Bright, C., 1986, 'On the road to war with the Soviet Union: strategic consensus for the 1990s', *Socialist Review*, 85, 7–43.

Brodie, B. (ed.), 1946, *The Absolute Weapon: Atomic Power and World Order* (New York: Harcourt Brace).

——, 1965, *Strategy in the Missile Age* (Princeton, NJ: Princeton University Press, original edition, 1959).

Brooks, L.F., 1986, 'Naval power and national security: the case for the maritime strategy', *International Security*, 11(2), 58–88.

Brunn, S.D. and K.A. Mingst, 1985, 'Geopolitics', in M. Pacione (ed.), *Progress in Political Geography* (London: Croom Helm) 41–76.

Brzezinski, Z., 1986, *Game Plan' a Geostrategic Framework for the Conduct of the US–Soviet Contest* (New York: Atlantic Monthly Press).

Bull, H., 1977, *The Anarchical Society: a Study of Order in World Politics* (London: Macmillan).

—— and A. Watson (eds), 1984, *The Expansion of International Society* (Oxford: Clarendon).

Bunge, W., 1988, *The Nuclear War Atlas* (Oxford: Blackwell).

Butterfield, H. and M. Wight, 1966, *Diplomatic Investigations: Essays in the Theory of International Politics* (London: Allen & Unwin).

Buzan, B., 1983, *People, States and Fear: the National Security Problem in International Relations* (Brighton, Sussex: Wheatsheaf).

——, 1984, 'Peace, power, and security: contending concepts in the study of international relations', *Journal of Peace Research*, 21(2), 109–25.

Calder, N., 1981, *Nuclear Nightmares: an Investigation into Possible Wars* (Harmondsworth: Penguin).

Calleo, D.P., 1987, *Beyond American Hegemony: the Future of the Western Alliance* (New York: Basic Books).

Carnoy, M., 1984, *The State and Political Theory* (Princeton, NJ: Princeton University Press).

Carr, E.H., 1946, *The Twenty Yeas Crisis: 1919–1939* (London: Macmillan).

——, 1966, *The Bolshevik Revolution: 1917–1923*, 3 vols (Harmondsworth: Penguin).

Caute, D., 1978, *The Great Fear: the Anti-Communist Purge Under Truman and Eisenhower* (New York: Simon & Schuster).

Cave-Brown, A. (ed.), 1978, *Dropshot: the American Plan for World War III Against Russia in 1957* (New York: Dial).

Centre for Contemporary Cultural Studies, 1977, *On Ideology* (London: Hutchinson).

Centre for Defence Information, 1980, 'Soviet geopolitical momentum: myth or menace? Trends of Soviet influence around the world from 1945 to 1980', *The Defence Monitor*, 9(1), 1–24.

Chace, J. and C. Carr, 1988, *America Invulnerable: the Quest for Absolute Security 1812 to Star Wars* (New York: Summit).

Chatterjee, P., 1986, *Nationalist Thought and the Colonial World: a Derivative Discourse* (London: Zed).

Chilton, P., 1985, 'Words, discourse and metaphors: the meanings of deter, deterrent and deterrence', in P. Chilton (ed.), *Language and the Nuclear Arms Debate: Nukespeak Today* (London: Pinter).

——, (ed.), 1985, *Language and the Nuclear Arms Debate: Nukespeak Today* (London: Pinter).

Chomsky, N., 1982, *Towards a New Cold War: Essays on the Current Crisis and How We Got There* (New York: Pantheon).

Clark, M.G. and L. Lange (eds), 1979, *The Sexism of Social and Political Theory: Women and Reproduction from Plato to Nietzsche* (Toronto: University of Toronto Press).

Clark, W. and J. Page, 1981, *Energy, Vulnerability, and War: Alternatives for America* (New York: Norton).

Clausewitz, C., 1968, *On War*, edited by A. Rapoport (Harmondsworth: Penguin, original *Vom Kriege*, 1823).

Cline, S., 1980, *World Power Trends and US Foreign Policy for the 1980s* (Boulder: Westview).

Coate, R. and C. Murphy, 1985, 'A critical science of international relations', *International Interactions*, 12(2), 109–32.

Cockburn, A., 1983, *The Threat: Inside the Soviet Military Machine* (New York: Random House).

Cockle, P., 1978, 'Analysing Soviet defence spending: the debate in perspective', *Survival*, Sept/Oct.

Cohen, R., 1979, *Threat Perception in International Crisis* (Madison: University of Wisconsin Press.

Cohen, S., 1963, *Geography and Politics in a World Divided* (New York: Random House).

Cohen, S.F., 1985, *Rethinking the Soviet Experience: Politics and History Since 1917* (New York: Oxford University Press).

Cohn, C., 1987, 'Sex and death in the rational world of defense intellectuals', *Signs: Journal of Women in Culture and Society*, 12(4), 687–718.

Collins, R., 1981, 'Does modern technology change the rules of geopolitics?', *Journal of Political and Military Sociology*, 9(2), 163–77.

Colton, T.J., 1986, *The Dilemma of Reform in The Soviet Union* (New York: Council for Foreign Relations).

Committee on the Present Danger, 1984, *Alerting America: The Papers of the Committee on the Present Danger* (Washington: Pergamon Brasseys).

Connell, J., 1986, *The New Maginot Line* (London: Secker & Warburg).

Connolly, W.E., 1984, 'The politics of discourse', in M.J. Shapiro (ed.), *Language and Politics* (Oxford, Basil Blackwell), 139–67.

——, 1989, 'Identity and difference in global politics', in Der Derian J. and M.J. Shapiro (eds), *International/Intertextual Relations: Postmodern Readings of World Politics* (Lexington, Mass.: Heath), 323–42.

Cox, A.M., 1980, 'The CIA's tragic error', *New York Review of Books*, 6 November, 21–4.

——, 1982, *Russian Roulette: the Superpower Game* (New York: Times Books).

Cox. M., 1984, 'From detente to the "New Cold War": the crisis of the Cold War System', *Millennium: Journal of International Studies*, 13(3), 265–91.

——, 1985, 'The rise and fall of the "Soviet Threat", *Political Studies*, 33(3), 484–98.

Cox, R.W., 1983, 'Gramsci, hegemony and international relations: an essay in method', *Millennium: Journal of International Studies*, 12(2), 162–75.

——, 1984, 'Social forces, states, and world orders: beyond international relations theory', in Walker, R.B.J. (ed.), *Culture, Ideology and World Order* (Boulder: Westview), 258–99.

Dallek, R.A., 1983, *The American Style of Foreign Policy: Culture, Politics and Foreign Policy* (New York: Mentor).

——, 1984, *Ronald Reagan: the Politics of Symbolism* (Cambridge, Mass.: Harvard University Press).

Daly, M. 1973, *Beyond God the Father* (Boston: Beacon Press).

DeBlij, H., 1981, *Geography: Regions and Concepts*, 3rd edition (New York: Wiley).

deCerteau, M., 1986, *Heterologies: Discourse on the Other*, translated by B. Mazzumi and Wlad Godzich (Minneapolis: University of Minnesota Press).

Der Derian, J., 1987, *On Diplomacy: a Genealogy of Western Estrangement* (Oxford: Basil Blackwell).

——, and M.J. Shapiro (eds), 1989, *International/Intertextual Relations: Postmodern Readings in World Politics* (Lexington, Mass.: Lexington Books).

Derrida, J., 1977, *Of Grammatology*, translated by G.C. Spivak (Baltimore: Johns Hopkins University Press).

——, 1981, *Dissemination*, translated by B. Johnson (Chicago: University of Chicago Press).

De Tocqueville, A., 1969, *Democracy in America*, edited by J.P. Meyer, (New York: Doubleday).

Deterrence and Survival in the Nuclear Age, 'The Gaither Report', 1957 (Washington: US Government Printing Office, 1976).

Deudney, D., 1983, *Whole Earth Security: a Geopolitics of Peace* (Washington: World Watch Institute).

Dibb, P., 1988, *The Soviet Union: the Incomplete Superpower* (Chicago: University of Illinois Press).

Dillon, M., 1988, 'Security and modernity', paper for the University of California, Institute of Global Conflict and Cooperation: second annual conference on Discourse, Peace, Security and International Society, Ballyvaughan, Ireland.

Dossa, S., 1987, 'Political philosophy and orientalism: the classical origins of a discourse', *Alternatives*, 12(3), 343–58.

Douglas, J.D. Jr and A.M. Hoeber, 1979, *Soviet Strategy for Nuclear War* (Stanford, Calif.: The Hoover Institution).

Douhet, G., 1942, *The Command of the Air*, translated by D. Ferrari (New York: Coward McCann).

Draper, T., 1983, *Present History* (New York:Random House).

——, 1986, 'Neoconservative history', *The New York Review of Books*, 32(21/2), 5–15.

Dumont, L., 1977, *From Mandeville to Marx: the Genesis and Triumph of the Economic Ideology* (Chicago: Chicago University Press).

Earle, E.M. (ed.), 1944, *The Makers of Modern Strategy* (Princeton: Princeton University Press).

Easlea, B., 1983, *Fathering the Unthinkable: Masculinity, Scientists and the Nuclear Arms Race* (London: Pluto).

Easterbrook, G., 1986, 'Ideas move nations: how conservative think tanks have helped to transform the terms of political debate', *The Atlantic Monthly*, January, 66–80.

Emmerson, D.K., 1984, "'Southeast Asia': what's in a name', *Journal of Southeast Asia studies*, 15, 1–21.

Enggass, P.M., 1984, *Geopolitics: a Bibliography of Applied Political Geography* (Monticello, Ill.: Vance Bibliographies, Public Administration Series P-1438).

Enloe, C., 1983, *Does Khaki Become You? the Militarization of Women's Lives* (London: Pluto).

Erickson, P.D., 1985, *Reagan Speaks: the Making of an American Myth* (New York: New York University Press).

Ermath, F.W., 1978, 'Contrasts in American and Soviet strategic thought', *International Security*, 3(2), 138–55.

Escobar, A., 1984–5, 'Discourse and power in development: Michel Foucault and the relevance of his work to the Third World', *Alternatives*, 10(3), 377–400.

Esteva, G., 1987, 'Regenerating people's space', *Alternatives*, 12(1), 125–52.

Etzold, T.H. and J.L. Gaddis (eds), 1978, *Containment: Documents on American Policy and Strategy 1945–50* (New York: Columbia University Press).

Evangelista, M., 1986, 'The new Soviet approach to security', *World Policy Journal*, 3(4), 561–99.

Fabian, J., 1983, *Time and the Other: How Anthropology Makes its Object* (New York: Columbia University Press).

Fairgrieve, J., 1915, *Geography and World Power* (London: University of London Press).

Falk, R.A., 1983, *The End of World Order* (New York: Holmes and Meier).

——, 1987, *The Promise of World Order* (Brighton, Sussex: Wheatsheaf).

—— and M. Kaldor, 1987, 'Introduction' in M. Kaldor and R. Falk (eds), *Dealignment: A New Foreign Policy Perspective* (Oxford: Blackwell), 1–27.

Farrell, J.C. and A.P. Smith (eds), 1968, *Image and Reality in World Politics* (New York: Columbia University Press).

Finlay, D.J., O.R. Holsti and R.R. Fagan, 1967, *Enemies in Politics* (Chicago: Rand McNally).

Fisher, C.A. (ed.), 1968, *Essays in Political Geography* (London: Methuen).

Foucault, M., 1972, *The Archaeology of Knowledge* (New York: Pantheon).

——, 1973, *The Order of Things: an Archaeology of the Human Sciences* (New York: Vintage).

——, 1977, *Language, Counter-Memory, Practice* (Ithaca: Cornell University Press).

——, 1980, *Power/Knowledge* (Brighton, Sussex: Harvester).

——, 1986, 'Of other spaces', *Diacritics*, 16(1), 22–7.

Franck, T.M. and E. Weisband, 1972, *Word Politics: Verbal Strategies among the Superpowers* (New York: Oxford University Press).

Frank, A.G., 1983, 'From Atlantic alliance to pan European entente: political economic alternatives', *Alternatives*, 8(4), 423–82.

Freedman, L., 1983, *The Evolution of Nuclear Strategy* (New York: St Martin's).

——, 1986, *US Intelligence and the Soviet Strategic Threat* (London: Macmillan).

Friedberg, A.L., 1980, 'A history of the US strategic "Doctrine": 1945 to 1980', *Journal of Strategic Studies*, 3(3), 37–71.

Frow, J., 1985, 'Discourse and power', *Economy and Society*, 14(2), 193–214.

Gaddis, J.L., 1978, *Russia, the Soviet Union and the United States: an Interpretative History* (New York: Wiley).

——, 1980, 'NSC68 and the problem of means and ends', *International Security*, 4(4), 164–70.

——, 1982, *Strategies of Containment* (New York: Oxford University Press).

Gallie, W.B., 1978, *Philosophers of Peace and War* (London: Cambridge University Press).

Galtung, J., 1981, 'Social cosmology and the concept of peace', *Journal of Peace Research*, 18(2), 183–99.

Garrison, J. and P. Shivpuri, 1983, *The Russian Threat: its Myths and Realities* (London: Gateway).

Gartoff, R.L., 1953, *Soviet Military Doctrine* (Glencoe, Ill.: Free Press).

——, 1978, 'Mutual deterrence and strategic arms limitation in Soviet policy', *International Security*, 3(1), 112–47.

——, 1980, 'The death of Stalin and the birth of mutual deterrence', *Survey*, 25(2), 10–16.

——, 1982a, 'Mutual deterrence and strategic arms limitation in Soviet policy', *Strategic Review*, 10(4), 36–57.

——, 1982b, 'A rebuttal by Ambassador Garthoff', *Strategic Review*, 10(4), 58–63.

——, 1985, *Detente and Confrontation: American–Soviet Relations from Nixon to Reagan* (Washington: Brookings Institution).

George, S., 1988, *A Fate Worse than Debt* (Harmondsworth: Penguin).

Gervasi, T., 1984, *America's War Machine: the Pursuit of Global Dominance: Arsenal of Democracy III* (New York: Grove Press).

——, 1986, *The Myth of Soviet Military Supremacy* (New York: Harper & Row).

Gill, S., 1986, 'Hegemony, consensus and trilateralism', *Review of International Studies*, 12, 205–22.

Gilpin, R., 1975, *US Power and the Multinational Corporation* (New York: Basic Books).

——, 1981, *War and Change in International Politics* (Cambridge: Cambridge University Press).

——, 1988, *The Political Economy of International Relations* (Princeton, NJ: Princeton University Press).

Goldstein, J.S., 1988, *Long Cycles: Prosperity and War in the Modern Age* (New Haven: Yale University Press).

Goure, L., 1976, *War Survival in Soviet Strategy: USSR Civil Defence* (Washington: University of Miami Centre for Advanced International Studies).

Gramsci, A., 1971, *Selections from the Prison Notebooks* (New York: International Publishers).

Gray, C.S., 1971a, 'What RAND hath wrought', *Foreign Policy*, 4, 111–29.

——, 1971b, 'Strategists: some views critical of the profession', *International Journal*, 26(4), 771–90.

——, 1971c, 'The arms race phenomenon', *World Politics*, 24(1), 39–79.

——, 1973, 'Of bargaining chips and building blocks: arms control and defence policy', *International Journal*, 28(2), 266–96.

——, 1974a, 'Mini nukes and strategy', *International Journal*, 24, 216–41.

——, 1974b, 'The practice of theory in international relations', *Political Studies*, 22, 129–46.

——, 1975a, 'SALT and the American mood', *Strategic Review*, 3, 41–51.

——, 1975b, 'SALT II and the strategic balance', *British Journal of International Studies*, 1(3), 183–208.

——, 1975c, 'New weapons and the resort to force', *International Journal*, 30(2), 238–58.

——, 1975d, 'Hawks and doves: values and policy', *Journal of Political and Military Sociology*, 3, 85–94.

——, 1976a, 'Foreign policy—there is no choice', *Foreign Policy*, 24, 114–27.

——, 1976b, 'SALT: time to quit', *Strategic Review*, 4(4), 14–22.

——, 1976c, 'Detente, arms control and strategy: perspectives on SALT', *American Political Science Review*, September.

——, 1976d, 'Theatre nuclear weapons: doctrines and postures', *World Politics*, 28(2), 300–14.

——, 1976e, *The Soviet–American Arms Race* (Lexington: Mass.: Lexington).

——, 1977a, *The Geopolitics of the Nuclear Era: Heartlands, Rimlands, and the Technological Revolution* (New York: Crane, Russack & Co).

——, 1977b, 'Across the great divide: strategic studies, past and present', *International Security*, 2(1), 24–46.

——, 1977c, 'Arms control in a nuclear armed world?', *Annals of the American Academy of Political and Social Science*, 430, 110–21.

——, 1977d, 'The end of SALT? Purpose and strategy in US–USSR negotiations', *Policy Review*, 2, 31–45.

——, 1977e, 'Who's afraid of the cruise missile?', *Orbis*, 21(3), 517–31.

——, 1977f, *The Future of Land Based Missile Forces* (London: International Institute for Strategic Studies, Adelphi Paper 140).

——, 1977-8, ' "Think tanks" and public policy', *International Journal*, 33(1), 177–94.

——, 1978a, 'Force planning, political guidance and the decision to fight', *Military Review*, 58(4), 5–16.

——, 1978b, 'The strategic forces triad: end of the road?', *Foreign Affairs*, 56(4), 771–89.

——, 1978c, 'Does theory lead technology', *International Journal*, 33(3), 506–23.

——, 1979a, 'Nuclear strategy: the case for a theory of victory', *International Security*, 4(1), 54–87.

——, 1979b, 'The military requirements of US strategy', *Military Review*, 59(9), 2–13.

——, 1979c, 'SALT II: the real debate', *Policy Review*, 10, 7–22.

——, 1979d, 'The SALT II debate in context', *Survival*, 21(5), 202–5.

——, 1979e, 'NATO strategy and the "Neutron Bomb" ', *Policy Review*, 7, 7–26.

——, 1980a, 'Targeting plans for central war', *Naval War College Review*, 33(1), 3–21.

——, 1980b, 'Strategic forces and SALT: a question of strategy', *Comparative Strategy*, 2(2), 113–28.

——, 1980c, 'Strategic stability reconsidered', *Daedalus*, 109(4), 135–54.

——, 1980d, *Strategy and the MX* (Washington: Heritage Institute).

——, 1981a, 'The most dangerous decade: historic mission, legitimacy and dynamics of the Soviet Empire in the 1980s', *Orbis*, 25(1), 13–28.

——, 1981b, 'Understanding Soviet military power', *Problems of Communism*, 30(2), 64–7.

——, 1981c, 'Strategic forces, general purpose forces, and crisis management', *Annals of the American Academy of Political and Social Science*, 457, 67–77.

___, 1981d, *The MX ICBM and National Security* (New York: Praeger).

___, 1981e, 'National style in strategy: the American example', *International Security*, 6(2), 21–47.

___, 1981f, 'A new debate on ballistic missile defence', *Survival*, 23(3), 60–71.

___, 1982a, 'Reflections on empire: the Soviet connection', *Military Review*, 62(1), 2–13.

___, 1982b, *Strategic Studies: a Critical Assessment* (Westport, Conn.: Greenwood Press).

___, 1982c, *Strategic Studies and Public Policy; the American Experience* (Lexington, Ky.: University of Kentucky Press).

___, 1982d, *America's Military Space Policy: Information Systems, Weapons Systems, and Arms Control* (Cambridge, Mass.: Abt).

___, 1982e, 'Dangerous to your health: the debate over nuclear strategy and war', *Orbis*, 26(2), 327–49.

___, 1982f, 'NATO's nuclear dilemma', *Poicy Review*, 22, 97–116.

___, 1983, 'Space is not a sanctuary', *Survival*, 25(5), 194–204.

___, 1984a, *Nuclear Strategy and Strategic Planning* (Philadelphia, Pa.: Foreign Policy Research Institute).

___, 1984b, 'War fighting for deterrence', *Journal of Strategic Studies*, 7(1), 5–28.

___, 1984c, 'Deterrence, arms control and defence transition', *Orbis*, 28(2), 227–39.

___, 1984d, 'Moscow is cheating', *Foreign Policy*, 56, 141–52.

___, 1985a, 'A case for strategic defence', *Survival*, 27(2), 50–5.

___, 1985b, 'The nuclear winter thesis and the US strategic policy', *Washington Quarterly*, 8(3), 85–96.

___, 1986a,'The transition from offence to defence', *Washington Quarterly*, 9(3), 59–72.

___, 1986b, *Nuclear Strategy and National Style* (Lanham, Md: Hamilton Press).

___, 1986c, *Maritime Strategy, Geopolitics and the Defence of the West* (New York: National Strategy Information Centre).

___, 1988, *The Geopolitics of Superpower* (Lexington, Ky: University of Kentucky Press).

___ and J.G. Barlow, 1985, 'Inexcusable restraint: the decline of American military power in the 1970s', *International Security*, 10(2), 27–69.

___ and K. Payne, 1980, 'Victory is possible', *Foreign Policy*, 39, 14–27.

___ and ___, 1983, 'Nuclear strategy: is there a future?', *The Washington Quarterly* 6(3), 55–66.

Grayson, B.L. (ed.), 1978, *The American Image of Russia 1917–1977* (New York: Ungar).

Gregory, D. and J. Urry (eds), 1985, *Social Relations and Spatial Structures* (London: Macmillan).

Griffiths, F., 1984, 'The sources of American conduct: Soviet perspectives and their policy implications', *International Security*, 9(2), 3–50.

___, 1985, 'Through the oneway glass: mutual perception in relations between the U.S. and S.U.', paper presented at the Third World Congress of Soviet and East European Studies, Washington, DC.

Gross, D., 1981–2, 'Space, time and modern culture', *Telos*, 50, 59–78.

Haglund, D.G., 1984, *Latin America and the Transformation of US Strategic Thought, 1936–1940* Alberquerque: University of New Mexico Press).

___, 1986, 'The new geopolitics of minerals', *Political Geography Quarterly* , 5(3), 221–40.

Hall, F., 1983, 'The United States' search for security: a psychotherapist's viewpoint', *Journal of Peace Research*, 20(4), 299–309.

Halliday, F., 1982, *The Threat from the East?* (Harmondsworth: Penguin).

——, 1983, *The Making of the Second Cold War* (London: Verso).

Halperin, M., 1961, 'The Gaither Committee and the policy process', *World Politics*, 13, 360–84.

——, 1962, *Limited War* (Cambridge, Mass.: Harvard University Centre for International Affairs).

Halsell, G., 1986, *Prophecy and Politics: Militant Evangelists on the Road to Nuclear War* (Toronto: NC Press).

Hanson, D.W., 1982–3, 'Is Soviet strategic doctrine superior?', *International Security* 7(3), 61–83.

Henrikson, A.K., 1975, 'The map as an idea: role of cartographic imagery during the Second World War', *The American Cartographer*, 2(1), 19–53.

——, 1980, 'The geographical "Mental Maps' of American foreign policy makers', *International Political Science Review*, 1(4), 495–530.

Hepple, L.W., 1986, 'The revival of geopolitics', *Political Geography Quarterly*, 5(4), Supplement, S21–S36.

Herken, G., 1980, *The Winning Weapon: the Atomic Bomb and the Cold War, 1945–1950* (New York: Knopf).

——, 1987, *Counsels of War* (New York: Oxford University Press, 2nd edition).

Herman, E., 1982, *The Real Terror Network* (Boston: South End).

Herz, J.H., 1957, 'Rise and demise of the territorial state', *World Politics*, 9(4), 473–93.

Heske, H., 1987, 'Karl Haushofer: his role in German geopolitics and in Nazi politics', *Political Geography Quarterly* 6(2), 135–44.

Hettne, B., (ed.), 1988, *Europe: Dimensions of Peace* (London: Zed).

——, 1988, 'Transcending the European model of peace and development', in Hettne B. (ed.), *Europe: Dimensions of Peace* (London: Zed), 181–203.

Hewitt, K., 1983, 'Place annihilation: area bombing and the fate of urban places', *Annals of the Association of American Geographers*, 73(2), 257–84.

Hilgartner, S., R.C. Bell and R. O'Connor, 1983, *Nukespeak: the Selling of Nuclear Technology in America* (Harmondsworth: Penguin).

Hobbes, T., 1968, *Leviathan* (Harmondsworth: Penguin).

Hoffman, G.W., 1982, 'Nineteenth century roots of American world power relations: a study in historical political geography', *Political Geography Quarterly*, 1(3), 279–92.

Hoffman, S., 1977, 'An American social science: international relations', *Daedalus*, 51, 41–59.

——, 1978, *Primacy or World Order?: American Foreign Policy Since the Cold War* (New York: McGraw Hill).

——, 1983, *Dead Ends: American Foreign Policy in the New Cold War* (Cambridge, Mass.: Ballinger).

Hogan, R., 1985, 'The frontier as social control', *Theory and Society*, 14(1), 35–51.

Holloway, D., 1983, *The Soviet Union and the Arms Race* (London: Yale University Press).

Holsti, K.J., 1971, 'Retreat from Utopia: international relations theory, 1945–70', *Canadian Journal of Political Science*, 4(2), 165–77.

——, 1985, *The Dividing Discipline: Hegemony and Diversity in International Theory* (London: Allen & Unwin).

Holsti, O.R., 1967, 'Cognitive dynamics and images of the enemy: Dulles and

Russia', in Finlay, D.J., O.R. Holsti and R.R. Fagan, *Enemies in Politics* (Chicago: Rand McNally), 25–96.

Holzman, F., 1980, 'Are the Soviets really outspending the US on defence?', *International Security*, 4(4), 85–104.

Hook, G., 1984, 'The Nuclearisation of language: nuclear alergy as political metaphor', *Journal of Peace Research*, 21(3), 259–75.

___, 1985, 'Making nuclear weapons easier to live with: the political role of language in nuclearisation', *Bulletin of Peace Proposals*, 16(1), 67–77.

Howard, M.E., 1981, 'On fighting a nuclear war', *International Security*, 5(4), 3–17.

___, 1984, *The Causes of Wars* (London: Unwin).

Hughes, T., 1975, 'Liberals, populists and foreign policy', *Foreign Policy*, 20, 98–137.

___, 1976, 'Unreal-Politik', *Foreign Policy*, 24, 127–38.

Hulsberg, W., 1988, *The German Greens* (London: Verso).

Independent Commission on Disarmament and Security Issues, 1982, *Common Security: a Programme for Disarmament* (London: Pan).

Institute for Strategic Studies, annual, *The Military Balance* (London).

JanMohammed, A.R., 1985, 'The economy of Manichean allegory: the function of racial difference in colonialist literature', *Critical Inquiry*, 12, 59–87.

Jay, P., 1979, 'Regionalism as geopolitics', *Foreign Affairs*, 58,(3), 485–514.

Jervis, R., 1970, *The Logic of Images in International Relations* (Princeton: Princeton University Press).

___, 1976, *Perception and Misperception in International Politics* (Princeton: Princeton University Press).

___, 1984, *The Illogic of American Nuclear Strategy* (Ithaca: Cornell University Press).

Joenniemi, P., 1988, 'Models of neutrality: the traditional and the modern', *Cooperation and Conflict*, 23(1), 53–67.

___, 1989, 'The peace potential of neutrality: a discursive approach', *Bulletin of Peace Proposals*, 20(1), 113–20.

Johansen, R.J., 1980, *The National Interest and the Human Interest: an Analysis of US Foreign Policy* (Princeton: Princeton University Press).

___, 1987, 'Global security without nuclear deterrence', *Alternatives*, 12(4), 435–60.

Johnson, B., 1981, 'Translators introduction', in Derrida, J., *Dissemination* (Chicago: University of Chicago Press).

Johnston, R.J. and P.J. Taylor (eds), 1986, *A World in Crisis? Geographical Perspectives* (Oxford: Basil Blackwell).

Johnstone, D., 1984, *The Politics of EuroMissiles: Europe's Role in America's World* (London: Verso).

Jones, S.B., 1954, 'A unified field theory of political geography', *Annals of the Association of American Geographers*, 44(2), 111–23.

___, 1955, 'Global strategic views', *Geographical Review*, 45(4), 492–508.

Jones, T.K. and W.S. Thompson, 1978, 'Central war and civil defence', *Orbis*, 22, 681–712.

Jungk, R., 1979, *The Nuclear State* (London: John Calder).

Kahler, M., 1979, 'Rumors of war: the 1914 analogy', *Foreign Affairs*, 58(2), 374–96.

Kaku, M. and D. Axelrod, 1987, *To Win A Nuclear War: the Pentagon's Secret War Plans* (Boston: South End).

Kaldor, M., 1978, *The Disintegrating West* (Harmndsworth: Penguin).
—, 1982, *The Baroque Arsenal* (London: André Deutsch).
—, 1983, 'Defending Europe the political way', *World Policy Journal*, 1(1), 1–21.
—, 1986, 'The global political economy', *Alternatives*, 11(4), 431–60.
—, 1987, 'The Atlantic technology culture', in Kaldor, M. and R. Falk (eds), *De-Alignment: a New Foreign Policy Perspective* (Oxford: Basil Blackwell), 143–62.
— and P. Anderson (eds), 1986, *Mad Dogs: the US Raids on Libya* (London: Pluto).
— and R. Falk (eds), 1987, *De-Alignment: a New Foreign Policy Perspective* (Oxford: Basil Blackwell).
Kampleman, M., 1984, 'Introduction', to Tyroler, C. (ed.), *Alerting America: the Papers of the Committee on the Present Danger* (New York: Pergamon Brassey), xv–xxi.
Kaplan, F., 1980, *Dubious Spectre: a Skeptical Look at the Soviet Nuclear Threat* (Washington: Institute for Policy Studies).
—, 1983, *The Wizards of Armagedon* (New York: Simon & Schuster).
Kaplan, S.S., 1981, *Diplomacy of Power: Soviet Armed Forces as a Political Instrument* (Washington: Brookings Institution).
Kaufman, W. (ed.), 1956, *Military Policy and National Security* (Princeton: Princeton University Press).
Kazanzadeh, F., 1980, 'Afghanistan: the imperial dream', *New York Review of Books*, 21 February, 10–14.
Kearns, G., 1984, 'Closed space and political practice: Frederick Jackson Turner and Halford Mackinder, *Society and Space*, 1, 23–34.
Keen, S., 1986, *Faces of the Enemy* (New York: Harper & Row).
Kemp, P., 1984, Review Essay of H.L. Dreyfus and P. Rabinow, *Michel Foucault Beyond Structuralism and Hermeneutics* in *History and Theory* , 23(1), 84–105.
Kennan, G., 1946, 'Moscow Embassy Telegram No. 511', in Etzold, T.H. and J.L. Gaddis (eds), *Containment: Documents on American Policy and Strategy 1945–50* , 50–63.
—, (alias 'X'), 1947, 'The sources of Soviet conduct', *Foreign Affairs*, 25(4), 566–82.
—, 1983, *The Nuclear Delusion: Soviet–American Relations in the Atomic Age* (New York: Pantheon).
Kennedy, P., 1987, *The Rise and Fall of the Great Powers* (New York: Random House).
Keohane, R.O., 1984, *After Hegemony: Cooperation and Discord in the World Political Community* (Princeton, NJ: Princeton University Press).
— (ed.), 1986, *Neorealism and its Critics* (New York: Columbia University Press).
Kiernan, V.G., 1969, *The Lords of Humankind: European Attitudes Towards the Outside World in the Imperial Age* (London: Wiedenfeld & Nicolson).
—, 1972, *Lords of HumanKind: European Attitudes to the Outside World in the Imperial Age* (Harmondsworth: Penguin).
Kissinger, H., 1957, *Nuclear Weapons and Foreign Policy* (New York: Harper & Row).
—, 1984, *The Report of the President's Bipartisan Commission on Central America* (New York: Macmillan).
Klare, M., 1981, *Beyond the Vietnam Syndrome: US Interventionism, in the 1980s* (Washington: Institute for Policy Studies).
— and P. Kornbluh (eds), 1988, *Low Intensity Warfare* (New York: Pantheon).

Klein, B.S., 1986, 'Beyond the Western Alliance: the politics of post Atlanticism', paper presented at the British International Studies Association Meeting, Reading.

——, 1987, *Strategic Discourse and its Alternatives* (New York Centre on Violence and Human Survival: Occasional Paper No. 3).

——, 1988, 'After strategy: the search for a post-modern politics of peace', *Alternatives*, 13(3), 293–312.

Knelman, F., 1985, *Reagan, God and the Bomb: from Myth to Policy* (Toronto: McLelland and Stewart).

Knorr, K. and J.N. Rosenau (eds), 1969, *Contending Approaches to International Politics* (Princeton: Princeton University Press).

Komer, R.W., 1985, 'What decade of neglect?', *International Security*, 10(2), 70–83.

Konrad, G., 1984, *Antipolitics* (New York: Harcourt Brace Jovanovich).

Kovel, J., 1983, *Against the State of Nuclear Terror* (Boston: South End).

Kramarae, C., M. Schulz and W.M. O'Barr (eds), 1984, *Language and Power* (Beverley Hills: Sage).

Krasner, S.D. 1978, *Defending the National Interest: Raw Materials Investments and US Foreign Policy* (Princeton, NJ: Princeton University Press).

Kress, G., 1985, 'Discourses, texts, readers and the pro-nuclear arguments', in Chilton P. (ed.), *Language and the Nuclear Arms Debate: Nukespeak Today* (London: Pinter), 65–87.

Kristof, L.K.D., 1960, 'The origins and evolution of geopolitics', *Journal of Conflict Resolution*, 4(1), 15–51.

Kumar, K., 1978, *Prophecy and Progress: the Sociology of Industrial and Post Industrial Society* (Harmondsworth: Penguin).

Laclau, E., 1977, *Politics and Ideology in Marxist Theory* (London: Verso).

—— and C. Mouffe, 1985, *Hegemony and Socialist Strategy: Towards a Radical Democratic Politics* (London: Verso).

Lambeth, B.S., 1979, 'The political potential of Soviet equivalence', *International Security*, 4(2), 22–39.

——, 1982, 'Uncertainties for the Soviet war planner', *International Security*, 7(2), 139–66.

Laquer, W., 1977, 'The spectre of Finlandisation', *Commentary*, 64, 37–41.

——, 1978, 'The psychology of appeasement', *Commentary*, 66(4), 44–50.

——, 1980, 'Containment for the 1980s', *Commentary*, 70(4), 33–42.

——, 1983, *America, Europe and the Soviet Union* (New Brunswick, NJ: Transaction).

Larrain, J., (1979), *The Concept of Ideology* (London: Hutchinson).

——, 1983, *Marxism and Ideology* (London: Macmillan).

Leaning, J. and L. Keyes (eds), 1983, *The Counterfeit Ark* (Cambridge, Mass.: Ballinger).

Lebow, R.N., 1988–9, 'Malign analysts or evil empire: Western images of Soviet nuclear strategy', *International Journal*, 44(1), 1–40.

Lee, W.T. and R.F. Staar, 1986, *Soviet Military Policy Since World War II* (Stanford: Hoover Institution Press).

Lefevre, H., 1976, 'Reflections on the politics of space', *Antipode*, 8(2), 30–7.

Leigh, M., 1976, *Mobilising Consent: Public Opinion and American Foreign Policy, 1937–1947* (Westport, Conn.: Greenwood).

Leitenberg, M., 1981, 'Presidential Directive (PD) 59: The United States Nuclear Weapon Targeting Policy', *Journal of Peace Research*, 18(4), 309–19.

Leites, N., 1950, *The Operational Code of the Politburo* (New York: McGraw Hill).

Levi, B.-H., 1979, *Barbarism with a Human Face* (New York: Harper & Row).

Levinas, E., 1969, *Totality and Infinity* (Pittsburgh: Duquesne University Press).

Levitas, R., 1986, *The Ideology of the New Right* (Cambridge: Polity).

Lichtheim, G., 1974, *Imperialism* (Harmondsworth: Penguin).

Liddell-Hart, B., 1968, *Strategy: the Indirect Approach* (London: Faber & Faber).

Liebowitz, R.D., 1983, 'Findlandization: an analysis of the Soviet Union's "Domination" of Finland', *Political Geography Quarterly*, 2, 275–88.

Lifton, R.J. and R.A. Falk, 1982, *Indefensible Weapons* (New York: Basic Books).

Linklater, A., 1982, *Men and Citizens in the Theory of International Relations* (London:Macmillan).

Lloyd, G., 1984, *The Man of Reason: 'Male' and 'Female' in Western Philosophy* (Minneapolis: University of Minnesota Press).

Loeb, P.R., 1987, *Hope in Hard Times: America's Peace Movement and the Reagan Era* (Lexington, Mass.: Lexington).

Lovins, A.B. and L.H. Lovins, 1982, *Brittle Power: Energy Strategy for National Security* (Andover, Mass.: Brick House).

Luckham, R., 1984, 'Armament culture', *Alternatives*, 10(1), 1–44.

Lukacs, G., 1973, 'On the responsibility of intellectuals', in Lukacs, G., *Marxism and Human Liberation* (New York: Delta), 267–76.

Luke, T.W., 1985, 'Technology and Soviet foreign trade: on the political economy of an underdeveloped superpower', *International Studies Quarterly*, 29, 327–53.

Luttwak, E., 1983, *The Grand Strategy of the Soviet Union* (New York: St Martin's).

Machiavelli, N., 1962, *The Prince* (Toronto: Mentor, original, 1532).

Mack, A., 1981, 'The Soviet threat: reality or myth?', *Politics and Power*, 4, 259–89.

Mackay, L. and M. Thompson (eds), 1988, *Something in the Wind: Politics After Chernobyl* (London: Pluto).

Mackinder, H.J., 1904, 'The geographical pivot of history', *Geographical Journal*, 23, 421–42.

——, 1919, *Democratic Ideals and Reality: a Study in the Politics of Reconstruction* (London: Constable).

——, 1943, 'The round world and the winning of the peace', *Foreign Affairs*, 21, 595–605.

MacNamara, R.S., 1983, 'The military role of nuclear weapons: perceptions and misperceptions', *Foreign Affairs*, 62(1), 59–80.

Magnusson, W. and R.B.J. Walker, 1988, 'Decentring the state: political theory and Canadian political economy', *Studies in Political Economy*, 26, 37–71.

Mandel, E., 1975, *Late Capitalism* (London: Verso).

Mani, L. and R. Frankenberg, 1985, 'The challenge of Orientalism', *Economy and Society*, 14(2), 174–92.

Markusen, A., 1986, 'The militarised economy,' *World Policy Journal*, 3(3), 495–516.

Marx, K. and F. Engels, 1976, *The German Ideology* (Moscow: Progress).

Matson, F.W., 1966, *The Broken Image: Man Science and Society* (New York: Doubleday).

May, B.,1984, *Russia, America, the Bomb, and the Fall of Western Europe* (London: Routledge & Kegan Paul).

May, E.T., 1988, *Homeward Bound: American Families in the Cold War Era* (New York: Basic Books).

Maynes, C.W., 1982, 'Old errors in the new Cold War', *Foreign Policy*, 46, 86–104.

Mayers, D., 1986, 'Containment and the primacy of diplomacy: George Kennan's views, 1947–8', *International Security*, 11(1), 124–62.

Mazrui, A.A., 1984, 'The moving cultural frontier of world order: from monotheism to North-South relations', in Walker, R.B.J. (ed.), *Culture, Ideology and World Order* (Boulder: Westview), 24–43.

McAllister, P., (ed.), 1982, *Reweaving the Web of Life: Feminism and Non-Violence* (Philadelphia: New Society).

MccGwire, M., 1984, 'Dilemmas and delusions of deterrence', *World Policy Journal*, 1(4), 745–67.

—, 1985–6, 'Deterrence: the problem—not the solution', *International Affairs*, 62(1), 55–70.

—, 1987a, *Military Objectives in Soviet Foreign Policy* (Washington: Brookings Institution).

—, 1987b, 'Update: Soviet military objectives', *World Policy Journal*, 4(4), 723–31.

McColl, R.W., 1983, 'A geographic model for international behaviour', in Kliot, N. and Waterman, S. (eds), *Pluralism and Political Geography* (London: Croom Helm), 284–94.

McNair, B., 1988, *Images of the Enemy* (London: Routledge).

McMahan, J., 1985, *Reagan and the World: Imperial Policy in the New Cold War* (New York: Monthly Review Press).

McMurtry, J., 1984, 'Fascism and neo-conservatism: is there a difference?', *Praxis International*, 4(1), 86–102.

Mearsheimer, J.J., 1982, 'Why the Soviets can't win quickly in Central Europe', *International Security*, 7(1), 3–39.

—, 1986, 'A strategic misstep: the maritime strategy and deterrence in Europe', *International Security*, 11(2), 3–57.

Melman, S., 1988, *The Demilitarised Society* (Nottingham: Spokesman).

Melskins, G., 1987, 'War of the worlds?' *New Left Review*, 162, 100–11.

Mendlowitz, S. and R.B.J. Walker (eds), 1987, *Towards a Just World Peace: Perspectives from Social Movements* (London: Butterworth).

Merchant, C., (1980, *The Death of Nature* (New York: Harper & Row).

Miliband R., J. Saville and M. Liebman (eds), 1984, *Socialist Register 1984: the Uses of Anti-Communism* (London: Merlin).

Modelski, G., 1978, 'The long cycle of global politics and the nation-state', *Comparative Studies in Society and History*, 20(2), 214–35.

Moffitt, M., 1987, 'Shocks, deadlocks and scorched earth: Reagonomics and the decline of US hegemony', *World Policy Journal*, 4(4), 553–82.

Moi, T., 1985, *Sexual/Textual Politics: Feminist Literary Theory* (New York: Methuen).

Morgenthau, H., 1977, 'The pathology of American power', *International Security*, 1(3), 3–20.

—, 1978, *Politics among Nations: the Struggle for Power and Peace* (New York: Knopf, 5th edition).

Mouffe, C., 1979, 'Hegemony and ideology in Gramsci', in Mouffe, C. (ed.), *Gramsci and Marxist Theory* (London: Rouledge & Kegan Paul), 168–204.

—, (ed.), 1979, *Gramsci and Marxist Theory* (London: Routledge & Kegan Paul).

Motyl, A.J., 1987, *Will the Non Russians Rebel? State, Ethnicity and Stability* (Ithaca: Cornell University Press).

Munck, R., 1986, *The Difficult Dialogue: Marxism and Nationalism* (London: Zed).

Nandy, A., 1980, *At the Edge of Psychology: Essays in Politics and Culture* (New

Delhi: Oxford University Press).

——, 1983, *The Intimate Enemy: Loss and Recovery of Self under Colonialism* (New Delhi: Oxford University Press).

——, 1984, 'Oppression and human liberation: towards a Third World utopia', in Walker, R. (ed.), *Culture Ideology and World Order* (Boudler: Westview), 149–79.

——, 1984–5, 'Reconstructing childhood: a critique of the ideology of adulthood', *Alternatives*, 10(3), 359–75.

——, 1987, 'Cultural frames for social transformation: a credo', *Alternatives*, 12(1), 113–24.

Nelkin, D. and M. Pollak, 1981, *The Atom Besieged* (Cambridge, Mass.: MIT Press).

New Left Review (ed.), 1982, *Exterminism and Cold War* (London: Verso).

Nitze, P.H., 1956, 'Atoms, strategy and policy', *Foreign Affairs*, 34(2), 187–98.

——, 1974–5, 'The strategic balance between hope and skepticism', *Foreign Policy*, 17, 136–56.

——, 1975, 'The Vladivostok accord and SALT II', *Review of Politics*, 37, 147–60.

——, 1976, 'Assuring strategic stability in an era of detente', *Foreign Affairs*, 54(2), 207–32.

——, 1976–7, 'Deterring our Deterrent', *Foreign Policy*, 25, 195–210.

——, 1977, 'The relationship of strategic and theatre nuclear forces', *International Security*, 2(2), 122–32.

——, 1978a, 'The global military balance', *Proceedings of the Academy of Political Science*, 33(1), 4–14.

——, 1978b, *SALT II—the Objective vs the Results* (Washington: Committee on the Present Danger).

——, 1980a, 'Strategy for the 1980s', *Foreign Affairs*, 59(1), 82–101.

——, 1980b, 'The development of NSC68', *International Security*, 4(4), 170–6.

Nye, J., 1984, 'The domestic roots of American policy', in Nye, J. (ed.), *The Making of American's Soviet Policy*, 1–9.

——, (ed.), 1984, *The Making of America's Soviet Policy* (New Haven: Yale University Press.

O'Loughlin, J., 1986, 'World power competition and local conflicts in the Third World', in Johnston, R.J. and P.J. Taylor (eds), *A World in Crisis* (Oxford: Basil Blackwell), 231–68.

Osgood, R.E., 1981, *Containment, Soviet Behaviour, and Grand Strategy* (Berkeley: University of California, Institute of International Studies, Policy Paper in International Affairs 16).

O'Sullivan, P., 1982, 'Antidomino', *Political Geography Quarterly*, 1(1), 57–64.

——, 1985, 'The geopolitics of detente', in Pepper, D. and A. Jenkins (eds), *The Geography of Peace and War* (Oxford: Basil Blackwell), 29–41.

——, 1986, *Geopolitics* (London: Croom Helm).

O'Toole, M., 1985, 'Disarming criticism', in Chilton, P. (ed.), *Language and the Nuclear Arms Debate: Nukespeak Today* (London: Pinter), 183–95.

O'Tuathail, G., 1986, 'The language and nature of the "New Geopolitics" – the case of US–El Salvador relations', *Political Geography Quarterly*, 5(1), 73–85.

——, 1987, 'The geopolitics of Southern Africa: the US State Department and the scripting of Southern Africa, 1969–1986', paper presented at the annual meeting of the Association of American Geographers, Portland, April.

——, 1988, 'Critical Geopolitics: the Social Construction of Space and Place in the Practice of Statecraft', unpublished Ph.D. dissertation, Syracuse University.

Oye, K.A., 1983, 'International systems structure and American foreign policy', in Oye, K.A., R.J. Lieber and D. Rothchild (eds), *Eagle Defiant: United States Foreign Policy in the 1980s* (Boston: Little Brown), 3–32.

Oye, K.A., R.J. Lieber and D. Rothchild (eds), 1983, *Eagle Defiant: United States Foreign Policy in the 1980s* (Boston: Little Brown).

Paggi, L. and P. Pinzauti, 1985, 'Peace and security', *Telos*, 63, 3–40.

Parker, G., 1985, *Western Geopolitical Thought in the Twentieth Century* (London: Croom Helm).

Parker, W.H., 1968, *An Historical Geography of Russia* (Chicago: Aldine).

Parker, W., (1982), *Mackinder: Geography as an Aid to Statecraft* (Oxford: Clarendon Press).

Pasquinelli, C., 1986, 'Power without the state', *Telos*, 68, 79–92.

Paterson, J.H., 1987, 'German geopolitics reassessed', *Political Geography Quarterly*, 6(2), 107–14.

Payne, K.B. and C.S. Gray, 1984, 'Nuclear policy and the defensive transition', *Foreign Affairs*, 62(4), 820–42.

___ and (eds), 1984, *The Nuclear Freeze Controversy* (Cambridge, Mass: Abt).

Peet, R., 1985, 'The social origins of environmental determinism', *Annals of the Association of American Geographers*, 75(3), 309–33.

Pepper, D., 1986, 'Spatial aspects of the West's "Deep Strike" doctrines', *Political Geography Quarterly*, 5(3), 253–66.

___ and Jenkins, A., 1984, 'Reversing the nuclear arms race: geopolitical bases for pessimism', *Professional Geographer*, 36(4), 419–27.

___ and (eds), 1985, *The Geography of Peace and War* (Oxford: Basil Blackwell).

Perle, R., 1979, 'Echoes of the 1930s', *Strategic Review*, 7(1), 11–15.

Peterson, J. (ed.), 1983, *The Aftermath: the Human and Ecological Consequences of Nuclear War* (New York: Pantheon).

Pipes, R., 1960, *A History of Russia* (Cambridge, Mass.: Harvard University Press).

___, 1963, *Social Democracy and the St Petersburg Labour Movement 1885–1897* (Cambridge, Mass.: Harvard University Press).

___, 1964, *The Formation of the Soviet Union: Communism and Nationalism 1917–1923* (Cambridge, Mass.: Harvard University Press, first edition, 1953).

___, 1973, 'Some operational principles of Soviet foreign policy', in Confino, M. and S. Shamir (eds), *The Soviet Union and the Middle East* (New York: Wiley).

___, 1974, *Russia Under the Old Regime* (London: Wiedenfeld and Nicolson).

___, 1976, 'Detente: Moscow's view', in Pipes, R. (ed.), *Soviet Strategy in Western Europe* (New York: Crane Russak), 3–44.

___ (ed.), 1976, *Soviet Strategy in Western Europe* (New York: Crane Russak).

___, 1977, 'Why the Soviet Union thinks it could fight and win a nuclear war', *Commentary*, 64(1), 21–34.

___, 1979, 'Why the Soviet Union wants SALT II', Washington: Committee on the Present Danger, reprinted in Tyroler, C. (ed.), 1984, *Alerting America*, 166–9.

___, 1980a, 'Militarism and the Soviet state', *Daedalus*, 109(4), 1–12.

___, 1980b, 'Soviet global strategy', *Commentary*, 69(4), 31–39.

___, 1981, *US–Soviet Relations in the Era of Detente* (Boulder: Westview).

___, 1982, 'Soviet strategic doctrine: another view', *Strategic Review*, 10(4), 52–8.

___, 1984, *Survival Is Not Enough: Soviet Realities and America's Future* (New York: Simon & Shuster).

Plous, S., 1985, 'Perceptual illusions and military realities: the nuclear arms race', *Journal of Conflict Resolution*, 29(3), 363–89.

Podhoretz, N., 1976, 'Making the world safe for communism', *Commentary*, 61(4), 31–41.
——, 1980a, 'The present danger', *Commentary*, 69(3), 27–40.
——, 1980b, *The Present Danger* (New York: Simon & Schuster).
Pollard, R.A., 1985, *Economic Security and the Origins of the Cold War 1945–1950* (New York: Columbia University Press).
Posen, B.R., 1987, 'Competing images of the Soviet Union', *World Politics*, 39(4), 579–97.
Prados, J., 1982, *The Soviet Estimate* (New York: Dial).
Pringle, P. and W. Arkin, 1983, *S.I.O.P.: the Secret US Plan for Nuclear War* (New York: Norton).
Prins, G. (ed.), 1983, *Defended to Death* (Harmondsworth: Penguin).
—— (ed.), 1984, *The Choice: Nuclear Weapons Versus Security* (London: Chatto & Windus).
Ratzel, F., 1892, *Anthropogeographie* (Stuttgart: Engelhorn).
Rearden, S.L., 1984, *The Evolution of American Strategic Doctrine: Paul H. Nitze and the Soviet Challenge* (Boulder: Westview).
Record, J., 1983–4, 'Jousting with unreality: Reagan's military strategy', *International Security*, 8(3), 3–18.
Report of the President's Commission on Strategic Forces, 1983, ('The Scowcroft Commission') (Washington: Government Documents).
Report by the Secretaries of State and Defence on 'United States Objectives and Programs for National Security', 1950 (Washington: NSC68, declassified 1975).
Richelson, J., 1980, 'The dilemmas of counterpower targeting', *Comparative Strategy* 2(3), 223–37.
——, 1983, 'PD-59, NSDD-13 and the Reagan strategic modernisation program', *Journal of Strategic Studies*, 6(2), 125–46.
Riesman, P., 1976, 'A comprehensive anthropological assessment', in Noel, D.C. (ed.), *Seeing Castaneda* (New York: Putnam), 46–53.
Rosecrance, R., 1986, *The Rise of the Trading State: Commerce and Conquest in the Modern World* (New York: Basic Books).
Rostow, E.V., 1968, *Law, Power and the Pursuit of Peace* (Lincoln: University of Nebraska Press).
——, 1972, *Peace in the Balance: the Future of American Foreign Policy* (New York: Simon & Schuster).
—— (ed.), 1976, *The Middle East: Critical Choices for the United States* (Boulder: Westview).
——, 1976, 'The safety of the republic: can the tide be turned?', *Strategic Review*, 4(2), 12–25.
——, 1979, 'The case against SALT II', *Commentary*, 67(2), 23–32.
Rostow, W.W., 1960, *The United States in the World Arena: a Study in Recent History* (New York: Harper & Row).
Ruggie, J.G., 1983, 'Continuity and transformation in the world system: toward a neo-realist synthesis', *World Politics*, 35(2), 261–85.
Ryan, M., 1982, *Marxism and Deconstruction: a Critical Articulation* (Baltimore: Johns Hopkins University Press).
Sack, R.D., 1980, *Conceptions of Space in Social Thought* (London: Macmillan).
——, 1986, *Human Territoriality: its Theory and History* (New York: Cambridge University Press).
Said, E., 1979, *Orientalism* (New York: Vintage).
——, 1982, 'Opponents, audiences, constituencies, and community', *Critical*

Inquiry, 9(1), 1–26.
——, 1985a, 'Orientalism reconsidered', Race and Class, 27(2), 1–15.
——, 1985b, 'An ideology of difference', Critical Inquiry, 12, 38–58.
Sahlins, M., 1972, Stone Age Economics (Chicago: Aldine-Atherton).
Saloma, J.S., 1984, Ominous Politics: the New Conservative Labyrinth (New York: Hill and Wang).
Sanders, J., 1983, Peddlars of Crisis: the Committee on the Present Danger and the Politics of Containment (Boston: South End).
Sartre, J.-P., 1966, Being and Nothingness (New York: Philosophical Library).
Schapiro, L., 1985, 1917: the Russian Revolutions and the Origins of Present Day Communism (Harmondsworth: Penguin).
Scheer, R., 1983, With Enough Shovels: Reagan, Bush and Nuclear War (New York: Vintage, 2nd edition).
Schurmann, F., 1974, The Logic of World Power (New York: Pantheon).
Segal, G., 1986, 'Nuclear strategy: the geography of stability', Political Geography Quarterly, 5(4), supplement, S37–S47.
Shapiro, M.J. (ed.), 1984, Language and Politics (New York: New York University Press).
——, 1988, The Politics of Representation (Madison: University of Wisconsin Press).
——, 1989, 'Representing world politics: the sport war intertext', in Der Derian, J. and M.J. Shapiro (eds), International/Intertextual Relations: Postmodern Readings of Global Politics (Lexington, Mass.: Lexington Books), 69–96.
Sharp, G., 1985, Making Europe Unconquerable (London: Taylor and Francis).
Sheridan, A., 1980, Michel Foucault: the Will to Truth (London: Tavistock).
Sherrill, R., 1979, 'Gene Rostow's propaganda club', The Nation, 11/18 August, 106–10.
Shiva, V., 1988, Staying Alive: Women, Ecology and Development (London: Zed).
Shoup, L.H. and W. Minter, 1977, Imperial Brain Trust: the Council on Foreign Relations and United States Foreign Policy (New York: Monthly Review Press).
Shulman, M.D., 1984, 'Tell me, daddy, who's the baddy?', Proceedings of the Academy of Political Science, 35(3), 177–83.
Simes, D., 1979–80, 'The anti-Soviet bridgade', Foreign Policy, 37, 28–42.
Singer, J.D., 1979, Explaining War: Selected Papers from the Correllates of War Project (Beverly Hills: Sage).
—— and M.D. Wallace, 1979, To Auger Well: Early Warning Indicators in World Politics (Beverly Hills: Sage).
Sklar, H. (ed.), 1980, Trilateralism: the Trilateral Commission and Elite Planning for World Management (Boston: South End).
Sloan, G.R., 1988, Geopolitics in US Strategic Policy 1890–1987 (Brighton, Sussex: Wheatsheaf Books).
Slocombe, W., 1981, 'The countervailing strategy', International Security, 5(4), 18–27.
Smith, A., 1980, The Geopolitics of Information: How Western Culture Dominates the World (London: Faber & Faber).
Smith, D., 1978, 'Domination and containment: an approach to modernisation', Comparative Studies in Society and History, 20(2), 177–213.
—— and E.P. Thompson (eds), 1987, Prospectus for a Habitable Planet (Harmondsworth: Penguin).
Smith, G., 1980, Doubletalk: the Story of the First Strategic Arms Limitation Talks (New York: Doubleday).
Smith, G.E., 1985, 'Ethnic nationalism in the Soviet Union: territory, cleavage and

control', *Environment and Planning C: Government and Policy*, 3(1), 49–73.

Smith, N., 1984, *Uneven Development* (Oxford: Basil Blackwell).

Smoke, R., 1987, *National Security and the Nuclear Dilemma: an Introduction to the American Experience* (New York: Random House).

Snow, D.M., 1983, *The Nuclear Future: Toward a Strategy of Uncertainty* (Alabama: University of Alabama Press).

Sohn-Rethel, A., 1978, *Intellectual and Manual Labour* (London: Macmillan).

Sokolovsky, V.D., ed., 1963, *Military Strategy: Soviet Doctrine and Concepts* (New York: Praeger).

Sondern, A., 1941, 'The thousand scientists behind Hitler', *Readers Digest*, 38 (June), 23–7.

Spender, D., 1984, 'Defining reality: a powerful tool', in Kramarae, C., M. Shulz and W.M. O'Barr (eds), *Language and Power* (Beverly Hills: Sage), 196–205.

Sprout, H., 1968, 'Political geography', *International Encyclopedia of the Social Sciences*, vol. 6, 116–22.

—— and M. Sprout, 1965, *The Ecological Perspective on Human Affairs* (Princeton: Princeton University Press).

Spruyt, H., 1985, 'Misconstruing the first image: the fallacy of US vulnerability', *Journal of Peace Research*, 22(4), 365–70.

Spykman, N., 1942, *America's Strategy in World Politics* (New York: Harcourt Brace).

——, 1944, *The Geography of the Peace* (New York: Harcourt Brace).

Strause-Hupe, R., 1942, *Geopolitics: the Struggle for Space and Power* (New York: Putnam).

Steele, J., 1985, *The Limits of Soviet Power* (Harmondsworth: Penguin).

Stockholm International Peace Research Institute (annual), *Yearbook* (London: Taylor and Francis).

Strode, R.V., 1982, 'Soviet strategic style', *Comparative Strategy*, 3(4), 319–39.

—— and C.S. Gray, 1981, 'The imperial dimension of Soviet military power', *Problems of Communism*, 30(6), 1–15.

Stubbs, R. and R. Ranger, 1978. 'Mechanistic assumptions and United States strategy', *International Journal*, 33(3), 557–72.

Sumner, C., 1979, *Reading Ideology* (New York: Academic Press).

Talbott, S., 1979, *Endgame: the Inside Story of SALT II* (New York: Harper & Row).

——, 1985 *Deadly Gambits: the Reagan Administration and the Stalemate in Nuclear Arms Control* (New York: Vintage).

Tatchell, P., 1985, *Democratic Defence: a Non-Nuclear Alternative* (London: GMP).

Taylor, C., 1979, *Hegel and Modern Society* (Cambridge: Cambridge University Press).

Taylor, P.J., 1985, *Political Geography: World Economy, Nation State and Locality* (London: Longman).

Tetlock, P.E., 1983, 'Policy-makers' images of international conflict', *Journal of Social Issues*, 39(1), 67–86.

Theunisson, M., 1984, *The Other: Studies in the Social Ontology of Husserl, Heidegger, Sartre and Buber*, translated by C. Macann with an introduction by F.R. Dallmyr (Cambridge, Mass.: MIT Press).

Thompson, E.P., 1982, *Beyond the Cold War* (New York: Pantheon).

——, 1985a, *The Heavy Dancers* (London: Merlin).

——, 1985b, *Double Exposure* (London: Merlin).

Thompson, J.B., 1984, *Studies in the Theory of Ideology* (Berkeley: University of California Press).

Thompson, W.R. and G. Zuk, 1986, 'World power and the strategic trap of territorial commitments', *International Studies Quarterly*, 30, 249–67.

Thucydides, 1954, *The Peloponnesian War* (Harmondsworth: Penguin).

Todorov, T., 1984, *The Conquest of America: the Question of the Other* (New York: Harper & Row).

Tonelson, A., 1979, 'Nitze's world', *Foreign Policy*, 35, 74–90.

Trofimenko, G., 1986, *The US Military Doctrine* (Moscow: Progress).

Turner, B.S., 1978, *Marx and the End of Orientalism* (London: Allen & Unwin).

Turco, R., O.B. Toon, T.P. Ackerman, J.B. Pollack and C. Sagan, 1983, 'Nuclear winter: global consequences of multiple nuclear explosions', *Science*, 222, 1283–92.

—, —, —, — and —, 1984, 'The climatic effects of nuclear war', *Scientific American*, 251(2), 33–43.

Van den Wusten, H., J. Nijman and R. Thijsse, 1985, 'Security policies of European countries outside the Soviet sphere', *Journal of Peace Research*, 22(4), 303–19.

Vertzberger, Y., 1982, 'Misperception in international politics: a typological framework for analysis', *International Interactions*, 9(3), 207–34.

Vincent, R.J., 1984, 'Race in international relations', in Walker, R.B.J. (ed.), *Culture Ideology and World Order* (Boulder: Westview), 44–59.

Virilio, P., 1986, *Speed and Politics* (New York: Semiotexte).

— and S. Lotringer, 1983, *Pure War* (New York: Semiotexte).

Visvanathan, S., 1986, 'Bhopal: the imagination of a disaster', *Alternatives*, 11(1), 147–65.

—, 1987, 'From the annals of the laboratory state', *Alternatives*, 12(1), 37–60.

Vitkovskiy, V., 1981, 'Political geography and geopolitics: a recurrence of American geopolitics', *Soviet Geography*, 22, 586–93.

Walker, R.B.J., 1980, *Political Theory and the Transformation of World Politics* World Order Studies Program, Occasional Paper 8, Princeton University Centre of International Studies.

—, 1983–4, 'Contemporary militarism and the discourse of dissent', *Alternatives*, 9(3), 303–22.

—, 1984, 'The territorial state and the theme of Gulliver', *International Journal*, 34, 529–52.

—, (ed.), 1984, *Culture, Ideology and World Order* (Boulder: Westview).

—, 1986, 'Culture, discourse, insecurity', *Alternatives*, 11(4), 485–504.

—, 1987, 'Realism, change and international political theory', *International Studies Quarterly*, 31(1), 65–86.

—, 1988a, *The Concept of Security and International Relations Theory* University of California, Institute of Global Conflict and Cooperation, Working Paper No. 3.

—, 1988b, *One World, Many Worlds: Struggles for a Just World Peace* (Boulder: Lynne Rienner).

—, 1988c, *State Sovereignty, Global Civilisation, and the Rearticulation of Political Space* Princeton University Center of International Studies, World Order Studies Program Occassional Paper No. 18.

—, 1989, 'The prince and the pauper', in Der Derian, J. and M.J. Shapiro (eds), *International/Intertextual Relations: Postmodern Readings in Global Politics* (Lexington, Mass.: Lexington), 25–48.

Wallensteen, P., J. Galtung and C. Portales (eds), 1985, *Global Militarisation*

(Boulder: Westview).
Wallerstein, I., 1979, *The Capitalist World Economy* (New York: Cambridge University Press).
——, 1984, *The Politics of the World Economy* (Cambridge: Cambridge University Press).
Walters, R.E., 1974, *The Nuclear Trap: an Escape Route* (Harmondsworth: Penguin).
Waltz, K.N., 1959, *Man, the State and War: a Theoretical Analysis* (New York: Columbia University Press).
——, 1979, *Theory of International Relations* (Reading, Mass.: Addison-Wesley).
Weeks, A.L., 1983, 'The Garthoff-Pipes debate on Soviet doctrine: another perspective', *Strategic Review*, 11(1), 57–64.
Weigert, H.W., 1942, *Generals and Geographers: the Twilight of Geopolitics* (New York: Freeport, Essay Index Reprint Series).
Weigley, R.F., 1973, *The American Way of War* (New York: Macmillan).
Welch, W., 1970, *American Images of Soviet Foreign Policy: an Inquiry into Recent Appraisals from the Academic Community* (New Haven: Yale University Press).
Wells, S.F., 1979, 'Sounding the Tocsin: NSC68 and the Soviet threat', *International Security*, 4(1), 116–58.
Wertsch, J.V., 1987, 'Modes of discourse in the nuclear arms debate', *Current Research on Peace and Violence*, 10(2–3), 102–12.
Whitaker, A.P., 1954, *The Western Hemisphere Idea: its Rise and Decline* (Ithaca: Cornell University Press).
Whitaker, R., 1984, 'Fighting the Cold War on the home front: America, Britain, Australia and Canada', in Miliband, R., J. Saville and M. Liebman, (eds), *Socialist Register 1984* (London: Merlin), 23–67.
Whittlesey, D., 1942, *German Strategy of World Conquest* (New York: Farrer and Rinehart).
Whitworth, W., 1970, *Naive Questions About War and Peace: Conversations with Eugene V. Rostow* (New York: Norton).
Wiarda, H.J., 1981, 'The ethnocentrism of the social sciences: implications for research and policy', *Review of Politics*, 43(2), 163–97.
Wight, M., 1966, 'Why is there no international theory?', in Butterfield, H. and M. Wight (eds), *Diplomatic Investigations: Essays in the Theory of International Politics* (London: Allen & Unwin), 17–34.
——, 1979, *Power Politics* (Harmondsworth, Penguin).
Williams, P., 1985, 'Detente and US domestic politics', *International Affairs*, 61(3), 431–47.
Williams, R., 1973, 'Base and superstructure in Marxist cultural theory', *New Left Review*, 82, 3–16.
——, 1977, *Marxism and Literature* (Oxford: Oxford University Press).
Williams, W.A., 1959, *The Tragedy of American Diplomacy* (New York: World Publishing Company).
Wilson, P., 1985, 'The President's foundering strategic modernisation plan', *Strategic Review*, 13(3), 9–13.
Wimbush, S.E., 1985, *Soviet Nationalities in Strategic Perspective* (London: Croom Helm).
Witheford, N., 1987, 'Nuclear Text', unpublished M.A. thesis, Burnaby, British Columbia, Simon Fraser University.
Wittfogel, K., 1957, *Oriental Despotism* (New Haven: Yale University Press).
Wohlstetter, A., 1959, 'The delicate balance of terror', *Foreign Affairs*, 37, 211–34.

——, 1968, 'The illusions of distance', *Foreign Affairs*, 46, 242–55.

——, 1974a, 'Is there a strategic arms race?', *Foreign Policy*, 15, 3–26.

——, 1974b, 'Rivals but no race', *Foreign Policy*, 16, 48–81.

——, 1975, 'Optimal ways to confuse ourselves', *Foreign Policy*, 20, 170–98.

Wolf, C., 1985, 'The costs of the Soviet Empire', *Science*, 230, 997–1002.

Wolf, E.R., 1982, *Europe and the People without History* (Berkeley: University of California Press).

Wolfe, A., 1984a, *The Rise and Fall of the Soviet Threat* (Boston, Mass.: South End).

——, 1984b, 'The irony of anti-communism: ideology and interest in post-war American foreign policy', in Miliband, R., J. Saville and M. Liebman, (eds), *Socialist Register 1984* (London: Merlin), 214–29.

——, 1984c, 'Nuclear fundamentalism reborn', *World Policy Journal*, 2(1), 87–108.

——, 1986, 'Crackpot moralism, neo-realism and US foreign policy', *World Policy Journal*, 3(2), 251–75.

Yergin, D.H., 1977, *Shattered Peace: the Origins of the Cold War and the National Security State* (Boston, Mass.: Houghton Mifflin).

Zeebroek, X., 1984, 'Soviet expansionism and expansive anti-Sovietism', in Miliband, R., J. Saville and M. Liebman, (eds), *Socialist Register 1984* (London: Merlin), 278–98.

Zoppo, C.E. and C. Zorgbibe (eds), 1985, *On Geopolitics: Classical and Nuclear* (Dordrecht: Martinus Nijhoff).

Index